POPE PIUS VII

OTHER WORKS BY THE AUTHOR

Rome Churches for English-Speaking People
The Quiet Grave (Journals)
St. Pius V
Between Two Wars—The Life of Pius XI
Gleams of English-Language Literature
Collected prose and poetry
Crisis Popes (private circulation)

POPE PIUS VII
1800 – 1823

HIS LIFE, REIGN AND STRUGGLE
WITH NAPOLEON IN THE AFTERMATH
OF THE FRENCH REVOLUTION

Professor Robin Anderson

*"For the foolishness of God is wiser than men;
and the weakness of God is stronger than men."*
—1 Corinthians 1:25

TAN BOOKS AND PUBLISHERS, INC.
Rockford, Illinois 61105

TAN BOOKS AND PUBLISHERS, INC.
P.O. Box 424
Rockford, Illinois 61105
2001

Dedicated
with respect and affection
to the late
John J. Cardinal Wright,
who asked me to write about
Pope Pius VII.

CONTENTS

General overview of Italy and eastern France (with modern boundaries), showing the cities that figured so prominently in the life of Pope Pius VII: Venice, Rome, Savona, Fontainebleau and Paris.

PROLOGUE

A Glance Back at the 18th Century

The conclave had dragged on for nearly four months in the Venetian island Abbey of St. George (*San Giorgio*), where the electing cardinals had assembled because of political conditions in Rome and Europe on the death of Pope Pius VI. On March 15, 1800, the Benedictine Cardinal Gregory Barnabas Chiaramonti accepted election and, out of gratitude to his predecessor and benefactor, took the name of Pius VII.

Venice was then under the government of Austria, whose rulers, members of the house of Hapsburg, had from medieval times held the title of Holy Roman Emperor.[1] The Austrians would not permit the new Pope to be crowned in St. Mark's Basilica. The Emperor Francis II had paid most of the conclave expenses but was disappointed with the election. He knew Pius VII would not be the Pope he had wanted to favor his policies. So the coronation ceremony had to take place in the modest abbey church. Nor would the Austrian government permit Pius VII to make the journey to his capital, Rome, through the Papal States.[2] Pius was obliged to go much of the way by sea in a dilapidated, badly equipped old boat, escorted by the Emperor's envoy.

But by the time Pius VII would be able to enter his capital at the beginning of July, General Napoleon Bonaparte's victory over the Austrian forces at Marengo would have altered the European balance of power. The Pope would find himself no longer fettered by the Emperor Francis but rather

confronted by one other man—the general who had risen
to power in France, Napoleon, the " First Consul," who in
a few years was to become "Emperor of the French" and
lord of most of Europe.

Napoleon's fourteen-year rule (1799-1814) was to prove a
very mixed blessing for France and for the Church. A man
of military genius and amazing energy, he restored order after
the turmoil and bloodshed of the French Revolution, launched
in 1789; but Napoleon was to some extent imbued with the
tenets of the Revolution. His unbounded political ambition
further caused him to contest the sacred rights of the Pope
and the Church, rights which he endeavored to dominate and
use for ruling and extending his empire. The first half of Pius
VII's reign would be taken up by his struggle with Napoleon.

The death of Pope Pius VI in France in August 1799, a
prisoner of the French Revolutionaries, had left the Catholic
Church in an apparently catastrophic, not to say hopeless
plight. The Pope was sneeringly called "Pius VI the Last."
Many thought, not for the first time, that the papacy was
finished.

During the 18th century, just closing, things had gone from
bad to worse. Philosophies such as Kant's in Germany and
Hobbes' in England had discarded supernatural faith in divine revelation. They led the way to the so-called Illuminism
of the French philosophers and encyclopaedists who purported
to propagate modern science and culture. In fact, neither culture nor science were propagated. The Age of Reason was
proclaimed: mankind had been in its infancy, but was now
adult for the first time.

The writings of Rousseau and Voltaire had popularized notions of man's natural goodness with no need for authority
and law in Church or society. The way was paved for revolution. In 1786, the Illuminatist (not Illuminist) society, secretly
founded in Bavaria by Weishaupt with anarchical aims, was
discovered and banned. But some of the conspirators found
refuge in France, where Weishaupt managed to merge with
Masonry.

Any means were considered permissible for overthrowing monarchy and lawful government, and for abolishing private property, hereditary rights, patriotism and military obedience, the family and marriage. With Machiavellian duplicity, Illuminatism appeared to be serving cultural and social interests, while pursuing its secret ends. Robespierre, Talleyrand (before becoming a Constitutional bishop[3]), Mirabeau and the Duke of Orleans (who provided the money) were members, along with others who were to become leading protagonists of the French Revolution—including the half-mad Cagliostro, hater of priests and kings.

The pre-revolutionary movement was less a political and philosophical movement than a religious one. Jansenism,[4] originating with Jansenius, Bishop of Ypres (1585-1638), in the 17th century, was possibly the most formidable heresy that ever arose in the Church. Hostile to Rome and papal authority, and to the Jesuits in particular, it contested the Church's magisterium and power of jurisdiction, but hid its true nature under various reforming ideals.

Even after Pope Clement XI's definitive condemnation in 1713, Jansenism found ways of surviving. Benedict XIV (1740-1758), called "the Protestant Pope" by some of his cardinals for his over-conciliatory policy, was lenient with the Jansenists. The next Pope, Clement XIII (1758-1769), protested in vain to the Catholic sovereigns of Europe, who were being influenced by Jansenist counselors to banish the Jesuits, strongest defenders of the papacy and leaders in evangelization, missionary work and education. At length the succeeding Pope, Clement XIV, threatened on all sides by powerful princes and for the sake of peace, as he said, in 1773 decreed the suppression of the Society of Jesus throughout the Church.

Impartial historians admit that in bringing about the suppression of the Society of Jesus, the enemies of Christianity intended to strike the Catholic Church. They knew that it would hardly have been possible otherwise to accomplish the destruction of throne and altar.

As in every age, saints were not lacking to counter by heroic penances and action the evils that authority seemed power-less to deal with. The Redemptorist missions founded by St. Alphonsus Liguori undid much of the harm done by the Jan-senists; primary education was carried on with great sacrifice by the Brothers of St. John Baptist de la Salle; the retreats given by the Passionists founded by St. Paul of the Cross led many back to the practice of true religion. But the gap left by the Jesuit suppression in higher education was not filled. Clement XIV is said to have admitted that he had cut off his right hand by his act of 1773.

In northern Italy, the saintly priest Bruno Lanteri widely counteracted the false doctrine of the Jansenists and so-called enlightened philosophers by a chain of Christian Friends secretly printing and spreading books and pamphlets of true teaching.

A unique expiatory and prophetic mission was fulfilled in Rome by Bl. Anna Maria Taigi. A woman of the people, mar-ried and the mother of seven children, but at the same time a tertiary member of the Trinitarian Congregation, she was born in 1769, the same year as Napoleon and, as it happened, in Siena, geographically opposite the future Emperor's birth-place on the island of Corsica.

Almost immediately after the outbreak of the French Revo-lution, she had her first vision of a mysterious, thorn-crowned sun appearing above her. This never left her, and by a glance into it she could tell the state of people's souls, what would happen to them, what they ought or ought not to do, as well as every event taking place in the world. She foresaw and foretold the trials and sufferings to come upon the Pope, the Church and much of society, and she knew they were permitted by Divine Justice as chastisement and purification of sins, especially ambition and pride. Cardinals, bishops, priests and people of all kinds came to consult her. Like St. Catherine of Siena, she venerated the Pope as Christ on earth, and it was for him that her prayers, sufferings and expiations were principally offered.

The Assembly of the French Estates General that was

summoned in 1789 to deal with the national crisis was not anti-religious at the start. Although the need for general reform was admitted, revolutionary notions were not put forward. Reports on the condition of the poorer classes sent up to Paris from the provinces were exaggerated, as were the accusations of the King and Queen's extravagance. Some cause for real grievance came from privilege; almost all French bishops were of the nobility. Though they were on the whole good and charitable men, their revenues were disproportionately larger than the lower clergy's. Nor were the clergy and religious orders really united. There was rivalry and discord. The ideas of the Jansenists and "enlightened" philosophers had entered many heads and even seeped into the cloister. Monasteries, with some exceptions, had ceased to be power-houses of prayer and penance.

Other countries were not much better. Even before the general suppression, Spain had banished the Jesuits. Pacca, papal envoy in Portugal (and future Cardinal Secretary of State of Pius VII), reported movements hostile to the papacy, as well as the clergy's almost total detachment from the Holy See. Holland had become a hotbed of unorthodox opposition and a refuge for Jansenists, unwelcome elsewhere. German Catholics were beset by a kind of Protestantism that had caught hold of many bishops and clergy. Italy ought to have given better example, but in the North, dominated by Austria, the local Synod of Pistoia (1786) introduced a Jansenist catechism, ordered the destruction of statues, side altars and relics, forbade traditional devotions and made Italian the liturgical language.

Even when Pope Pius VI (1775-1799) traveled to Vienna to protest to the Emperor in person, he received honorable welcome but was conceded little or nothing.

The times were ripe for drastic upheaval. Few of the revolutionaries themselves, though, foresaw the magnitude and iniquity of the events to come.

Far from being closed to proper reforms, Church and State representatives of the French Estates General were open to it and had no thought of changing—still less of abolishing—the old order. But from the start, too great attention was paid to the spirit of innovation. It was this, Burke noted in his famous *Reflections,*[5] that in a short time turned against the perpetrators and ended in their own destruction.

Bishops and clergy were taken by surprise as unsuspected purposes and aims showed themselves. But none proposed that the Pope, the Head of the Church, be consulted. In Rome, few were expecting such an upheaval in France; most were bewildered when nationalization of Church property was followed by suppression of religious orders and when a Civil Constitution of the clergy withdrew allegiance from the Holy See.

Pius VI did penance, prayed and caused prayers and penances to be offered to turn away God's anger. The Pope declared: "Men averse to true Catholic principles, claiming to restore simplicity to corrupt religion, have been wretchedly deluded by an empty phantom of liberty, ensnared by false philosophers that contradict one another."[6]

Pressed by some of his ministers to approve the Civil Constitution of the clergy, King Louis XVI appealed to the Pope for advice, but the warning reply came too late; the King had meanwhile reluctantly signed the Constitution.

Pius VI condemned the Civil Constitution and, in a letter to the French bishops, clergy and people, denounced the consecrations of new bishops by Bishop Talleyrand—who was thus creating a schismatic national church headed by the Jansenist Abbé Grégoire. The Pope further refused to recognize the French National Convention which legalized divorce and issued edicts against private property.

Louis XVI then had the courage to renounce all connection with the revolutionary government. But his attempted flight failed, and he was taken back to Paris, imprisoned and executed, as was Queen Marie Antoinette soon afterward.

Pius VI compared the fate of the French sovereigns guillotined in 1793 to that of Mary Queen of Scots, with whom they deserved to be called martyrs for the Faith, and he stigmatized those responsible for the crime of regicide.

The Church in France had been turned upside-down, despoiled and nationalized. Priests and religious were persecuted, deported or killed for refusing to adhere to the Civil Constitution. Altars, statues and paintings were destroyed or sold, the liturgy altered beyond recognition, celibacy derided and clerical dress forbidden. The humanistic cult of Reason culminated in the horror of an actress of loose morals enthroned as a goddess near the high altar of Notre Dame Cathedral amidst an orgy of dancing, blasphemy and obscenity. The streets of Paris ran with the blood of thousands who were beheaded as enemies of the people.

But in 1795, the Revolution was forced to come to terms with the people of the Vendée and other regions where the true spirit of Catholic France remained unbroken. The new Parisian government, the more moderate "Directory," still felt secure enough, after defeating the first Austro-Prussian allied coalition, to send its armies into Northern Italy, under the command of the young General Napoleon Bonaparte.

Napoleon had distinguished himself early as a daring and resourceful young officer. After the abolition of the French monarchy in 1793, the National Convention (third revolutionary government), which had taught the people to rebel, itself lived in constant fear of popular rebellion. Bonaparte was put in command of troops ordered to quell the mob risings. His success made him Commander-in-chief of the Army of the Interior. His marriage in 1796 to Josephine Beauharnais, who had friends in the fourth revolutionary government, the Directory, led to his being put in charge as commander-in-chief of the army that was to invade Italy and take possession of the fertile lands of Lombardy ruled by Austria. General Bonaparte's repeated victories revealed his military and organizational genius.

Napoleon's Italian successes emboldened the Directory. He was ordered to march on Rome and overthrow the temporal power of the papacy. But he did not immediately do so, already filled with his own ideas. Even when the Austrian-held key fortress of Mantua fell to him and left the way open, he still did not proceed to Rome. He first ordered the Pope, by the Treaty of Tolentino, to pay an enormous sum and hand over the better part of the Church's territories, the Papal Legations. Then, on his own account, he set up the "Cis-Alpine Republic," modeled on the French Constitution.

Two archbishops opposed this "Republic" as incompatible with Catholic principles. Others left it.

The Cardinal-Bishop of Imola, Chiaramonti, stayed and found ways of accepting the *régime de facto,* while not sacrificing Catholic principles. He even told his clergy and people, when pressed to do so, that it was a form of democracy not incompatible with Christianity.

Pius VI had himself told the clergy of France to submit to the new government, the Directory, when there seemed no hope of renewing broken-off diplomatic relations.[7]

Cardinal Chiaramonti aimed to go along with the Republican *régime,* as far as possible, for the sake of preserving calm and order in the essential interests of religion. This was counter-matched by General Bonaparte's policy of going along with the Church, for all intents and purposes, but for exactly opposite reasons: he saw in Catholicism a force too powerful to eliminate (although that was the goal of the revolutionaries), and a subduable system necessary for achieving the conquest of Catholic peoples.

Cardinal and General—the two future protagonists as Pope and Emperor—were not yet destined to meet; for when in 1797 the General descended on occupied Imola and stayed in the episcopal palace, the Cardinal-Bishop was on his way to Rome, where Pius VI had summoned him out of danger.

The Pope also particularly valued Chiaramonti, a co-citizen of his own native Cesena, as an experienced and prudent adviser in the increasingly difficult circumstances. He further asked him to be ready to go with him into exile, if need be. The need did not arise, since Pius determined at all costs to remain in Rome, and Chiaramonti was able to return to his diocese, where he was regarded with general affection.

It has been surmised that the Pope chose Chiaramonti as his companion in the event of exile also because he considered the Cardinal a likely successor.

Meanwhile, a young Frenchman had been shot by papal guards in a skirmish, providing a pretext for the French Directory to renew orders for invading Rome. With Bonaparte in Egypt, General Berthier was given command, and early in 1798 he obeyed. Concealing his real intentions and promising to respect religion, he obtained the City's surrender. Representatives of the French Directory then decreed that, "by an act of the Sovereign People," the Pope's temporal power was ended; they declared the ancient Roman Republic reestablished. But within a year the French would be driven out by the Neapolitans and allied armies.

Pius VI had refused the British offer to help him escape from Rome. He was now told he must leave the city in three days to go to Siena; he was eventually taken to France, where he died.

Some cardinals were induced to sing a *Te Deum* of thanksgiving in St. Peter's for the "Roman Republic" for fear of what might happen if they refused. Others were imprisoned, exiled or forced to take flight—as did the English Cardinal York, Bishop of Frascati, who sought refuge in the kingdom of Naples.

Italian "patriots," revolutionaries and Jansenists, rejoiced over the suppression of papal temporal power. The head of the French schismatic Constitutional Church, Abbé Grégoire, proclaimed his satisfaction that the Pope would be free to carry on his pastoral ministry according to primitive tradition.

Napoleon, meanwhile, had maneuvered himself (not without some shady dealings) into becoming First Consul (1799) with practically sovereign powers. In this position he was to put order again into the administration of the French nation. In 1802 he would be proclaimed Consul for life, and in 1804 he would be asked by the Senate to adopt the title of Napoleon I, Emperor of the French.

★   ★   ★

The news of Pius VI's death in Valence in August, 1799 reached Imola in October. Meanwhile, the Revolution had been driven out of Italy by the Austrians, and Rome had been occupied by Neapolitan troops, with Lord Acton Prime Minister for the Bourbon King of Naples.

Pius VI had provided against the danger of the French holding a schismatic conclave by laying down that the true conclave electing his successor would be the one convoked by the Cardinal Dean of the Sacred College within the domains of a Catholic ruler. Venice was chosen, under Austrian protection, where already a number of cardinals, led by the Dean Albani and the English Cardinal York, had assembled. The Benedictine island Abbey of St. George provided necessary isolation and seclusion.

For Venice, then, Cardinal Chiaramonti would set out in December 1799. Impoverished by deprivation of revenues and personal charities, he would have to borrow money for the journey. Little would he foresee that the prayers he directed to be offered throughout his diocese to the Holy Spirit for a worthy successor to Pius VI were to result in his own election.

Just how providential this election was to be can be seen from his early training, experience and career as monk of St. Paul's in Rome, professor of theology at Parma and at the Roman University of St. Anselm, as Bishop of Tivoli and then Cardinal-Bishop of Imola in the thick of the fray during the time of the revolutionary Cis-Alpine Republic.

NOTES

1. The Holy Roman Empire was initiated on Christmas Day of the year 800 with Pope Leo III's coronation of King Charles of France—"Charlemagne"—as "Emperor of the Romans." Under the successors of the Emperor Charlemagne," France, Germany, Italy and Savoy constituted this empire—the "Holy Roman Empire." In 962 the King of the Germans, Otto I, was crowned Emperor by Pope John XII. From the 13th century until the 19th, almost all the Emperors were of the Austrian House of Hapsburg. The Holy Roman Emperor was, at least

nominally, the protector of the Church. The title was abolished by Napoleon in 1806, the Emperor Francis II taking the title of Emperor of Austria.

2. The Papal States or States of the Church were the territories ruled by the popes as temporal sovereigns. They began with the "Patrimony of Peter" after the Peace of Constantine in 313. The district around Rome, then the Romagna and Northern Duchies of Parma, Modena, Spoleto and the March of Ancona, and the provinces of Bologna, Perugia and Orvieto came to be included. In 1870 all these territories were seized by Italy, and the Papal States ceased to exist. The "Legations" were those provinces of the Papal States—such as Bologna, Ferrara, Romagna and Imola—which were governed by a papal legate.

3. The French Revolution passed through the following stages:

    a) The *National* or *Constituent Assembly* of 1789 confiscated ecclesiastical goods, suppressed religious orders, and in 1790 the clergy were required to take an oath of loyalty to the so-called "*Civil Constitution.*" Bishop Talleyrand took the oath and consecrated the Abbé Grégoire and other priests constitutional bishops, forming a national, schismatic French church; this schism was not healed until the Concordat of 1801. The *Civil Constitution of the Clergy* was condemned by Pope Pius VI and the clergy forbidden to take the oath by the papal brief *Quod aliquantum*, 1791. Some of the constitutional clergy abandoned the Faith altogether.

    b) The *Legislative Assembly* (second revolutionary government, 1791) legalized divorce, suppressed charitable associations and began the banishment or massacre of bishops, priests, men and women religious remaining faithful to the Holy See.

    c) The *National Convention* (third revolutionary government, 1792-1795) issued edicts against family life and private property, abolished the French monarchy and proclaimed a *Republic* in 1793. The execution of King Louis XVI and Queen Marie Antoinette in 1793 was followed by the "Reign of Terror." The Christian calendar was changed to one without holy days, saints' days or even Sunday. Notre Dame Cathedral was turned into a "Temple of Reason," other churches were desecrated or destroyed. Thousands of people were killed.

    d) The *Directory* (fourth revolutionary government, 1796), with the advent of Napoleon Bonaparte as First Consul in 1799, pursued a milder policy and bloodshed ceased, though the Catholic religion was in practice forbidden until the 1801 Concordat, which restored the Church's worship and government in France.

4. Jansenism was similar to Calvinism in denying free will and in teaching that neither divine grace nor human concupiscence could be resisted. These false teachings, and harsh over-emphasis on the fear of God, found their way into Catholic theology and fueled Febronianism, Josephism and French Gallicanism, all of which attempted to limit, or usurp, the authority of the Pope and the Holy See.
5. Edmund Burke, great orator and writer, *Reflections on the Revolution in France,* London, 1982 (first edition 1790).
6. Consistory of 1790.
7. The papal brief *Quod aliquantum,* 1791.

POPE PIUS VII

Northern Italy in the 18th and 19th centuries, showing the Legations and the Papal States (see page xxi, note 2), as well as the Republic of Venice and the various duchies. The Italian territories were united into the nation of Italy by Victor Emmanuel II in 1870.

EARLY YEARS

Benedictine Monk—Professor of Theology—
Abbot—Bishop of Tivoli

Barnabas Chiaramonti was born on the eve of the Feast of the Assumption of the Blessed Virgin Mary, 1742, in Cesena, not far from Bologna. The reigning Pope was Benedict XIV. His grandfather, Count Scipione Chiaramonti, related to the Clermonts of France, was a well-known mathematician and philosopher, friend of Galileo and fellow of several European universities, including Paris and Oxford. He became a priest late in life and founded the Oratorians of St. Philip Neri in Cesena.

Barnabas' father died when he was eight years old. His mother, the Marchioness Giovanna Ghini, brought up her five children—two sons older than he, one younger and a younger sister—strictly and piously. When he was 12, she entrusted him to the Benedictines of Mount St. Mary's Abbey just outside Cesena and is said to have foretold that he would become pope. She herself later retired to the Carmelite convent at Fano, where she died in 1777, after 15 years of exemplary religious life.

Not much is known of the boy Barnabas' early training. He was high-spirited, high-strung and not at first able to adapt himself to monastic discipline. He tried to set fire to his mattress in protest for being severely punished and rode a donkey up the main stairway to the upper story of the abbey, causing consternation among the monks resting in their cells.

Soon, though, he settled down and submitted to the Benedictine Rule under the gentle but firm guidance of his novice-master and experienced educators. After two year's trial, he was allowed to take the religious habit, with the name of Gregory, and was professed two years later in 1758.

Three years of studying for the priesthood at St. Paul's Abbey, Rome, culminated in a successful public debate before his being sent after ordination in 1761 to pursue philosophical studies at St. Justa's Abbey, Padua. St. Justa's had been a famed center of true reform and learning. The rule was well kept, with accompanying works of charity, but poverty imperfectly observed. Personal allowances were received from relatives for extras such as books, journeys and food to supplement the fare served in the refectory. Fr. Gregory's family had been obliged to move from their ancestral mansion to a smaller residence, and the little they could send him went mostly for books that formed the beginning of his private library.

A few years before his arrival, the germs of Jansenism had entered St. Justa's Abbey. The Venetian Inquisition discovered meetings held by a French Dominican in one of the monk's cells. There was no condemnation as the culprits had been careful to avoid any explicitly heretical opinions, but the damage was done. The false teaching spread to others of the community, and before long Venice itself was affected and infected. Material and political interests soon began to predominate over spiritual ones.

It was something of a miracle of grace that at this stage the future Pope remained immune from unorthodox tendencies and did not himself absorb the Jansenist views of some of his teachers, who looked askance at Rome and were hostile to the Jesuits. His experience at St. Justa's certainly afforded him first-hand knowledge of the Jansenist mentality, as well as its protean tactics of disguising itself and changing to suit all places and circumstances.

Fr. Gregory—or Dom Gregory, in the Italian usage—was

recalled to Rome in 1763 in order to complete his theological formation with a view to professorship at St. Anselm's College (at that time under the wing of St. Paul's Abbey), founded expressly to counteract Jansenist ideas that were penetrating Rome and religious life there.

Then from 1766 to 1775, Dom Gregory was professor of theology at St. John the Evangelist's College, Parma. Here he gained direct experience in what was practically a small-scale pre-experiment of the French Revolution. Voltaire was played in the theaters; the works of Locke, Hume, Rousseau and the French *"philosophes,"* sold in all the shops, were read and discussed in private and public.

Dom Gregory made full use of Parma's Palatine Library, one of the largest and most up-to-date of Italy. He was librarian of St. John's Abbey and caused eyebrows to be raised by altering the motto *Initium salutis sapientia et scientia* ("Wisdom and learning are the beginning of salvation") to *Initium salutis scientia et sapientia* ("Learning and wisdom are the beginning of salvation"). He felt this reversal of the last words was more in keeping with an age avid for learning. It also denoted his own teaching program. Putting learning before wisdom would not seem quite consonant with the Augustinian dictum and Anselmian philosophical principle, "Believe in order to understand," that he was later to profess and teach in Rome; yet if learning be truly grounded on moral norms, wisdom may certainly follow.

Dom Gregory's personal library included the complete works of St. Augustine, St. Basil, St. Athanasius, St. Gregory the Great, St. Jerome, St. Hilary and Lactantius. He had the works of other Fathers of the Church in critical editions brought out by the French Benedictine Maurists (founded in 1618 by St. Maur). The copy he acquired of the *Dictionnaire raisonné des Sciences, des Arts et des Métiers* by Diderot and his French *"philosophes"* collaborators (put on the Index of Forbidden Books by Clement XIII) was only for the Abbey library, which he felt ought to contain so famous a contemporary work whose shafts against faith and Christian morality, slipped into informative articles of considerable utility and interest, did much in disposing people's minds for revolution.

The young theological professor of St. John's, Parma, kept abreast of the times and must also have studied the famous work of the Abbé Condillac,[1] adopting what was good in his new psychological methods. But he distinguished between these and his faulty philosophical system that suppressed reflection in favor of ideas, all coming, according to Condillac, from experience or external sensations, the human mind being only a sort of mosaic.

Modernization of the little Duchy of Parma was carried out according to the physiocratic theory of "government by natural order," putting the cart before the horse, giving primacy to economy. Despite Pope Clement XIII's condemnation, reforms ill-suited to local conditions were hurried through. Writings from abroad (meaning Rome) were forbidden, the Jesuits expelled (before the general suppression) and foreign priests and religious banished. The people were assured that nothing was being changed essentially—only abuses being eliminated. The real defenders of Catholicism were "the friends of truth" (one title given by the Jansenists to themselves) and the "enlightened" governors of Parma— not the Pope, his medieval court and Roman immobilism.

The result was a short-lived disaster.

Upon the death of Clement XIV and accession of Pius VI, Dom Gregory was again called back to Rome and appointed to the highest teaching chair of his congregation, that of professor of theology at St. Anselm's. The College, founded in 1687 and opened by Innocent XI, aimed at remedying intellectual decadence in Benedictine monasticism, as well as counteracting Jansenism by the teaching of Anselmian philosophy.[2]

The loss of the archives taken in Napoleonic times to Paris leaves no data concerning the life of Dom Gregory Chiaramonti at this period. But known results of his professorship reflect the worth of the teacher: many of his students became, in turn, holders of highest university chairs or renowned for their lectures and writings.

Dom Gregory's great personal and intellectual gifts and outstanding success made him a sign of contradiction among some of his brethren. Besides this, he disapproved of the harsh punishments given by superiors for offenders against the Rule. The latter often came to him for help and consolation, and he was accused of inciting insubordination. He defended himself by quoting St. Bernard's maxim that a superior ought to be more loved than feared.

The matter came to the attention of Pius VI, and Dom Gregory was asked to explain himself. Hearing what he had to say so increased the Pope's already existing esteem that he made him an honorary abbot—having the title but not the government—of Mount St. Mary's, Cesena.

But here the same contradictions continued—what is known as persecution of the good by the good. Pius VI, on his way to Vienna in 1782, paid a personal visit to Mount St. Mary's. It was summer, and the Pope found his protégé's cell extraordinarily hot. He remarked on this and was told it was because the kitchen chimney passed through one of the walls.

The Pope went to see the Abbot, found him occupying a cool and spacious apartment and ordered him to change places with Dom Gregory, recalling the monastic duty of perfect mutual charity. But returning to Rome from Vienna in 1783, the Pope put an end to any further unpleasantness by withdrawing Dom Gregory from monastic life and appointing him Bishop of Tivoli.

The monks of St. Paul's Abbey, as well as Cesena, proffered their apologies to the newly elected Bishop, admitted they had been wrong and, in true Benedictine spirit, tried to make up for the past. Bishop Gregory had only words of forgiveness, charity and peace for all.

The new Bishop's ancient aristocratic family background assured him the most respectful welcome from clergy, city governors and people of all classes who still respected time-honored traditional standards. They were astonished to see their pastor as simple and cordial as he was distinguished and cultured and were moved to admiration by his being at all times available.

Bishop Chiaramonti's time was passed in prayer, spiritual exercises, diocesan business and pastoral visitations. He lived with utmost simplicity and frugality, as was always his custom. No archives of his bishopric are still in existence, but details are available concerning his inspection of churches in which he personally ordered redecoration and repairs in minutest detail: walls to be white-washed, tiles of roofs and floors to be replaced, vestments mended, windows cleaned, candlesticks cleaned and polished, missals renewed and worn missal-markers changed for new ones. He took away the benefice of a chaplain whose altar was in a state of neglect until the chaplain had carried out restoration work.

The new Bishop visited his diocese three times in one and a half years. He had to go to some parishes on foot, others on horseback or riding a mule where there was only a rocky and steep track.

Bishop Chiaramonti, for all his mildness and gentleness, showed absolute firmness, even righteous anger, where his episcopal rights were concerned.

Soon after he took possession of his diocese, a picture of Pope Clement XIV (who had suppressed the Jesuit Order) with a halo around his head had appeared posted on the cathedral wall. (The new Bishop was aware that his predecessor had avoided publishing the papal bull suppressing the Jesuits by temporarily retiring and leaving his vicar general to read it. This had scandalized the local Jansenists, loud in their defense of papal authority—in this particular case.) The picture of Clement XIV had appeared without the Bishop's knowledge or permission, was implicitly pro-Jansenist and explicitly anticipated the canonical judgment of the Church with regard to the sanctity of this Pope. Bishop Chiaramonti therefore had the picture removed, but he found that reproductions were being distributed for sale with permission of the Dominican Holy Office official in Tivoli, an ardent advocate of the cause of Clement XIV.

The official refused to withdraw the pictures, and Bishop Chiaramonti was obliged to insist on recognition of his rights as local Ordinary, under threat of ecclesiastical sanctions.

Meanwhile the Bishop became aware that the Dominican official in Tivoli was being underhandedly supported by a colleague holding a key post in Rome in the papal administration. He also suspected that the whole affair had been started by the Jansenists. They still had their spies everywhere, probably knew of his former anti-Jesuitical teachers and now wanted to provoke him, as Bishop, into taking an open stand.

This conviction grew as the Tivoli official, with the backing of the Roman one, continued to resist and defy the authority of Bishop Chiaramonti. The only thing to do was to lay the matter directly before Pius VI—which he did, humbly offering, if justice were not done and his juridical rights not respected, to resign.

The Pope pronounced Bishop Chiaramonti fully in the right and ordered the matter settled accordingly.

The incident is told in considerably more detail by the great papal historian von Pastor,[3] naming all persons concerned, which would not be within the compass of this work.

Pius VI several times invited Bishop Chiaramonti to stay in Rome at the Quirinal Palace. But much as he revered and was grateful to the Pope who had so benefited him, he did not feel at ease in the grand life of the papal court. Personal letters of his reveal how much his simple and frank nature disliked the petty calculations of the "clerical labyrinth," as he called it.

The Pope was informed of the Bishop's constant zeal and good works; Bishop Chiaramonti was loved by the people whom he governed, and he taught and sanctified with rare intelligence and fatherly goodness. In 1785, Pius VI created him cardinal and appointed him to the vacant bishopric of Imola.

When he took leave of the clergy and people of Tivoli, after only a year and a half as their Bishop, many wept to lose him, and some predicted he would become Pope.

Chiaramonti waited in Rome for a while at St. Paul's Abbey, where he wrote his first pastoral letter to the clergy and people of his new diocese. Directly and frankly, avoiding the formal style in vogue with many bishops of the time, he asked the secular clergy in particular to preach less by words than by example, warned them against the false worldly spirit of the times and told them that if any committing faults paid no heed to his fatherly correction, he would show himself to be a severe judge and spare no effort in seeing that the prescriptions laid down by the Council of Trent regarding the clergy be exactly enforced.

NOTES

1. Etienne de Condillac (1715-1780), a priest who never exercised his priestly powers, tutor of Louis XV, friend of Rousseau and disciple of Locke. The Italian translation of his *Origins of Human Knowledge* was dedicated, with critical introduction, to Chiaramonti when he became Bishop of Tivoli.
2. St. Anselm, Archbishop of Canterbury (1033-1109), followed St. Augustine's dictum *Crede ut intelligas*—"Believe in order to understand." Faith, obtained from Christ and His Church, is the source of all knowledge leading to infallible truth. The moral and reasoning effort needed for possession of truth through mastery of Anselmian philosophy was considered the most efficacious means for rectifying the warped pseudo-Augustinian teachings of Jansenism's originator, Bishop Jansenius of Ypres (1585-1638), which, among other errors (and purporting to remedy ecclesiastical laxity) gave undue regard to political and temporal matters at the expense of spiritual and supernatural ones.
3. Ludwig von Pastor, *History of the Popes*, vols. 39 and 40.

~ 2 ~

CARDINAL CHIARAMONTI OF IMOLA

The Future Pontiff
Faces the Revolution

Dom Gregory Chiaramonti is recorded as having assumed the cardinalate with such outward indifference as to seem unreal. Nonetheless, the monks of St. Paul's fêted their newly created cardinal in grand style on the day of his taking possession of his titular Roman Church of St. Calixtus.

To avoid too much fuss being made, he chose not to publish the date of his entering Imola and did so unnoticed after nightfall. He would not at once receive the official visits of clergy and civil and military public authorities but, saying he was tired, kept them waiting a couple of days. Then all were struck by the new Cardinal-Bishop's extreme simplicity and dignified amiability.

Cardinal Chiaramonti was now forty two. The portrait of him painted by the Roman artist Millione shows a man of upright bearing: deep, dark eyes under thick, sweeping brows and high, limpid forehead crowned by dark, flowing locks; an expression of great determination and firmness, the full-lipped mouth ready to break into a smile—face and figure eminently reflecting gentleness and serenity.

His ancestors of Cesena had for generations been prominent in religious and civil affairs, so he was quite at home among all classes of people in Imola, a neighboring city, and knew just how to speak to them: Imola recognized in him a true and worthy pastor.

His first pastoral letter had been welcomed—his putting all on guard against the false spirit of the times and denunciation of its dangers: "The shades of darkness have much overrun almost every epoch, but their obscuring of ours is almost beyond description. The furious persecutions, schisms and heresies in the history of the Church have surely been outpassed—it is evident to anyone who soundly reflects—by a philosophical method insinuating and masking itself by every sort of guile. To destroy from top to bottom the religion established by God and ruin traditional standards and moral customs, the new ideas are daily spread among the masses by perverted and depraved men, in reality feeblest among others, but deluding themselves they are strongest."

Chiaramonti knew that to win these compatriots of his, whom he regarded with fatherly love, and who in turn were ready to look to him with affectionate respect, he had to speak to their hearts. He begged them "not to follow the standards of unbelievers who, with their shallow-thinking pamphlets and deceiving conversation, mingle daily with you propagating disastrous ideas." He bade them all beware of false persons here, there and everywhere undermining right notions, and be obedient to superiors, submissive to those in authority and available for every kind of good work.

The Cardinal-Bishop was made a patrician and magistrate of the city council but was careful not to take direct part in any administrative business. He regarded his position as honorary and held himself aloof from civil and temporal affairs.

How necessary the warnings in his pastoral letter had been soon became apparent. During the years before the outbreak of the French Revolution, more and more of its agents were discovered entering Italy, and passport controls were tightened up. They came disguised as commercial travelers, tourists and pilgrims, some even masquerading as priests. In Imola, a revolutionary agent was discovered working unsuspected as a ladies' hairdresser.

Whether he wanted to or not, the Cardinal-Bishop in his

judicial capacity soon found himself dealing with a serious violation of papal authority and corruption amounting to an organized mafia on the part of a lay administrator.[1] Several times summoned to appear before Chiaramonti, the culprit refused, flouted his authority and went to Rome to justify himself before the papal court. Great courage and firmness were needed to deal with the case. The previous bishop had either been ignorant of the matter or failed to act, and it fell to Chiaramonti to inform Rome of the enormity of what had been going on and fearlessly reveal the lies and cunning. He finally succeeded in ridding the diocese of the corrupt administrator, whom the long-exploited and terrorized inhabitants of the region had not dared accuse and bring to justice.

After the outbreak of the Revolution hundreds, then thousands of French emigrants, many of them priests and religious, began arriving in Northern Italy and the Papal States to escape persecution. Imola was a small city; there had been bad harvests, and it was all the people could do to find food and shelter for the refugees, deprived of everything and with no resources.

One of these was brought before the Cardinal as suspected of being a spy, and he admitted having spoken of a planned French landing at Ancona. But closely questioned, it turned out he had read of this as a maneuver actually proposed by Voltaire with the idea of looting the nearby Sanctuary of the Holy Family, the Holy House of Loreto, for its supposed vastly rich treasure.

Then in 1791, a well-known citizen of Imola was accused and found implicated, as a French agent, in a large-scale conspiracy from Bologna to overthrow the papal government. Tension became acute and Rome was alarmed. Pius VI refused to receive the French ambassador and recalled the nuncio from Paris; diplomatic relations were broken off. A French invasion of the Papal States was feared. A pretext for such a threat was afforded by the arrest in Rome of two French art students for having made and exhibited a statue of *Fanaticism* (papal government) overthrown by *Reason* (Revolutionism).

The Pope was threatened that if he refused to release the students, justice would be done and his States invaded.

Nothing came of the threat, but in 1793 a far more serious pretext was provided by the death of a young French embassy official in a scuffle which he himself had provoked. The young official's death was doubly heinous in the eyes of the French government: he had been fired on by the papal police and, with his dying breath, had renounced the Republican Civil Constitution of the Clergy,[2] asking for a "proper priest" to give him the Last Sacraments.

Cardinal Chiaramonti happened to come to Rome shortly after the incident on an *ad limina* visit to the tombs of the Apostles. He found the city still in ferment, though order was gradually returning with severe police measures and the clergy preaching calm and tranquility in the public squares.

But almost immediately, news came of the guillotining of Louis XVI. The Pope refrained from making an immediate public announcement. Nor was the French government, forced to come to terms with popular armed uprisings in the Vendée and other regions where priests and people were demanding liberty for religion and the Church, in a strong enough position to follow up further threats of invasion.

The Pope was advised by the Spanish ambassador in Rome to come to terms with the French Republic, as Spain was doing. But Pius VI declined the advice, saying he felt reassured by Britain's joining the First Allied Coalition[3] and by the presence in the Mediterranean of an English fleet. Pius VI convoked a secret consistory of the Sacred College and condemned the regicidal crime of the French government. Cardinal Chiaramonti would certainly have been present at the consistory.

Returning to Imola, he found things fairly quiet. The fall of Robespierre, the end of the Reign of Terror in France and the toleration of religious practice by the new government, the milder Directory, gave hopes of better days. But the financial crisis of 1794 and 1795 in Rome and many regions of Italy had caused widespread misery and discontent. Rising prices, speculation, inflation and devaluation obliged the papal government to have recourse to base coin. Popular uprisings, hitherto anti-French, became anti-papal. Agitators had fertile ground for sowing seeds of unrest.

Then early in 1796, news suddenly reached Rome that a French army of 10,000 strong was advancing from the North. The next thing known was that Bonaparte had entered Milan, where the victorious General proclaimed his intention of marching on Rome to "liberate the people from their long enslavement." The French Directory had ordered him personally to conduct the invasion, so as "to overthrow the last of the popes and take the tiara from the pretended Head of the universal Church."

Bonaparte was in a position to march on Rome after the fall of the key fortress city of Mantua. But he did not move at once, wanting rather to use Catholicism to conquer the Italians. After biding his time, he ordered two of his generals to begin by overrunning the Romagna. Imola was one of the first cities to be occupied, offering little or no resistance.

Cardinal Chiaramonti went to meet the French General Augerau and offer him hospitality in the episcopal palace. Mastering his natural feelings, he knew it was in the best interests of his defenseless flock to show courtesy toward the French invaders. The General, a magnificent figure of a man but a rough and hardened soldier, could not help responding to the simple grandeur and gentleness of this Prince of the Church. Seeing the example set by their Bishop, the people stifled their indignation and behaved with the same moderation and courtesy—all except a band of latent sympathizers with the Revolution, some lawyers and doctors and a conventual Franciscan. A few priests favored the new democratic ideas, but most of the clergy and people were united.

A large ransom payment was demanded as Imola's contribution to the war of "liberation," but it could not be raised. The Cardinal eventually managed to find the money and thus save the situation. But not satisfied, the French occupiers went on to requisition goods and food for the soldiers quartered in the city. The Cardinal intervened by ordering inventories to be submitted to him of all goods and provisions possessed by the clergy, monasteries, convents and sanctuaries of the diocese under pain of sanctions for any not complying. He gave himself no rest day and night until he saw his orders carried out, then ordered reasonable amounts to be collected and handed over. Serious trouble for his people and threatened suspension of public services in protest were avoided.

Thus far, the Cardinal had succeeded in rallying clergy and people, though not without some individual complaint, in a situation of great, general emergency. Other cities such as Ravenna and Lugo, subjected to similar demands, had refused and were on the verge of insurrection, to their much heavier cost.

But when in due course the French demanded from Imola still more goods and sums of money, and these could not be supplied, they threatened to break into and plunder the pawnbroking establishment. Many of the poorer people had been obliged, through want, to pawn their modest valuables, and this proved too much. Free rein was given to popular indignation. Housewives surged into the streets armed with sticks, rolling pins and kitchen implements and surrounded the French officers before the building. Swelled by husbands and men at work in various parts of the city, the mob grew so menacing that one of the officers drew his sword; blood would have been shed but for the Cardinal's appearance on the scene at that moment.

His stern appeal for order calmed the people. But one of the younger officers was foolish enough to step forward with drawn sword and threaten the Cardinal. The fury of the crowd broke out again, and the officer would have been lynched if the Cardinal had not commanded the people to draw back. Overwhelmed by the bravery of the man who had saved his life, the young soldier went up before all and tearfully embraced him. He became the Cardinal's guest in the episcopal palace and, after the French had withdrawn, returned to pay him a visit.

Thanks to Cardinal Chiaramonti, Imola for the most part remained calm; but other occupied cities did not. Lugo was particularly known for its religious conservatism and fidelity to the papal government. All classes of clergy and people abhorred the Revolution, and armed resistance had for some time been thought of. A demand for silver ornaments to be given up from the churches caused an outcry, and when commissioners arrived to take away the statue of the city's patron, St. Hilary, they were set upon. The people took up arms, recovered the statue and were momentarily masters of the situation. They stirred up the inhabitants of neighboring cities to drive the French out. Emissaries were sent to Rome to obtain the Pope's blessing on the holy war.

Cardinal Chiaramonti foresaw certain defeat and terrible consequences from such an undertaking. He was determined to intervene, confident that his authority would persuade the insurgents. But the people of Imola would not let their indispensable protector go, and blocked all ways out of the city so that the Cardinal had to resign himself to sending messengers—but to no avail. The people of Imola were insulted and injured, and Chiaramonti was called a sympathizer with the French.

He managed to send a second and severer appeal for calm and order, this time in the name of the Sovereign Pontiff, who, far from giving his blessing on the "holy war," had expressed his strong disapproval. But this too failed.

The distraught Cardinal learned of Bonaparte's threats and of his orders to General Augerau to march and take the city of Lugo. But Augerau hesitated. The thought of innocent blood having to be shed—the insurgents were only a minority—and above all the Cardinal's entreaties obtained a counter-order on condition of surrender.

But it was too late: another column of the French army was already moving toward Lugo. The city was sacked. The soldiers rode on horseback into the churches and grabbed any precious objects they could find—ornaments, chalices and monstrances. When they left, the devastated city was without police or military protection. Brigands from the surrounding countryside swooped down and pillaged all that the French had not been able to take. Nothing remained when those returned who had fled before the battle, having refused to heed the Cardinal's appeals for calm and order.

The situation throughout the Papal States had become increasingly alarming. Coming from Milan, Bonaparte had arrived in Bologna and arrested the Cardinal-legate governor, holding him hostage. Pius VI, fearing the same fate for Cardinal Chiaramonti, ordered him to seek temporary refuge in his home city of Cesena and from there to prepare to come to Rome. In fact, Bonaparte had formed a mobile column for invasion of the Papal States, proclaiming as justification the "provocations of the papal court."

The Cardinal got away just in time. At 5:00 in the morning of the following day, Bonaparte descended on Imola and took up his quarters in the episcopal palace. He had evidently counted on the cooperation of Chiaramonti, whom the French Directory had listed as a "patriot" because of his frequent appeals for submission in regard to the French conquerors. Bonaparte was surprised to find the Cardinal gone and the diocese governed by the Vicar General, an unyielding aristocrat.

So Bonaparte acted on his own. He gathered all the priests and religious of the diocese and told them in Italian that priests must mind their own business, not busy themselves with political affairs, and must preach the Gospel and inculcate obedience, docility and peace. He himself had wanted peace, but the Pope had repulsed him. Bonaparte left Imola a few days later and repeated the same words to the clergy of Cesena—but again, the future Emperor and future Pope were not yet destined to meet, for by that time Cardinal Chiaramonti was on his way to Rome.

He had traveled quickly, while the way was still free, hearing of the lightning advance of the French armies. Reaching Rome, where he stayed at St. Paul's Abbey, he was told by the Pope to be ready to accompany him into exile at Terracina, on the borders of the kingdom of Naples. But after a long and laborious night discussion, the Pope and cardinals decided to ask for an armistice. When Chiaramonti came to the Quirinal Palace the next morning, he was told the Pope had changed his mind.

The Treaty of Tolentino was concluded with the French invaders in 1797, and there was interim peace of a kind—but Pius VI was obliged to cede all his rights over the papal territories known as "the Legations," that is, Bologna, Ferrara, Imola and the Romagna, as well as pay an enormous sum and hand over priceless manuscripts and works of art.

Before leaving for his Egyptian campaign, Bonaparte proclaimed from Milan the setting up of a "Cis-Alpine Republic"[4] modelled on the French Revolution's Constitution of 1790. Among other things this meant that the Papal Legations, removed from the Church's temporal domains and government, were to be ruled by Italian mandatories under the control of the French. It was supposed to be a democracy, run on anti-aristocratic, anti-hierarchical, egalitarian lines. Ecclesiastics were deprived of their titles and revenues. But Italian and French Republicans alike realized that the changeover from a theocracy to a "Republic" based on revolutionary principles would be slow and difficult.

A "Tree of Liberty" was planted in the two main squares of Imola to the ringing of bells, rolling of drums, the playing of violins and a fireworks display at which all the civil and religious authorities were obliged to be present. However, during the transition of government, the Cardinal-Bishop's presence and guiding hand were needed, in social as well as religious matters. The Catholic religion was proclaimed official; but convents and monasteries were closed, their property confiscated and religious processions prohibited.

Chiaramonti was loved by his people and valued and respected by the French occupiers. A letter was addressed to "Citizen Cardinal" in Rome by the members of the new Imola city council, asking him to return: ". . .We are your sons and you our Father. We know your heart and have recourse to you, certain that we shall see you again without delay. . ." ran part of the letter.

The Cardinal's appreciative and affectionate reply announcing his return—which in fact he had already, God willing, decided upon—was accompanied by a further pastoral letter emphasizing the need for Christian charity and humility in submitting to the new Republican order established by the victorious commander-in-chief of the French army in Italy, Napoleon Bonaparte.

"Citizen" Chiaramonti was welcomed back by all. Nevertheless, he was shortly afterwards enjoined by the new Minister of Police to order the suppression of prayers for the Emperor and princes and to substitute prayers "for all in authority and the good of the people in the Cis-Alpine Republic." He was next required to suppress the Good Friday and Holy Saturday prayers *pro perfidis Judaeis.*[5]

Then "Citizen Cardinal" was informed by the local commissars of the Parisian Directory that "a religion such as that of Christ, founded on humility, is incompatible with pomp and display." So as once again "to put into force the simple maxims of the Gospel," the Cardinal-Bishop was invited to remove from the altars every sign of ecclesiastical and aristocratical distinction, diametrically opposed to principles of Republican equality, and to take away the dais, steps and baldequin of the episcopal throne. "Seeing you more humble, the people will respect you more and you will gain the confidence of a government that does not allow distinctions among citizens."

Unlike the Cardinal-Archbishop of Bologna, Mattei, who hotly replied to such a request by stating that the Church's government is not democratic and popular but monarchical and aristocratic, calling to witness the Saints and Fathers of the Church, Chiaramonti calmly replied that he would have the baldequin taken down, although he was persuaded that, from the study of the history of sacred rites, his enlightened citizen commissars would admit that what they complained of had a different origin and purpose from pomp and pride.

He was equally sure they would not confuse worldly aristocratic family lineage with hierarchical degrees in the Church instituted by Christ.

"Citizen Cardinal" further begged leave not to remove the dais and steps of the throne for the time being, as he found that in other cities of the Republic these had been conserved, and wondered why Imola should in this matter be so distinguished. Also, he did not see why, on principles of equality, the elevation of university professors' chairs above the students should be viewed with complacency, while the cathedral chairs of Christ's ministers so raised should be objected to.

The egalitarian, Republican motto of the new rulers, *Liberty, Equality, Fraternity,* had the Cardinal's compliance in all things possible without betraying Christian principles. This was adroitly reflected in a genial manner by the new heading which the "Citizen Bishop" put on his writing paper: *Liberty* was printed at the top lefthand corner, *Equality* to the right, but instead of *Fraternity,* there was printed in the middle *And Peace in Our Lord Jesus Christ,* preserving the religious principle.

Before long, Chiaramonti was approached by the new rulers concerning the composing of a special pastoral letter. He was presented with a copy of one written by his brother citizen Bishop of Pavia that was very favorable to the Republican government and was asked to publish another on similar lines. The Cardinal demurred. The invitation became an order. "The duties of your ministry require it. It is time the people understood that the Catholic religion is conformable to the principles of Republican *Liberty, Equality and Fraternity."* None could explain this better than Citizen Cardinal Chiaramonti. He was required to make clear that the spirit of the Gospel is founded on these maxims.

Obliged to comply, the Cardinal agreed, but set out his reasons for composing and delivering a homily instead of a pastoral: "Churches are places particularly consecrated to the worship of God, where the faithful go to pray and procure the help of God's grace and hear the Gospel of Jesus Christ, where the Sacraments are administered and the people instructed in the mysteries of Faith and Christian duties.

"The holy Catholic Religion is the perpetual and unique source of true happiness, of public tranquility, of peace and of that submission to government without which social order cannot be conserved."

As for himself, he had not ceased to inculcate, in such terms as were laid down by General Bonaparte, that the clergy should not meddle with politics, and he hoped that the promised pastoral letter he had drafted in the form of a homily and intended to deliver at Christmas would serve further to animate clergy and people.

The Cardinal had been ordered to show that the Gospel is based on the Republican motto *Liberty, Equality, Fraternity,* and in no way opposed to democracy. He turned the tables on the Republican democrats by implying that *true* liberty, equality and fraternity are based on the Gospel.

The famous Christmas homily first views God's gifts of the Creation, the Law of Moses and the Incarnation and shows our chief duty to God to be one of gratitude, obedience and humility. It goes on to state that true *liberty* is also God's gift—the power to do, or not to do, His will and the will of men: free correspondence with divine grace, without which all on earth is servitude and sin. Abuse of liberty contradicts God's sovereign and temporal laws. Social duties require obedience to civil authority just as religious ones do toward the spiritual. Does this precept apply to all forms of government? To monarchy, no doubt. But may a Christian in conscience submit to democracy? Is democracy incompatible with the Catholic Church?

The Republican form of democratic government is not incompatible with the Gospel of Christ and His Church. But to be true it needs those virtues that are only acquired in the school of Christ. In other words, if there is no virtue, there is no true democracy.

Equality is unknown to philosophy. True equality is revealed in the Gospel of Christ, who told His followers to renounce themselves, so that St. Paul made himself "all things to all." But equality of natural and intellectual powers, wealth, character and virtues does not, never has and never can exist. Such arithmetical equality would end by upsetting both the physical and moral order. True equality is not a relationship limited to human beings, but is a relationship among them toward God the Creator, who alone is their true reward—the God of pure, disinterested love, who wills the salvation of all.

Fraternity—charity, brotherly love—is the soul of Christianity. This cannot be attained except by prayer and the interior, spiritual life. By charity, Christ wills to unite all, in the freedom of love and mutual respect. This is impossible without humility—"the humility and obedience of the Saviour Himself."

These are the main points in outline of Cardinal Chiaramonti's 1797 Christmas homily—unique among others of the time in tone, form and content—which was immediately published by the Republican press and distributed to the civil authorities and clergy of the diocese. It was inevitably criticized as having been influenced by liberal movements in Europe and America. But the homily was in time forgotten, deliberately by some, after Napoleon became Emperor and Chiaramonti Pope.

Bishop Grégoire, former head of the French Constitutional Church, was to translate and publish the homily in 1814. He praised the Cardinal for his "love of religion and liberty, and overwhelming charity," but suppressed certain phrases. The partisans of the Italian *Risorgimento*[6] tried to use the homily. In 1836, a liberal priest of the movement requested a copy from Cardinal Mastai, then Bishop of Imola and future Pope Pius IX, but was firmly refused. The original Italian text was not republished until 1859, with an editorial note that "the great Homily will speak to the heart of all that have imprinted on their minds love of the faith of their fathers and of the common fatherland."

The Cardinal-Bishop had found a way of conforming to governmental requirements while keeping intact all the requirements of religion. But now he was faced with a

situation for which there could be no such solution: the com-
pulsory oath of fidelity to the Cis-Alpine Constitution and
of hatred for sovereigns, which no Catholic could in conscience take.

The local commissaries used every argument to obtain the
head of the diocese's acceptance of the oath, but were courteously though firmly told it was incompatible with Catholic
principles and belief. Such was the respect amounting to veneration for the Cardinal felt by the government officials and
even by members of the French Directory itself that for the
time they did not insist.

Imola, meanwhile, heard of the occupation of Rome by
General Berthier at the beginning of February, 1798, and the
abduction of Pius VI, causing the greatest grief for the Cardinal
personally, as well as for the Church. But life in his diocese
continued little affected outwardly as part of a Republic become independent of papal administration. Nor did Cardinal
Chiaramonti, a Benedictine monk, mind being reduced to
complete poverty, deprived of his revenues. He was only distressed at being powerless to help others hard hit by high
taxation, rising costs and scarcity of necessary goods.

Vexatious laws for religious and civil life continued to be
passed. The *Corpus Christi* procession that year was reluctantly allowed to go through the streets, crowds following
the Cardinal carrying the Blessed Sacrament. But the Milan
Directory soon afterward prohibited any future manifesta-
tions of religious worship outside church precincts, including
burial services in the cemetery. The clergy were forbidden
to ring bells, hold up the crucifix, chant prayers for the dead,
incense the coffin or bless the grave.

The city council attempted to make up for the curtailing
of religious rites, which the people were devoutly attached
to, by giving free public concerts, operatic performances and
"patriotic" banquets with ballroom dancing. At first many
succumbed to these attractions. But the Cardinal retaliated
by singing Vespers every evening in the cathedral with great
solemnity and beauty. This gradually drew more people than

those attending government concerts, shows, banquets and dancing. People came to the cathedral also in prayerful and silent protest for the arrest and imprisonment of the cathedral chapter clergy for the sole crime of wearing their violet hoods, which had been forbidden because they denoted canonical dignity and distinction.

The Republican fidelity oath continued to cause division and discord among most of the clergy and people of all classes, especially teachers and students. A youth club had been started and was presided over by a conventual Franciscan, an enthusiastic supporter of the French Republican régime. His daily harangues had persuaded a good many of the young people of the need for being "patriots." But their parents and teachers mostly remained adamant in refusing to take the oath. So the government's only recourse was to dismiss and replace them with others "more worthy of confidence." Among these was the Franciscan youth club leader, who was given the chair of philosophy newly established in the city hall.

The young people of the youth club said they thought the "red Franciscan," as he came to be called, was a very remarkable president and preached better than anyone else. Others were shocked to hear a priest holding forth against religious devotions, the saints and even the Pope. He would sometimes be seen in his Franciscan habit and sometimes fashionably dressed. When some ventured to express pained surprise at seeing a priest attired like that, they received the reply: "I dress like this for going to the theater!"

The Franciscan "red monk" was something of an enigma, for in spite of these revolutionary habits, he was acknowledged a gifted, genuinely religious person. He said Mass every morning and was regularly present in his stall for the recital of the Divine Office in his monastery, one of the only ones not suppressed.

The Cardinal would say no more than that he was "a bit of a rebel—but a son all the same." This in spite of knowing that sometimes after haranguing the youth club the Franciscan would go about the streets in lay dress accompanied by young "patriot" friends shouting "Long live the Republic!" and "Death to princes and kings!" He and his group would occasionally gather after dark below the windows of the episcopal palace, sing profane songs and call the Cardinal names. Once a voice was heard crying, "Death to Chiaramonti!"

Later when normal times returned, the "red Franciscan" admitted having insulted the Cardinal, but denied he had himself used or been a party to these words. He excused his collaboration with the French Republicans by declaring he had only "accepted what was acceptable" of the Revolution, as had many other clergy and lay persons.

Months went by and more and more citizens, who had at first been glad to shake off the yoke of papal government, longed to have it back and be liberated from their liberators. The Cardinal celebrated midnight Mass of that year, 1798, with no ringing of bells and no outward signs of the festivity now forbidden by law, leaving a void in many hearts. Some may have thought rather ruefully of the Christmas homily their bishop had delivered the year before, declaring the Gospel compatible with Republican democracy. For the new régime had ignored his counsels, oppressed the Church, and made all but vain his efforts toward coexistence and reciprocal understanding. It had taken advantage of his leniency and goodness by increasing government control based on antireligious principles. Far from lending itself to a "baptism" which should have made virtuous Catholics good democrats, the régime had betrayed the Cardinal's confidence and systematically diminished Catholicism in the name of democracy.

Everything had to be modelled on Paris in what, for all intents and purposes, had become a French colony, offending the people as much in their national pride as in their Religion.

Most rejoiced when news reached Imola of the Austro-Russian allies of the second anti-French coalition occupying Verona, and some emboldened extremists in the spring of 1799 uprooted the Tree of Liberty in the piazza.

General Hulin, more terrible than Augerau, threatened from Bologna to raze the city of Imola. But the people in

mountainous regions, fired by Imola's example, uprooted their
Trees of Liberty and came down to the city. Soon there
gathered a howling mob that French democratic bayonets
could not check. The "red monk" and his friends fled to
the episcopal palace and implored the Cardinal's protection.

Hulin was prevented from entering Imola by an advance
guard of Austrians and a band of armed local (anti-Republican)
insurgents who appeared as he approached.

Feelings exploded, church bells were rung, people danced
around a bonfire made from the Tree of Liberty. The houses
of Italian "patriots" were assaulted, the prison forced open
and political prisoners released.

The city councillors were powerless. The one person able
to intervene was "Citizen Chiaramonti," who appealed for
calm and order—more necessary than anyone realized. For,
after doing their liberating work, the Austrian forces retired
and so did the local insurgents. Imola was left defenseless
and in fear of reprisals.

Hulin once again was approaching. The Cardinal had publicly declared he would be ready, in case of need, to mediate
in any way, go anywhere and meet anyone in any emergency.
So a delegation was formed, headed by the Cardinal, and
set out in the middle of the night in the hope of forestalling
the formidable General.

Dawn was breaking as the party arrived at a Sanctuary
Church of the Blessed Virgin. The group halted, the Cardinal went in to worship and was soon lost in prayer. But Hulin
swiftly drew near, scoffing at the delegates' cries for clemency
and in a stentorian voice ordered his men to march on.

The Cardinal heard and hurried out of the church from
praying to Our Lady to supplicate with Hulin: on his knees,
his voice choked with sobs, he pleaded that he had always
enjoined submission and preached calm and order. He begged
for the lives of the majority of innocent citizens not guilty
of the excesses of those who had not listened to the voice
of their pastor.

Touched, and finally moved, the terrible Hulin condescended, demanded a war payment of shirts and shoes and told the Cardinal they could proceed to Imola together, but he would not be responsible for what might occur if any signs of resistance were seen on entry.

Early in the morning, the people of the city anxiously waiting were amazed at the sight of the formidable French general and his mounted troops peacefully riding through the streets accompanied by the Cardinal-Bishop, clergy and nobles. But the Cardinal had hardly time to get back to his residence, giving thanks to God, overcome more by emotion than fatigue, than news was brought him of Hulin's order for a band of insurgents, captured as they tried to get away, to be shot in the main square. He set out again in all haste to intercede for them, but too late. The sounds of shooting came to him before he could arrive to see the blood-spattered Tree of Liberty being replanted over the fallen bodies.

A few days later, the Austrians returned, struck down the Tree of Liberty and once more withdrew.

But soon the local insurgents came back down from the mountains, better armed and in greater numbers, and took possession of the city. Their triumph was now lasting, for the Austrians were pouring into the country from the North. Imola's "patriot" citizens with the "red monk" and his friends were put under guard. Handed over to the Austrian authorities and brought before the imperial court of justice at Bologna, they escaped the death penalty, thanks to the Cardinal's further appeal for clemency.

These appeals of his for submission and mercy earned Chiaramonti the reputation of being a friend of the Revolution—so much so that, although he never lost the respect and affection of most of his people, he felt obliged to justify his attitude and conduct, with due dignity and in due measure, in a pastoral letter.

Among the Cardinal's accusers were some who had benefited from his forbearance, counsel, prestige and clemency, and had forgotten. But his knowledge and experience of human nature were too great to leave room for resentment; his supernatural charity at once completely pardoned, although his sensitive and loving nature suffered from the veiled or open reproaches. He had, though, the supreme consolation of knowing that, as father and head of his flock, he had only tried on all occasions to make himself, in Christ, all things to all. He had done his best to do his duty as a bishop, without giving way on Christian principle. His own natural gaiety, too, made him rise above human pettiness.

Life returned to normal in Imola. The Austrian Emperor's troops were firmly installed in the Romagna and other Legations. The singing of a *Te Deum* of thanksgiving in the cathedral, presided over by the Cardinal, was followed by a procession led by him of all the clergy, religious orders, confraternities and civil authorities through the festooned streets to the ringing and chiming of church bells, with the armed forces rendering military honors.

Outwardly, order as in the past was reestablished. Inward pacification and reconciliation of minds and hearts after the crisis and bitter experience had still to be effected. The Cardinal waited for the first excitement to die down, then let his voice be heard, giving clergy and people renewed guidelines by a forceful reminder of the first and foremost duty of Christian charity. It was hardly a year since his Christmas homily, and his task was a delicate one.

"Our sins provoked God's anger, our faults and failings drew down on us the divine chastisement," he told his people: "days of sorrow and darkness seen from a human standpoint, yet proving us in fidelity by resisting, with Christian constancy and humility, the assaults of a mutilated philosophy, the insults of incoherent fanaticism, the threats and ill-treatment of those that could not succeed in otherwise dictating unjust laws to human consciences."

Putting all on guard against temptations of pride and revenge after the scourge had passed, the Cardinal inculcated the duties of forgiveness and penance for those who had failed in the time of trial. Only iniquity is to be hated. The evildoer is distinct from the evil and must be shown mercy and love, with justice. This was the constant and unalterable teaching of the Church, in accord with which St. Augustine said: "The devil and his angels are shown in Holy Scripture as destined to eternal fire and punishment. For them alone is no amendment to be hoped."

The pastoral letter ended with an exhortation to pray for Pius VI suffering in exile, and for the Austrian Emperor Francis II—not without a reminder to His most pious Apostolic Majesty that spiritual concerns and the Church's freedom are to be regarded before temporal matters of State: the Altar comes before the Throne.

The reminder was most necessary. The new Austrian rulers before long began to neglect justice and equity. Germanic domination in Italy, though it lasted but briefly, was to bear consequences in some ways not much less lamentable than those caused by French Republican occupation.

NOTES

1. Rome and the Papal States were a clergy-ruled theocracy.
2. See Note 3, p. xxi.
3. The First Allied Coalition against France (1792-1797) consisted of Austria, Prussia, Sardinia, England, Spain, Portugal and Holland, together with Naples, Tuscany and the Papal States.
4. Cis-Alpine Republic: territory within boundaries created by Bonaparte and the Directory between the Alps and Rome. (*Cis* is Latin for "on this side of"; it is the opposite of *trans*.)
5. The Latin word *perfidus* has not the sense of "perfidious" but rather "lacking in faith," on account of many Jews failing to perceive the Messias.
6. *Risorgimento*: the nationalist, unifying movement among Italian states which was to culminate in the establishment of the Kingdom of Italy under the House of Savoy (Victor Emmanuel II) in 1870. (*Risorgimento* is Italian for "Resurrection.")

~ 3 ~

THE CONCLAVE OF 1800

Cardinal Chiaramonti Is Elected
Pope Pius VII—Entry into Rome—
Napoleon Rises to Power·

The news of Pius VI's death at the end of August in Valence, France, reached Cardinal Albani, Dean of the Sacred
College, during mid-September in Venice, where he, Cardinal York and some other cardinals had gathered. Venice had
for two years been subject to Austria, and Pius VI had had
this city in mind as the best place for the conclave electing
his successor; but he had left the cardinals free to decide on
whatever place their greatest number, together with the Cardinal Dean, would be found gathered at the time.

Venice was therefore decided on, and the agreement of
the Emperor Francis II was sought. The island Abbey of
St. George guaranteed absolute separation from the outside
world. The Benedictine monks moved out into temporary
quarters, and troops garrisoned in part of the buildings were
evacuated, leaving only a small guard. Cardinal York shared
responsibility for overseeing material arrangements; his
young protégé, Msgr. Consalvi, was appointed conclave
secretary in charge of practically all else. The College of
Cardinals was without funds, and most expenses were borne
by the Austrian government, although Spain sent a substantial contribution.

The evacuation of Rome by the remaining French Republi-

can forces and the city's occupation by Ferdinand II, King
of Naples, raised hopes that the conclave might yet be held
in the papal capital. But plans for St. George's Abbey were
too far advanced to be changed; the Austrian Emperor's protection was of too great importance and the Holy See was
distrustful of the Neapolitan King's territorial intentions.

Cardinal Chiaramonti learned of Pius VI's death only at
the beginning of October. Ties of friendship had long linked
the noble Braschi and Chiaramonti families of Cesena; bonds
of personal affection and gratitude bound the Cardinal to the
late Pope, whom he referred to as his "most benign Father
and signal benefactor."

He set out for Venice without means, due to the suppression of his revenues by the French Republic and to his manifold charities. Bad roads prevented his reaching Ferrara before
late evening, when the coach was stopped at the city gates
and the guards asked to check his name and the identity of
fellow travelers—his conclavist and secretary, a servant and
a cook. As they continued along more bad roads after dark,
the coach sank into deep ruts, and they were unable to go
on until a peasant came to their rescue with a pair of oxen
and drew them out.

They stayed the night with the Bishop of Rovigo and were
on the road again at seven the next morning, reaching Padua
before noon. Here a great welcome awaited the Cardinal at
St. Justa's Abbey where, after singing Vespers with the monks,
he visited the city hospital. He left Padua early in the morning by boat from the river estuary, where the fishermen
brought a meal of differently cooked fish, with bread and
wine. Venice was sighted at four in the afternoon.

Gliding into the Venetian lagoons half an hour later, the
Cardinal and his fellow travelers disembarked on the quay
before the great Dominican Church of Sts. John and Paul,
where lodgings had been arranged. The Prior had moved out
of his own apartment for the Cardinal and came to meet him.
He personally made up his bed, provided supper and lavished
every possible attention upon him, insisting on accompany-

ing him everywhere he went until the opening of the Conclave.

Before the Conclave was begun, the Novendial, or Pope's Novena—nine days' public Masses for the repose of the soul of a deceased Pontiff—was held in St. Mark's Basilica. Chiaramonti's simple piety and great personal dignity were noted by many present, who wished he might be Pope.

Thirty-four of the forty-six cardinals then living were able to enter the Conclave on the appointed day, December 1, 1799. Some had traveled with considerable risk and difficulty. Cardinal Maury, representing King Louis XVIII in exile, had evaded the French Republican officials disguised. Three cardinals who had been disloyal during the revolutionary occupation of Rome, and had been secularized, were not called to the Conclave. It was at the precise moment of entering the Conclave in St. George's Abbey that Cardinal York, last of the royal Stuarts and claimant to the throne of England and Scotland, was informed of the pension handsomely granted him by George III of England, whose heart had been touched on hearing of the plight of the aged Cardinal and son of his predecessor, James III.

Little could be done while waiting for the arrival of the Austrian Cardinal Hertzan, who entered the conclave twelve days later. Mandatory of the Emperor Francis, he was given a magnificent welcome, but his intentions soon became clear to all: to secure election of a man compliant with the Emperor's policies—namely, Cardinal Mattei. Mattei had signed the Treaty of Tolentino handing over to France the Papal Legations, which had since been occupied by Austria, and it was surmised he would not, as pope, insist on their return to rightful papal sovereignty.

Daily voting took place in the upper chapel of St. George's Abbey. A near majority was had almost at once by Cardinal Bellisomi, Bishop of Cesena. Pius VI's nephew, Cardinal Braschi, headed a faction in his favor, which included the Dean of the Sacred College, Albani, Cardinal York and Cardinal Chiaramonti.

Braschi accordingly told Cardinal Hertzan that, if the

Emperor would not oppose it, his (Hertzan's) added vote might secure a prompt election. Hertzan assured Braschi he would have no difficulty, and it seemed certain that Bellisomi would soon be Pope.

But Hertzan had all along been secretly forming an opposing imperial faction in favor of Mattei. To gain time, he had made the irregular request for Bellisomi's election to be delayed until the Emperor had been consulted. The Cardinal Dean consented, not wanting to offend, but only after Hertzan had assured him he would give his vote to Bellisomi if no reply came from Vienna within reasonable time.

During the delay, Mattei's votes suddenly increased, while Bellisomi's diminished. Induced by Hertzan, various cardinals had deserted Braschi, justifying this by saying they felt bound to conform to the Emperor's wishes.

A two-and-a-half month deadlock followed, almost without record in conclave history: Braschi and his party declared they would rather die than vote for Mattei; the opposing faction protested they would remain in conclave till the Day of Judgment rather than vote for Bellisomi. The situation was only brought to an end by an act of the Spanish Sovereign, who vetoed the Austrian Emperor's candidate.[1]

Behind Spain's decisive intervention was Bonaparte's aim of also preventing the election of Mattei. As First Consul of France, he now had the powers of a king, but no ambassador or representative among the cardinals in conclave. To make a good impression at Rome and Venice, Bonaparte began by decreeing official honors to be paid to the mortal remains of Pius VI at Valence. Then he took advantage of the Spanish King's public congratulations on his becoming First Consul by inviting him to defend France's interests, as well as his own, against Austria's at the Conclave. The King agreed and vetoed Mattei's election.

With Austria's candidate eliminated and the stalement ended, the Pope still had to be found. Just how Cardinal Chiaramonti came to be elected has remained open to question.

Several diaries were kept during the Conclave, two officially:

Consalvi's (not tallying with the account he wrote in his
Memoirs) and that of Prince Chigi (marshal of the Conclave,
whose version differs from Consalvi's). A diary kept by Cardinal Flangini differs from both Consalvi and Chigi. The unofficial Spanish envoy at the Conclave, Archbishop Despuig, wrote
a day-to-day record in which he himself emerged as the person secretly promoting Chiaramonti, by roundabout ways
from outside the Conclave. Consalvi, however, made no men-
tion whatsoever of Despuig in his conclave diary or later
Memoirs, and Chigi gave him only a vague and inaccurate
passing reference. But from Consalvi's *Memoirs*, it discreetly
emerges that it was Despuig who suggested a way of ending
the deadlock.

Accounts of the Conclave electing Pius VII contained in
biographies and Church histories are all different, and there
are a great number.[2] Many make the Conclave Secretary, Consalvi, the chief actor, or the main instrument, in promoting
the election of Chiaramonti. In his *Life of Pius VII,* the French
Minister in Rome, Artaud de Montor, writing in 1836, even
makes Consalvi harangue the cardinals concerning the character and qualities of Chiaramonti, persuade them he is the right
person for the critical situation, then convince Chiaramonti
himself that he ought to accept election—all of which is shown
to be fantasy by the ecclesiastical historian Moroni,[3] who shows
that such conduct would have dishonored the Conclave Secretary, the Sacred College and Chiaramonti. Moroni bases his
account of what really happened on the account of one who
was present all the time as master of ceremonies, Msgr. Pietro
Baldassari, author of *The Glories of Pius VI*; Msgr. Baldassari
had accompanied Pope Pius VI into exile.

Baldassari's account is clear, direct and simple. According
to him, the sole credit for proposing Chiaramonti goes to
the Cardinal Dean, Albani. When the Cardinal Dean (fifty
years a cardinal with experience of three previous Conclaves)
saw that exhortations to his colleagues on the urgency of
agreeing on a speedy election were of no avail, he had the
crossed staves put up over the door of his cell, a recognized

sign of his withdrawal and wish not to receive anyone.

But Braschi, seeing his faction weakened by Hertzan, begged Albani to receive him. Albani consented. Albani asked Braschi if there were not other cardinals no less deserving than Bellisomi, and himself suggested some names, ending with Chiaramonti's. Braschi declared himself favorable and found all his party of the same mind—especially Bellisomi.

The cardinals of the opposing, imperial faction were then consulted and also found favorable to Chiaramonti, including Hertzan. So at last, on the evening of March 12, Feast of Pope St. Gregory, all were in favor of electing Gregory Barnabas Chiaramonti.

Baldassari's account continues by quoting the (unpublished) diary of the other master of ceremonies, Msgr. Speroni: "After the usual balloting [on March 13], which showed the same results as for the past weeks, the cardinals went out of the chapel, and the writer [Speroni] as usual locked the doors. He then saw and heard from the cardinals in the corridors it was indeed true that the next day Chiaramonti would be elected.

"The writer went in search of him, found him walking in another part of the Conclave and told him what he had seen and heard... His Eminence turned paler than usual, stopped walking but said nothing... The writer was the first to speak, excusing himself by adding it would be necessary to try on the white vestments: only two large-size ones had been provided, instead of the customary three (Chiaramonti was of smallish stature). His Eminence answered that the writer might come to him at the evening *Angelus*."[4]

As he was on his way that evening to keep the appointment, Msgr. Speroni met the Cardinal Dean leading the others to Chiaramonti's cell for the traditional act of kissing the hand of the cardinal whose election had been decided for the morrow. Chiaramonti's humility made it hard for him to accept this gesture, but Albani and his colleagues insisted.

Both vestments proved too large. The only tailor that could be found within the Conclave had to work during the night

making one to the right size. Chiaramonti also had to sit
up part of the night with his secretary drafting letters communicating his election to Catholic sovereigns and papal
nuncios.

All the cardinals went to Chiaramonti's cell at the customary
hour of voting the following morning and took him with
them to the chapel, which he entered hand in hand with Albani. Elected by almost unanimous vote—it was March 14,
1800—he had given his own vote to the Cardinal Dean, who
had been instrumental in promoting him.

Asked if he accepted, he requested (as is wont) a few minutes
to pray and remained alone in his stall on his knees. The
contented expression on the face of Cardinal Bellisomi and
the melancholy look of Mattei were noted. Chiaramonti then
replied that, though knowing himself unworthy, he adored
God's judgments in fear and trembling before so weighty
a responsibility and the thought of his own insufficiency. He
wished to be called Pius VII, in memory of his predecessor
and in gratitude to him.

While the new Pope was putting on the papal vestments,
a cardinal was heard to remark that the Sacred College had
just given proof their power was greater than the Pontiff's,
for they had changed black into white. The Cardinal's pleas-
antry referred to Chiaramonti's Benedictine habit being exchanged, by their vote, for white vestments. The Pope, because
of his supreme authority, is said to be able to make white
black; but to make black white is more difficult.

The rejoicings at Cardinal Chiaramonti's election inside and
outside the Conclave, Msgr. Consalvi noted in his diary, were
impossible to describe. After the traditional act of "adoration" on the part of the cardinals, then of all others in the
Conclave, the doors were unlocked and the people admitted
to kiss the foot of the Pope, as was then the custom.

The new Pope took his midday meal in the cell of Cardinal
Braschi, after which, seated on the portable throne or *sedia
gestatoria,* Pius VII was borne processionally to the altar of
the Abbey Basilica, where a second "adoration" took place

publicly. For the rest of the day, the Pope remained in prayer in the Basilica, where the immense crowds of people were admitted little by little—and so it continued for several days on end, the church doors being kept continually open.

Pius VII's coronation should have taken place in Venice's St. Mark's Cathedral. But this was not permitted by the Austrian authorities, who saw in the tiara a sign of the Pope's temporal sovereignty which, as occupiers of papal territory, they did not want recognized publicly. Rather than renounce the ceremony, Pius resolved to have it carried out with as much solemnity as possible in St. George's Abbey. The Basilica could not contain the numbers of people, and very many had to take part from the piazza outside. Thousands more witnessed the Pope's crowning on the outer balcony from boats anchored in the canal and from St. Mark's Square on the other side of the water.

The Pope spent the following days receiving delegations from Venice and from all over Italy and abroad, besides visiting churches, monasteries and convents of the city and other islands. He would leave St. George's in the gilded gondola put at his disposal and arrive unannounced in remote places, going on foot among the throngs of applauding people. He took part in the prayers of men's and women's religious orders and conversed with them. Gathered around him with special affection were the younger members, students, acolytes and children.

St. George's Island Abbey thus became, for a time, the heart and center of all Venice and of Christendom.

Within a few days of the new Pope's election, the Emperor Francis II, who had not been able to get the pope he wanted, attempted to entice Pius VII into being compliant to his policies by inviting him, through Cardinal Hertzan, to visit him in Vienna, as his predecessor Pius VI had done (to little or no advantage). Pius declined the invitation, aware of the Emperor's intentions, whereupon Francis sent a special envoy to communicate his wish that the Pope recognize Austria's possession of the Papal Legations.

Pius VII showed the steely firmness beneath the usual gentleness of his character by replying to the threats of the Emperor's envoy with disconcerting energy: "Let His Majesty beware of putting clothes that are not his into his wardrobe. . ." At this the imperial envoy ran off to Msgr. Consalvi—whom Pius had appointed pro-Secretary of State and created Cardinal—complaining that the new Pope was young and inexperienced.

Pius intended making the journey to Rome by way of Ravenna, Ferrara and Bologna—the Legations—but again, the Emperor intervened to prevent this. Determined to uphold his own rule over the papal dominions, he feared that the Pope's presence would provoke popular demonstrations. An itinerary by sea was imposed by the Austrian authorities as far as Pesaro on the Adriatic coast, whence the Pope could proceed by road to Rome. The boat put at his disposal was ill-manned and ill-equipped and took three weeks instead of three or four days to reach its destination, partly because of storms and partly because of the ineptness of the crew. The imperial envoy accompanied the Pope on the voyage as a mark of honor—but actually more as a jailer, Cardinal Consalvi noted.

Sadness could be read on all faces as the Pope left St. George's Abbey by gondola accompanied by some of the monks, the members of his little court and some cardinals.

Traveling from Ancona to Rome by road, Pius stopped at Fano, among other places, where his mother had passed her last years as a Carmelite. He celebrated Mass in the convent church in which his mother was buried. By chance, the pontifical throne had been set up over the place of the sisters' common grave below the flooring. One of the Pope's assistants apprised him of this, at which Pius grew pale and shed tears of emotion.

When the party reached Ancona, news had come of Bonaparte's victory over the Austrians at Marengo, in northwest Italy; soon the Austrians were withdrawing from the Papal Legations, Venice and all parts of Italy. By the time

Pius VII reached Rome, the European balance of power had changed: the papacy was no longer under the protection or patronage of the Emperor Francis II, but was confronted by Bonaparte, the all-powerful French First Consul.

NOTES

1. The right of exclusion, or veto, claimed by certain sovereigns and rulers to name one whom they wished to exclude from election to the papacy was never approved by the Holy See. It was finally prohibited by Pope Pius X (Constitution *Commissum nobis* of January 1, 1904).
2. See Bibliographical Notes.
3. G. Moroni, *Dictionary of Ecclesiastical History (Dizionario di erudizione storico-ecclesiastico)*, 1851, vol. 53.
4. Vatican Library, manuscripts: Vat. lat. 9894 (Italian).

~ 4 ~

THE NEW POPE AND NAPOLEON

First Acts of Pius VII—
The French Concordat—The Italian Concordat—
Napoleon Asks the Pope to Crown Him Emperor
of the French in Paris

Pius entered his capital fervidly acclaimed by clergy and people. He went, according to custom, to pray at the tomb of St. Peter, his first predecessor, in the Vatican Basilica, before proceeding to the Quirinal Palace.

But the very next day rejoicing changed to consternation: the French were once more advancing on Bologna. News followed that they had occupied the Adriatic port of Ancona, through which the Pope had lately passed. It looked as though Rome might again be invaded, with a repetition of the "Roman Republic" of two years before, when Pius VI had been abducted.

The new Pope determined to stay where he was, trusting in divine Providence. Just as he made this decision, Bonaparte's first proposals for a concordat[1] between France and the Holy See were communicated to him. The proposals were received with due reserve, but there were grounds for hope that an agreement could be reached that would lead to restoration of the Catholic religion in France, and an envoy was sent to Paris to negotiate.

Pius VII's first acts in Rome were the setting up of congregations to deal with the gigantic task of recovering order in every field. Religious affairs had become so confused and chaotic as to seem almost beyond repair. Speculators and profiteers abounded, taking advantage of the general impoverishment and counteracting the efforts of the religious authorities. Pius VII withdrew from circulation the base coin that had been damaging commerce and reintroduced free trade in grain. He pardoned disloyal subjects who had collaborated with the Revolution in various ways.

After some days of prayer and reflection, he drafted a reply to the proposals from Napoleon Bonaparte. The Pope was aware that the First Consul's attitude to religion and the Church was mainly political, and he had no illusion regarding the obstacles that would have to be overcome before reaching proper understanding and agreement, still more for putting such an agreement into practice once arrived at.

King Louis XVIII, in exile, also putting political and national interests before religious ones, did everything in his power, through his mandatory Cardinal Maury, to prevent an accord being reached between the Pope and Bonaparte that would strengthen the latter's régime. He even tried to enlist some of Europe's other sovereigns in the cause of the French monarchy. If His Holiness were so weak as to want a concordat, the French King said, the bishops of France should refuse to obey laws which the Pope and an unlawful régime might impose upon them. Many in Rome sympathized with the French monarch's attitude, and several cardinals refused to have anything to do with negotiations between the Holy See and France, in spite of Bonaparte's expressed good intentions. Cardinal Consalvi, however, was all in favor of negotiations.

In France, the chief opponent of the Concordat was the apostate Bishop Talleyrand—now married and Minister of Foreign Affairs—who had ordained the first bishops of the Constitutional French Church[2] and was intent on maintaining his and their schismatic position. Obliged to acquiesce in the First Consul's concordatory policy, he feigned collaboration while secretly doing his utmost to sabotage it.

Bishop Grégoire, head of this nationally constituted French Church, made constant war on those working for the Concordat. This revolutionary bishop, true to his anti-Roman, Jansenistic and Gallican[3] principles, assigned "a place of honor" to the Pope, but insisted that Pius VII must recognize the rights of the Constitutional Church, nationalized in its liturgy, prayers, rites, catechism and most else. His energetic campaign to impede the Concordat had such an effect that Bonaparte's own entourage became ill-disposed, and the papal envoy reported from Paris that there were none left who wanted the Concordat except Bonaparte—and he in his own way for his own ends.

The First Consul of France knew that more and more sincere Catholics were insisting on having "proper priests," and the Constitutionals were being discredited. He was aware that the majority of priests and people of France would never be submissive without his coming to some agreement with the Pope.

Napoleon saw the Church as something like an army, and bishops as generals whom he could command. His orderly military mind also recognized that bishops, as generals, have to be regularly appointed and put in command, otherwise there is indiscipline and chaos. He therefore went to any lengths to have the bishops whom he wanted, and whom he thought would be subservient to him in furthering his plans, regularly put in command by the Church's head. Pope Pius was equally determined on no account to cede in his right of ratifying bishops, which even the French Concordat explicitly recognized, well knowing that some of Napoleon's nominees might be persuaded to serve the all-powerful Emperor and self-styled Protector of the Church more than continuing to obey him, the rightful, God-given head. In the end, Napoleon became illogical and overstepped himself by trying to force and intimidate the Pope into ratifying his nominees; he even contradicted himself by insisting on his bishops' installment by any means.

Several drafts for a concordat were rejected either by

Bonaparte or by the papal representative. Some of the articles
had apparently been dictated by Bishop Grégoire. The First
Consul then dictated an unacceptable version of his own, in
military style, and sent it to Rome as final.

It was the end of Lent; Holy Week ceremonies and Easter
had to be celebrated, and Rome took time in replying. The
First Consul grew impatient and delivered an ultimatum: his
concordat had to be approved in five days or he would withdraw the French ambassador—and the papal government might
conclude what could follow.

Bonaparte's veiled threats and promises that, in return for
a concordat to his liking, he would give the Papal Legations
back to the Church were ignored. The French Ambassador
was instructed by the First Consul to deal with the Pope
"as though he had two hundred thousand bayonets behind
him." Pius VII gently told the Ambassador: "The soldiers
of Jesus Christ far outnumber those of the First Consul of
the French Republic."

In the end it was agreed that Cardinal Consalvi should
go to Paris himself and speak to Bonaparte. Before setting
out, Consalvi confided in a letter to Sir John Acton, Prime
Minister of the King of Naples: "The good of religion needs
a victim. I am on my way to a martyrdom—God's will be
done!..."

The Cardinal Secretary of State had his first audience with
Bonaparte at the Tuileries Palace the day after his arrival. He
found the main staircase lined with statesmen, senators,
ministers, generals and a host of troops as though his audience were a public one. Talleyrand personally led him to
the audience room, where Consalvi still hoped he might be
alone with the First Consul. The door was thrown open upon
a still more dazzling scene; members of the Senate, the
Tribunate, the Legislative Corps, the higher Magistracy filled
the hall with generals, officers and dignitaries of every rank.
Standing apart in their midst were the three Consuls of the
French Republic.

Bonaparte gave Consalvi no time to speak but began

haranguing him about having to sign a concordat at once, saying he had no need of Rome.

Consalvi's instructions from Pius VII were neither to break off negotiations nor refuse a concordat, even if it were not as favorable to the Church as hoped. During more than one all-night session with the French consular delegates, it looked as though there could be no agreement. Consalvi withstood the threats and blandishments, not yielding on any of the points the Pope had insisted on.

Bonaparte grew impatient, declaring that if things were not speedily settled he could, if he chose, follow the example of Henry VIII of England, than whom he was twenty times more powerful.

Consalvi told him outright that some of the provisions of the concordat were too bold. The First Consul yielded to the gracious and persuasive manner of Consalvi, and the articles were modified.

But the battle went on. It was not only Bonaparte who had to be reckoned with. "All the chief magistrates, all the philosophers, all the libertines, the majority of the military heads are thoroughly against restoration of the Catholic religion in the French Republic," Consalvi wrote in a report to Rome, "and they are very powerful."

When at last a compromise that could be accepted was reached and the moment came for signing, a draft was put before Consalvi which he was urged to sign. He at once perceived that it was different from the one agreed upon the day before, and refused. The attempted deception was the work of Talleyrand, but it was also typical of tactics Bonaparte was liable to resort to in order to gain his ends. So yet another draft was prepared. Bonaparte flew into a rage and tore it to pieces.

Unaccountably, however, he changed his mind and consented. One historian of the French Concordat, while giving Bonaparte his due and according Consalvi chief merit in the dealings, believed that the prayers of Pius VII in Rome were more efficacious than anything else, and that in the end, "The

Concordat with France was the work of a hero and a saint."[4]

Consalvi returned to Rome, where he met with a mixed reception. The Concordat articles were criticized at Rome as being too favorable to Napoleon. But in addition to stipulating that the Catholic religion was to be again made legal in France, the Concordat laid down that some restitution of confiscated Church property was to be made, and proper ecclesiastical government restored. Pius believed the best possible terms had, in the circumstances, been obtained and he ratified the Concordat, which was signed by the First Consul in September, 1801.

But now he who had been so imperious and impatient over requiring an immediate settlement delayed in having it promulgated. To work out ways and means of applying the terms of the Concordat, Bonaparte had requested a papal legate with fullest powers, asking for Cardinal Caprara, who had been nuncio at the court of the Emperor Francis II. Pius VII's way of dealing with Bonaparte was to yield in all things lawful and possible without sacrificing Catholic principles. He was aware from this Cardinal's over-conciliatory dealings in Vienna that the Holy See would not be represented to greatest advantage, but nevertheless agreed to send him.

The first need in reestablishing the Catholic religion in postrevolutionary France was the appointment of bishops. Many dioceses were vacant because of the death or exile of bishops; others were unlawfully in the hands of constitutional, schismatic pastors. The dioceses of France were now to be reorganized and greatly reduced in number. The Concordat gave the First Consul the right to appoint new bishops, but canonical institution[5] of the bishop as head of the diocese had to be granted by the Pope. Bonaparte planned to make a clean sweep of existing conditions, requiring the resignation of all the bishops of France and getting the Pope to install the new bishops appointed by himself. Pius VII reluctantly agreed.

To ask for the resignation of an entire episcopate was an act without precedent in Church history. Yet most of the bishops who were still resident in France or who had returned

there did resign. Certain of those exiled in London and elsewhere refused. All the constitutional bishops resigned. The
Holy See had striven to prevent Bonaparte from re-nominating
any of these to the new dioceses, but the Pope was once more
obliged to consent, provided they signed some formula of
reconciliation with Rome.

A political complication was now added to these ecclesiastical problems, delaying the Concordat's promulgation: the
French Republic required all treaties to be submitted to the
senatorial assembly, and the Senate withheld approval. Soon
however, the setting up of an "Italian Republic" with Bonaparte
as President, and the Treaty of Amiens making temporary
peace with the English, gave added prestige to the First Consul; as a result the Concordat was approved, and the celebration of political and religious peace was decided at Easter.

Nevertheless, not satisfied that the Concordat had given
him sufficient control over the Church and knowing it would
not please powerful sections of the government, Bonaparte
had drawn up a further set of regulations, reintroducing Gallican principles, that is, spiritual matters were made subject
to temporal concerns of state. These so-called "Organic Articles" were published as an appendix to the Concordat.

Bonaparte had ordered promulgation of the Concordat to
be celebrated in Notre Dame Cathedral (which only recently,
with the consecration of a new archbishop by Caprara, had
passed out of the hands of the constitutional clergy). Willingly or unwillingly, the civil and military authorities had
to follow the First Consul and members of his family in the
gala carriages of the court of Louis XVI.

Contemporary chronicles pictured the scene in Notre Dame:
the Cardinal Legate with the new Archbishop and bishops,
clergy and religious, members of the State Council, officials
and ministers, civil and military authorities—a gathering such
as had not been seen in the French capital for over a decade—
eagerly viewed by the people. But some government members showed little respect for the proceedings, and others
openly sneered. The First Consul appeared to be performing

a public duty, without a trace of recollection or piety. Nor did he receive the Sacraments.

Pius VII was shocked beyond words when he learned of the "Organic Articles." The dismayed and indignant Consalvi could scarcely believe that Bonaparte had arrogated to himself those powers of the State over Church affairs which Consalvi had so fought—and with seeming success—to prevent: briefs and bulls coming from Rome had to have governmental approval; no seminaries could be established without the First Consul's approval; the civil marriage contract was to have precedence over the religious. . . .The Pope spared no pains and gave himself no rest in endeavoring to bring about a revocation of the Articles, which even obliged the teaching of false doctrine—Gallicanism and Jansenism—in the training of future priests.

Bonaparte's victory over Austria at Marengo in 1800 had enabled him to reconstitute the former Cis-Alpine Republic in Italy. His next move after promulgation of the French Concordat was for the consolidation of the new Italian Republic through the drawing up of an Italian Concordat. He publicly gave repeated assurance that here the Catholic, Apostolic and Roman Religion would be recognized as that of the State, providing the clergy would show themselves "the docile instruments of his policy and ready to favor it. . ."

Pius stipulated in vain that ecclesiastical matters in the new Concordat should not be settled without the consent of the Holy See. "Bonaparte alone can save Italy from imminent ruin," the First Consul's Minister wrote from Paris. "None can calculate the extent of the disaster if His Holiness becomes inexorable and refuses to agree to a convention which would be the sole means of preserving the Holy See and Italy from a new catastrophe."

The Pope passed days of anxiety faced with the impossibility of avoiding the dilemma and at length, to avoid greater evil, wrote to Bonaparte that he would agree on all possible points, but that although France had had need of a concordat for the reestablishing of Religion, which had been suppressed but had remained hidden in the hearts of the people, there were not the same reasons for making a concordat with Italy. Nevertheless, Bonaparte pursued his intention of having a concordat concluded immediately, "to guarantee the stability of religious matters in Italy."

For the Pope, this meant just the opposite. "His Holiness is in great anguish over the situation concerning religious matters," wrote Consalvi in a letter to the nuncio in Paris. "It is truly terrifying. One feels oneself transfixed...The Holy Father's position is terrible, whether to grant or deny the demands...Really there has never been a worse situation for the Church, and there is extreme need for God to help us... I have almost lost courage..."

At length (as with the French Concordat), after many a draft had been discussed, rejected, revised and modified, the version changed by the First Consul himself was practically imposed by force, and the Pope had no choice but to ratify it. He wrote to Bonaparte expressing recognition of the benefit to Religion it was hoped would result from this concordat as from that with France, especially in view of the clause stipulating that any difficulties that might arise were to be dealt with directly between the Pope and the First Consul.

Yet almost immediately (as before), a set of articles was published by the Vice President of the new Italian Republic, with Bonaparte's express approval, termed "Executive Regulations." These, too, were Gallican and Jansenist, giving the State control over most Church matters. The Holy See was not consulted. What could have been a pact in some ways positively good for Religion in Italy had been vitiated from the start.

The Pope wrote directly to Bonaparte, saying he could not find words to express his amazement and grief. At the same time, he still trusted that as the First Consul had been the author of the Italian Concordat, he would nevertheless vindicate it by requisite measures. Bonaparte replied that the only remedy was indeed for he himself to take everything in hand. But he did nothing.

Pius told the French ambassador at Rome: "We find, alas, true peace and repose only in those governments where Catholics are subject to infidels and heretics. The Catholics of Russia, England, Prussia and the East cause no pain to Us. They ask for bulls, for necessary counsels, then go their way peaceably in conformity with the laws of the Church. But you know what Our Predecessor had to suffer through the changes brought about by the Emperor... At this present moment, no man is so unfortunate as the Sovereign Pontiff. He is the guardian and supreme head of religion and of its divine ordinances. But it is religion which men are seeking to demolish, although they say they respect it. They pretend to have need of Us to carry out their ever-recurring attempts at changes, without considering that Our conscience and honor make Us powerless to consent. Our objections are then passed over with ill-feeling and anger; and in nearly every case the demands made on Us are accompanied by threats...

"We had hoped that France, which possesses what other powers have the ambition to possess, would remain in harmony with the Holy See... But if the First Consul introduce innovations into Italy," Pius continued prophetically, "it will no longer be possible for Us to hold Our own at Rome."

But introducing innovations into Italy was just what Bonaparte, who did not forgive Pius for protesting against the "Organic Articles" and "Executive Regulations" in consistory, was now bent on doing.

Napoleon had meanwhile conceived the plan of getting the Pope to Paris to crown him Emperor of the French, as he had been proclaimed in May of that year, 1804. Caprara intimated that such a desire was perfectly legitimate, and that it would be highly inadvisable for the Pope to demur or risk offending the new Emperor by a refusal.

Thus yet a further major cause of anxiety was added to those already weighing on the Pope. For such a request, though not without precedent, gave rise to a host of difficulties, not the least being the offense to Louis XVIII and the Austrian

Emperor, who looked on Napoleon as an upstart, if not a usurper.

Pius VII had for some time felt that he needed to talk personally with the all-powerful Bonaparte concerning the French "Organic Articles," the bishops of France and the Italian "Executive Regulations." His desire for personal talks was increased by the new French ambassador in Rome, who was Napoleon's uncle, Cardinal Fesch. But it took him some months to decide on the momentous step of going to Paris to crown one who considered himself heir to Charlemagne.

Consultations with his cardinals resulted in multiple objections to the proposed coronation: the so-called "Organic Articles" and the laws of France that violated the Church's rights, the fact that some of the constitutional bishops had never signed a retraction of their errors and were still in formal schism, and the need for a clear justification on religious grounds of an act that could be attributed to merely human or other considerations.

Consalvi tried to get some assurance from Fesch on certain points regarding the Emperor's request and the proposed visit to Paris of Pius VII. But the French ambassador brusquely left the room, banging the door and exclaiming it would be easier to make an army of women see reason than to convince the Roman Curia.

All the while the Holy Father was in a growing state of renewed anguish over what decision he ought to make. "The Pope has been made ill," the Austrian Ambassador, Lebzeltern, reported. "Last Saturday morning, His Holiness was in such a state of prostration and physical weakness that he was unable to celebrate Mass. . ."

Pius had in fact been multiplying penances and fasts and spending hours in prayers begging God to enlighten him. Consalvi felt that the Pope should go to Paris, as did Pius himself. But one of the conditions insisted on by the opposing cardinals was that the Pope should obtain the promise of some definite concessions to the Church in return for so great and singular a service to the Emperor, about whose

motives for the request none were under any illusion. But
these concessions were not forthcoming. A vague and inconsistent letter from Napoleon caused the Pope fresh qualms
and doubts about his going.

"The Pope was so upset last Sunday," reported Lebzeltern
to the Court of Vienna, "that he could not say Mass without
mistakes at every moment, the words fading from his lips.
Only toward evening was he induced with the utmost difficulty to take a little food, having fasted all the previous day,
and passed the night in prayer. . . his health is feared for. . .
His *maestro di camera* told me personally he had several times
found him on his knees crying hot tears, his arms raised to
Heaven, and that he remained in this position for hours on
end imploring God to save him from this critical, crucial moment and send him light as to what decision to make."

All Europe had come to know of the discussions taking
place regarding the Pope's crowning of Napoleon. How could
he humiliate him by a refusal? Yet, what real grounds for
hope were there that the cause of religion would truly be
served, or that Catholicism in France would be strengthened?
This was in the end the sole justification for acceptance.

Finally Pius decided to go, whatever might be the consequences. And once resolved (Lebzeltern again reported), he
got back all his habitual serenity, even natural joviality. "After
all," Pius confided, smiling slyly, "I know how the French
need to be dealt with." The Austrian Ambassador was then
regaled with reminiscences of the Cis-Alpine Republic in the
days when he was Cardinal-Bishop of Imola. "So what are
We to do?" Pius ended. "The French are in such a hurry!"

Nevertheless, the note that contained Napoleon's formal
invitation was so curt, apart from the vague and inconsistent
promises, that in the moment of receiving it Pius felt inclined
not to answer.

In finally deciding to go and crown Napoleon, Pius VII
had also to consider that such an act would be giving added
strength and power (and apparent political support) to a man
who, all-powerful for the time, might not remain so in the

not far distant future. England was again at war with France and a third coalition was being prepared of Russian, Austrian and other allies. The Russian Czar had broken off diplomatic relations with Rome because of what he considered Pius VII's "shocking and excessive subservience" to Napoleon.

The famous French author De Maistre, then ambassador at St. Petersburg (Leningrad), went so far as to write: "The crimes of Pope Alexander VI were less revolting than this hideous apostasy on the part of his feeble successor Pius VII." Even as he was preparing to set out for Paris the pasquinade was heard in Rome, and it was placarded up in places that "Pius VI lost his throne to save his faith, but Pius VII has lost his faith to save his throne."

There was no precedent for the papal act of going abroad to crown a sovereign except for a thousand years back when Pope Stephen II had journeyed from Rome to crown Charlemagne's father, Pepin. Charlemagne himself had gone to Rome for his crowning by Pope Leo III in 800. Pius VII felt it necessary to justify his action before the cardinals in consistory, and to other European courts; he declared that Napoleon's request constituted a proof of his piety and also of his intentions to protect the holy Faith, whose ruins Bonaparte had so far undertaken to repair with such generous endeavors. But many of the cardinals were little reassured, especially concerning the kind of protection Napoleon had so far given to the Faith and might in the future be expected to give.

NOTES

1. A concordat is a treaty between the Holy See and a sovereign secular state, in the interests of religion. There have been many concordats in the history of the Church, but the term *"The Concordat"* denotes the one between Pius VII and Napoleon in 1801, reestablishing the Church in France.
2. The schismatic, national French church created by the Civil Constitution of the Clergy at the National Assembly in 1790 and condemned by Pope Pius VI. (cf. n. 3, p. xxi).

3. Gallican (from Gaul, France): exalting the prerogatives of the Church in France at the expense of the authority of the Holy See, in accord with the 1628 "Gallican Articles."

4. P. Ilario Rinieri on *The Concordat between Pius VII and the First Consul,* in the *First Centenary of the Death of Pius VII* (Ravenna, 1923—Italian).

5. Canonical *institution* is equivalent to *installation* of a new bishop before the canons of the cathedral, whereby he enters into his powers as head of the diocese. The Pope normally and freely appoints the bishop; but in the case of appointment by a ruler, institution (or installation) cannot lawfully take place without the consent (approval, confirmation or ratification) of the Pope.

~ 5 ~

THE POPE IN PARIS

Napoleon's Attempts to Overshadow the Pope—
The Coronation—Enthusiastic Reception
of Pius VII by the French People

After celebrating Mass in St. Peter's and praying at the tomb
of the Apostle, Pius VII set out for Paris on November 2,
1804, by way of Viterbo, Siena, Florence and Turin, crossing
the Alps over the Mount Cenis route. The papal convoy was
made up of some hundred persons. Napoleon had asked for
twelve cardinals including Consalvi. But Pius had decided
on only six going with him, to avoid the impression of part
of the Sacred College moving to Paris for the occasion. He
left the Cardinal Secretary of State, Consalvi, in Rome.

One of the most important questions, the regulation of
the coronation ceremony, was decided only at the last minute
and presented to the Pope for his agreement as he was nearing Paris. The use of the Roman ceremonial had been rejected
by Talleyrand, who maintained it had been invented at a time
when ecclesiastical authority still wanted to make believe it
was the Church that should invest the civil power. The ancient French ceremonial for the crowning of French kings
at Rheims was discarded for the same reason. A new rite
was therefore specially composed. The Pope accepted it, including its stipulation that he not place the crown on the
Emperor's head. The Emperor was to take the crown in his
own hands, and the formula *"Accipe coronam"* — "Accept the

crown" —was changed to *"Coronet vos Deus"* — " May God
crown you" —considered more appropriate for the times.[1]

Pius VII was, however, intransigent in opposing the Emperor's pronouncing the constitutional oath during the religious ceremony. It was agreed this should be done at the
end of the rite, when the Pope would leave the sanctuary
and retire to an adjoining chapel to take off the papal vestments and so avoid seeming to sanction by his presence an
oath unacceptable to the Church.

It was getting dark and raining as the papal convoy drew
near the forest of Fontainebleau on the outskirts of Paris. Suddenly there appeared Napoleon in hunting costume—booted,
spurred and surrounded by a pack of hounds. His first meeting with the Pope had been so arranged as to avoid the deferen-
tial act of homage demanded by formal custom, an act which
the Emperor felt would be publicly humiliating for himself.

The Holy Father's carriage stopped, and so did Napoleon's.
Pius had to walk some way in his white silk shoes in the
mud before Napoleon began to move toward him. Then Pope
and Emperor embraced.

The imperial carriage was waiting to take the Pope to Fontainebleau Palace. Here, too, Napoleon had contrived to as-
sert himself by not giving the Pope precedence. Getting into
the carriage not after but simultaneously with the Pope, he
seated himself on the right, leaving the left for the Pope.

These acts asserting the Emperor's precedence were the first
of a series of others, humiliating or insulting Pius VII throughout his stay in France—where he was made to feel like, and
publicly shown as, a personage of secondary importance. The
Emperor ceded the rightful place of honor to the Sovereign
Pontiff only on their way into Paris. But the city was purposely entered by night so that the people might not see their
temporal Sovereign's degradation (as he considered it).

Napoleon's attitude and behavior toward the Pope puzzled
many at the time and have puzzled many since. The man
whom he had summoned to crown him in Paris was not only
Head of the Catholic Church but also a temporal sovereign

having, by divine right and antiquity, precedence over every other. Napoleon's purpose of investing his imperial title, less than a year old, with divine authority before the world, should logically have led him to show the greatest possible respect for the Vicar of Christ and holder of highest spiritual authority and power on earth.

In his highly readable popular historical book, *Revolution and Papacy*, E. E. Y. Hales offers some explanation using the psychological speculations of the chief historian of the coronation, Frédéric Masson; the speculations are based on Napoleon's character and temperament. But, as Hales rightly remarks, the Emperor's consistent, studied discourtesy was a calculated policy, as ill-advised as it was ill-mannered. For the effect was just the opposite of making people feel that Napoleon, rather than the Pope, was master. Indeed, the Emperor himself was heard to complain that crowds flocked spontaneously to see the Pope, but only a few came to *him* even when summoned.

Pius VII had no sooner arrived at Fontainebleau than he was faced with unexpected difficulties. He was presented with an ambiguous document setting out the retraction he had insisted on from six remaining constitutional bishops; and it was revealed to him by Napoleon's consort Josephine that he and she had not been married in the Church. The religious ceremony was arranged to be performed privately by the Emperor's uncle, Cardinal Fesch, on the eve of the coronation. But Pius refused to be satisfied with mere promises of retraction on the part of the schismatic bishops; he risked the imperial wrath by requiring their submission, which was finally obtained after affecting scenes and conversations.

The Emperor kept the Pope waiting an hour and a half in Notre Dame Cathedral. Witnesses spoke of an expression of pain on the face of the Sovereign Pontiff. When the moment came for him to anoint the forehead and hands of the young Emperor and Empress, those nearest saw large tears running down the Pontiff's cheeks. Napoleon took the crown lying on the altar and placed it on his own head, then placed

Josephine's on hers, and the Pope accompanied them to the great throne set up in the midst of the cathedral. Then, embracing the Emperor, he exclaimed: *"Vivat imperator in aeternum!"*

When all was over and Napoleon and Josephine had left the cathedral with their court, the Pope remained there in the midst of the people, who came crowding around him to show their veneration and affection, so that it was with difficulty he was able to make his own way out. At the public banquet that followed, the Pope was given third place after the Emperor and Empress.

Then, breaking his promise that there would be no other civil ceremony, Napoleon had a second public coronation carried out. Yet, the day after, he was capable of declaring his coronation in Notre Dame "solemnized by the presence of our Lord and Pope Pius VII, visible head of the Universal Church," and that the acclamations of his subjects during the ceremony had "penetrated his soul with such deep sentiments as he would never be able to forget. . ."—words that had a ring of sincerity and truth.

The requests made by Pius in talks with the Emperor during his time in Paris met with fair promises, but little else. The Pope had purposely prolonged his stay until Easter. Getting ready to return to Rome, he was sounded out by a court official as to whether he might not consider the advantages of residing in France at Avignon under the Emperor's direct protection, or in Paris where His Majesty could put the Archbishop's palace at his disposal. Pius was bound to reply that the very idea was out of the question. In fact, to guard against all possibility of his being constrained to remain in France and prevented from peaceably returning to Rome, he had taken the precaution of signing a formal act of abdication that had been left with the Cardinal-Archbishop of Palermo on Italian territory not governed by the French. If the Emperor were now contemplating a plan to keep him in France, the Pope concluded, he would have as hostage not the Sovereign Roman Pontiff Pius VII, but only a poor monk called Gregory Chiaramonti.

This seems to have spurred the Emperor, himself preparing to leave Paris to be crowned "King of Italy" in Milan, to intimate to the Pope that his welcome had been outstayed.

Relations between Pope and Emperor had cooled since their initial meeting. Pius VII's popularity with the Parisians had so displeased Napoleon that Pius had been forbidden to celebrate pontifical Mass in Notre Dame on Christmas Day. The Emperor's attempts to degrade the Pontiff in the people's eyes failed signally, for everywhere he went he was surrounded by spontaneous popular affection, veneration and respect. The painter David, who depicted the coronation scene and was not himself devout, called Pius a "true priest." Even members of the Senate, Legislative Corps and Tribunate filled their official addresses of homage with expressions of deference and admiration.

The Pope gave Josephine and her ladies-in-waiting blessed rosaries which were eagerly accepted, worn around their necks and introduced to Parisian women who got the Pope to bless them as he passed. Many, grown frivolous and cynical, recognized again the truth of Religion—officially suppressed, but alive in consciences and flickering in hearts. Here and there, darkly hostile, hardened looks were not softened on the Pope's approach. To one who ostentatiously scowled and turned his back, Pius gently exclaimed: "Come, now! An old man's blessing does nobody any harm!. . ." The remark went the rounds of the French capital and increased the people's admiration.

A particularly warm and enthusiastic reception was given to the Pope visiting the Church of St. Germain-des-Près, cradle of the Benedictine Congregation in France, as old as the French monarchy. There he blessed and laid the first stone of a new altar to the Virgin Mary.

Pius VII was reported as saying: "To restore the Catholic religion in France I am ready to make any sacrifice. I would even go to the gates of Hell, but I do not want to enter them." When Fouché, Chief of Police, asked the Pope how he found France, Pius was, however, able to reply: "Thanks be to God! We have passed in the midst of a people on their knees. . ."

From a temporal viewpoint, the Pope obtained no advantage; from an ecclesiastical one, little; but from a spiritual and moral one, the prestige gained by Pius VII's sojourn in France proved inestimable. The coronation, calculated as a triumph for Napoleon, was a still greater one for the Pope—despite the former having planned to eclipse the latter.

Pius VII's journey to Paris, wrote a French chronicler of the time, Lanzac de Labori, initiated in France a renewed devotion to the Pope, a devotion destined to increase during the 19th century. Gallicanism, after condemning itself by the excesses of the French Revolution and of imperialism, was to enter its definitive decline, thanks largely to the sojourn in France of this Pope who had so nobly personified the dignity of the Roman Apostolic See.

NOTES

1. Despite this having been established, some historical manuals and authors erroneously continued to affirm that Napoleon crowned himself in defiance of the Pontiff.

Artist unknown. Portrait owned by the Chiaramonti family.

The future Pontiff, Cardinal Chiaramonti of Imola.

Benedictine Abbey of St. Mary of the Mount, Cesena, where young Barnabas Chiaramonti, the future Pope Pius VII, entered religion, being professed at age 16.

Portrait of Pope Pius VII by Lawrence. (*Copyright reserved to Her Majesty Queen Elizabeth II, and reproduced by permission of the Lord Chamberlain, St. James Palace, London, with grateful acknowledgment.*)

58-2

Portrait of Pope Pius VII done by Jacques Louis David at the time of Napoleon's coronation, 1804. This portrait brings out the kindness, simplicity and spirituality which so characterized this Pontiff.

Contemporary popular engraving published at the time of Pope Pius VII's coronation in Venice, 1800. St. George's Abbey is visible in the background.

Portrait of Pius VII shortly after his election.

The Coronation of Pope Pius VII on the outer balcony of St. George's Abbey. Because of political conditions the Conclave had been held in Venice, rather than in Rome. (*After a popular 19th-century engraving.*)

Engraving by Alessandro Contardi, Rome.

Pope Pius VII. (*Painting from life by G. B. Wicar.*)

The newly elected Pope Pius VII arrives in Rome from Venice in June of 1800. (*Engraving in the Vatican Library, Clementine Gallery.*)

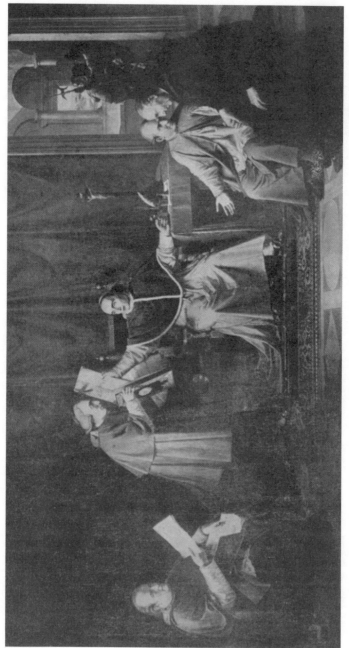

Painting by G.B. Wicar, in Castel Gandolfo.

58-6

Pope Pius VII approves "the French Concordat" between France and the Holy See in 1801. From left to right are Msgr. di Pietro, Cardinal Consalvi, Pius VII, Msgr. Spina, and Padre Caselli.

PIVS. PP. VII.

Contemporary engraving of Pope Pius VII with Cardinals Consalvi (left) and Pacca (right), at different times his Secretaries of State and overall his two chief advisors throughout his pontificate. Cardinal Pacca's approach to the rebuilding of the government of the city of Rome after the Revolution was to work to restore the former order virtually the same as before; Consalvi's was more flexible, as he felt that certain changes were inevitable and should be accepted.

58-7

The coronation of Napoleon and Josephine in Notre Dame, Paris, 1804. Pope Pius VII is seated to the right of Napoleon; Napoleon's mother is seated at upper left. (*Painting by Jacques Louis David, The Louvre, Paris.*)

Cav. Orlandini, Modena.

Statue of the Immaculate Virgin recalling the first stop of Pope Pius VII—May 4, 1805—on the occasion of his return from Paris after the coronation of Napoleon.

Engraving in the Vatican Library, Clementine Gallery.

The abduction of Pope Pius VII by order of Napoleon, carried out by the French General Radet. The Pontiff is led into the carriage which will take him to his place of exile in Savona, northern Italy. The abduction took place in July of 1809.

Pope Pius VII in Savona, where he was confined in the episcopal palace from 1809-1812.

The balcony of the episcopal palace in Savona from which Pope Pius VII used to bless the crowds every day.

At Napoleon's orders the Pope is moved from Savona to Fontainebleau, a town near Paris, in June of 1812. (*Engraving in the Vatican Library, Clementine Gallery.*)

Pope Pius VII and Napoleon at Fontainebleau in January of 1813. It was at this time that the exhausted Pontiff was pressured into signing a tentative agreement sometimes called "the Concordat of Fontainebleau." He soon retracted this agreement point by point.

The Duke and Duchess of Modena pay homage to the Pope on his way back to Rome after being freed from exile in 1814.

The Pope returns in triumph to his capital at Pentecost of 1814. (*Engraving in the Vatican Library, Clementine Gallery.*)

Blessed Anna Maria Taigi, wife, mother of seven children, mystic, seer and Trinitarian tertiary. She saw the famous events of the time, including the activities of Napoleon and Pope Pius VII, in a mysterious thorn-crowned sun, and she suffered in expiation for the evils of the time. Bl. Anna Maria Taigi suffered for Napoleon for 15 years.

~ 6 ~

THE DEEPENING CONFLICT

Pius' Return to Rome—Napoleon's Efforts to
Control Italy—French Occupation of Rome and Virtual
Imprisonment of Pius VII—Bull of Excommunication—
Arrest and Abduction of the Pope

All Rome welcomed the return of the Sovereign Pontiff
after Easter, 1805. Awaiting the Pope's arrival in St. Peter's
were the octogenarian Dean of the Sacred College, Cardinal
York, along with the cardinals, prelates of the Roman Curia,
the Senate, the nobility, the Vatican Basilica chapter and many
thousands of people.

The Cardinal Dean gave Benediction of the Blessed Sacrament, after which the Pope knelt at St. Peter's tomb where,
before leaving Rome for Paris six months previously, he had
prayed regarding his intentions on the journey to crown
Napoleon. Now the Pontiff gave thanks to his first predecessor, the Prince of the Apostles, for his preservation from the
many perils and mishaps that might have befallen him in his
undertaking.

It was growing dark, but the Pope remained kneeling deep
in prayer while the cardinals, clergy and people waited in
reverent silence. It grew darker and darker, but the Pope did
not rise from his knees. Lights were called for, and Cardinal
Consalvi approached the Pope to ask if perhaps he were not
feeling well. An affectionate clasp of the hand reassured the
Cardinal Secretary of State: the Pope's prolonged prayer had

come from excess of consolation on returning safe and sound to his capital.

Various members of the Curia, however, were not happy, and some cardinals were still critical concerning the visit to Paris and Napoleon's coronation. Pius told the cardinals of the Sacred College in a consistorial allocution—almost in spite of his own feelings—that he had brought back more than hopes from Paris. "Many things have really already been accomplished," he said, "preceding what has still to be done." He had, indeed, been personally able to reconcile the Constitutional, schismatic French bishops.

But Napoleon, meanwhile, after having himself crowned "King of Italy," had proceeded to reorganize Church matters without consulting Rome. In addition, the French civil code permitting divorce was causing utmost scandal in that Catholic land. To the Pope's vigorous protest the Emperor-King replied that the Roman Curia was behind the times and that it was no use following a policy that had held good for past centuries but was no longer suitable for the present one.

As though to emphasize the modernity of his legislative pretensions, Napoleon now demanded that the Pope declare invalid the marriage of his younger brother Jerome, a minor, to Elizabeth Patterson, daughter of a wealthy American Protestant family. Research ordered by the Pope proved there had been no invalidating impediments, the Emperor's claim to the contrary notwithstanding. Pius therefore had to inform him that although the Church did not approve of mixed marriages—which were all the more blameworthy if contracted without the knowledge or consent of parents—Jerome's marriage was a valid one. However much Pius desired to gratify the Emperor, particularly in things involving his person and family, he was in this case unable to do so without making himself guilty before God and the Church of the most crying abuse of his sacred ministry.

In France, the Feast of St. Napoleon—a martyr of uncertain authenticity, after whom Bonaparte had been named—was introduced and made a holy day of obligation by imperial decree, instead of the Assumption of Our Lady. The papal legate Caprara confirmed its observance by an apostolic indult, and a number of French bishops vied with one another in pastoral letters in extolling the rediscovered national saint. Special historical lessons on St. Napoleon's life and martyrdom were introduced into the breviary.

A single liturgy of the Mass was imposed for all France.[1] Further, an imperial catechism was composed on the Emperor's orders for use throughout the Empire. Rome could not approve; but the accommodating Cardinal Caprara gave it his approbation so that the new catechism looked as though it had the Holy See's approval. The French bishops adopted it, and before the *fait accompli* Rome was silent, unable to take action without discrediting the papal legate and the French episcopate.

Questions and answers such as these were typical of the imperial catechism:

> Q. What are the duties of Christians toward princes that govern them, and what, in particular, are our duties toward Napoleon I, our Emperor?
>
> A. Christians owe to them that govern them, and we, in particular, owe to Napoleon I, our Emperor, love, respect, obedience, loyalty, military service and the taxes ordered for the preservation of his empire and his throne.

Napoleon also set up an imperial university with a curriculum designed particularly for the middle classes to supply suitable officials in government and military administration. The university was not run on non-religious lines, as are most modern ones, but made use of religion as an essential basis in the formation of character and civic duty.

In 1806 the Third Coalition, composed of English, Russian, Austrian, Swedish and Prussian allies, engaged Napoleon in a campaign against the Austrians in Bavaria. From there he ordered occupation of the papal port of Ancona lest it leave a bridge for his enemies, in the event of a British landing, between Italy and Austria via the Adriatic. To be doubly sure, Napoleon then required the Pope to blockade English shipping.

Pius VII and his advisers saw from this latest move of the Emperor's that in the future no part of Italy might be safe from invasion. The Pope wrote personally to Napoleon sharply complaining of the occupation of Ancona and refusing to blockade English shipping. The letter ended with a kind of ultimatum: if Ancona were not evacuated of French troops, it would be difficult for the Pope to keep up relations with the French ambassador at Rome.

Napoleon was taken aback by the Pope's change of tone. He was accustomed to a resigned and compliant attitude, but now for the first time sensed Pius VII's potential firm resistance where a vital matter was at stake—a resistance which he was soon to show and which future years of captivity and persecution were never effectively to break. (In his memoirs written during his own imprisonment on St. Helena, Napoleon was to speak of Pius as having here taken up the pen of Gregory VII.)

The Emperor did not reply to the ultimatum at once, but waited until his victory over the Austrians left him in a strong enough position. He then wrote to Pius that he keenly resented the threat contained in his letter at a moment when all the allied powers in British pay were making unjust war on him. Was it not better for Ancona to be in the Emperor's hands than in those of Turkish infidels or English heretics? The Holy See's ingratitude to him, the Church's protector, and her bad policy were no doubt due to false counsellors. Consalvi was largely to blame for the ultimatum, and Fesch, the French ambassador, was ordered to tell him he had either to do as the Emperor wished or resign as Secretary of State.

Napoleon, now master of Venice as well as Northern Italy, next forced the King of Naples, Ferdinand II into exile for favoring the British landing there; he then put his own brother Joseph on the throne. The result was that Rome and the Papal States lay open to being caught in a pincer movement from north and south. Napoleon aimed to bring the whole of Italy into his political system. The Pope's main concern in the ensuing struggle was for his sovereign independence.

Pius claimed his traditional right of investing the Neapolitan king, Ferdinand II, but Napoleon replied that if the Pope refused to recognize his brother Joseph's kingship, he, the Emperor, would no longer recognize the temporal sovereignty of the Pope. He emphasized his point by ordering a further invasion of papal territory and by occupying Civita Vecchia, the Mediterranean seaport nearest to Rome. "All Italy will be under my law," the Emperor wrote. "I shall not interfere with the Holy See's independence... but on condition that Your Holiness show the same respect for me in the temporal sphere as I for you in the spiritual... Your Holiness is Sovereign of Rome, but I am Emperor... All my enemies must be yours. Enemy nationals must be banished and their ships excluded from the papal ports."

The Emperor concluded his conditions for respecting the Pope's temporal sovereignty with a lesson: "Your Holiness is surrounded by men who cause unreasonable delays. They think of worldly interests and the vain prerogatives of the tiara, while permitting souls to perish that are the true foundation of religion."

Pius replied by setting out the nature of the Church's mission, spiritual and universal, and the Pope's sacred charge of defending the unalterable rights of free sovereignty. He cannot banish allied nationals or exclude their ships—and this not because of temporal interests, but because he is the Vicar of Christ desiring peace for all. Only the need for countering hostile aggression against Christian civilization had on past occasions obliged certain of his predecessors, for just reasons, reluctantly to abandon a pacific policy. Hostile action of the kind demanded by the Emperor would cut the Holy See off from Catholics in the offended countries. There were many millions in the Russian and Austrian empires and in the lands ruled by the King of England. Pius affirmed that the Catholic Church could not take part in a temporal conflict between rival nations.

"You are immensely great," Pius went on to tell the Emperor. "But you have been elected, crowned and recognized Emperor of the French, not of Rome. There is no Emperor of Rome. . . There is indeed an Emperor of the Romans; but this title is recognized by all Europe, and by Your Majesty himself, as pertaining to the Austrian Emperor. It is a title of dignity and honor that in no way lessens the real or apparent independence of the Holy See. . ."[2]

Napoleon's only reply was a note announcing the replacement of Cardinal Fesch as ambassador to Rome by the ex-revolutionary regicide Alquier. When Alquier was presented to Pius by the retiring Fesch, the Pope told him that if the Emperor were to use force against him, he would be obliged to use the spiritual as well as the temporal means that God had given him. Fesch interrupted, saying that the Pope had no right to use his spiritual powers in a quarrel which concerned temporal matters. In righteous anger, Pius VII's voice rose to a shout as he asked where the Cardinal had gotten that idea.

Having practically forced Consalvi to retire from the Secretariat of State, Napoleon sent a second request, through his new ambassador, for the closing of the papal ports against English ships and for the Pope's support of his political system.

"Our determination is irrevocable," Pius answered. "And you may look on it as our testament; for we are ready to sign it with Our blood." To Caprara in Paris he wrote, "We are in God's hands. Who knows if the persecution His Majesty may be threatening Us with has not been decreed by Heaven for the bringing about of a revival of faith and reawakening of True Religion in the hearts of Christians."

A peremptory diplomatic note then arrived from the Emperor, who had announced he would no longer write directly to the Pope: either Pius VII must ally himself with Napoleon's enemies or lose the remainder of the Papal States. It was the Head of the Church's duty to make common cause with him in fighting infidels and English heretics, who were constituting a threat to world peace.

At the same time, a set of "proposals" arrived in Rome from Paris regarding matters to be regulated for the Italian Church: the creation of a number of French cardinals, dispensation of bishops from making their *ad limina* visits to Rome and the suppression of men's religious orders, because the Emperor disliked monks—who did not exist in the time of the Apostles—and above all, Jesuits.

Pius VII now deemed it time to have recourse to the most effective spiritual means in his power: refusal to grant canonical institution to bishops appointed by Napoleon for vacant French and Italian sees. He knew that from his refusal in so vital a matter he could expect the worst from the Emperor; Napoleon's immediate response was to occupy still more papal territory.

Pius then recalled the ambassador he had sent to Paris in an attempt at peaceful negotiations— "dialogue," as it is now termed—concerning affairs of the Church. The College of Cardinals in Rome was firmly behind the Pope in his determination to resist the Emperor's demands. One final effort was made for conciliation, by a diplomatic note, but the French ambassador Alquier declined to deliver it. He declared friendly relations with his government broken off, the time for negotiation past; it was now time for action.

Thus was the order given at the end of January 1808 for General Miollis to occupy Rome.

The French ambassador aimed a parting shot at Pius before he left, repeating that the Pope now had no alternative but to enter the imperial confederation against Napoleon's enemies if he did not wish to lose everything—and the sooner he yielded the better.

Pius replied: "You may tell them at Paris they may hack me to pieces or skin me alive, but we shall always say no to any suggestion of adhering to their political system or confederation. Our Predecessor had the strength of a lion. I have so far acted like a lamb. But I shall know how to defend myself and, if need be, die like a lion." The Pope's "fiery countenance, flashing eyes and vigorous words" so impressed Alquier that upon returning to France he informed his court that nothing would overcome the Pope's obstinacy, adding, "You do not know this man."

The French troops entered Rome at the beginning of February. First disarming the papal guards, whom the Pope had forbidden to offer any resistance, they occupied Castle St. Angelo opposite the Vatican.

It was tactically announced that a portion of the French army was making a temporary halt in Rome since the English, in league with the exiled Neapolitan King, were on the march toward Naples. But this announcement was belied by the cannon stationed in front of the Quirinal Palace, its barrel pointed up at the windows of the papal apartment.

Pius at once had a protest affixed in public places of the City. At the same time, he addressed a brief to the College of Cardinals saying he was ready to shed his blood in defense and support of Religion and the Holy See.

General Miollis requested an audience for himself and his officers. It was granted by the Holy Father, who spoke words of marked kindness for the French people and complimented the General on the discipline he maintained among his soldiers.

Miollis had set about winning the favor of the people of Rome, especially the most influential, by inviting them to magnificent receptions, banquets and balls in the Doria Palace where he had taken up residence. But on hearing of this, the Pope ordered that none should frequent them; and soon the General's banqueting halls and ballrooms were deserted. Also, when the Governor of Rome issued an appeal to all citizens to forego the carnival customarily celebrated during the days preceding Lent, the people willingly complied.

After Consalvi's forced resignation, Pius had named Cardinal Pacca Secretary of State. Miollis knew him to be an intransigent enemy of the Revolution and sent men to arrest him in his office at the Quirinal Palace. Pacca refused to obey any orders other than his Sovereign's and managed to get a note to the Pope—who came into the room, his hair literally standing on end (as Pacca described it). In holy wrath Pius cried out to Miollis' official that he could go and tell his general that the Pope was tired of putting up with so many outrages and insults from one still calling himself a Catholic but whose plan was to take away the Pope's ministers in order to prevent him from exercising his Apostolic charge and temporal sovereignty. He commanded Pacca not to obey the General's orders but to follow him, the Pope, to his apartments and share his imprisonment. If the General still had it in mind to take the Cardinal away from him, he would have to do so by breaking in the doors and be responsible for every consequence of such unheard-of violation.

"Let us go, my Lord Cardinal," Pius ended, taking Pacca by the hand and leading him out of the room up the main stairs, on whose either side applauding members of the papal household had gathered with cries of *"Bravo il Papa!"*

The cry was taken up in the streets outside where Miollis had tried in vain to make the people arrange a carnival procession. Instead, they had succeeded in getting the neighborhood and most of Rome specially illuminated to celebrate the eighth anniversary of Pius VII's election.

Pacca had to bear the reproof for not having thought of any plan to allow the Pope to escape from Rome by sea to safety in one of the allied lands that were France's enemies. But such a plan had been thought of, a plan involving the Scottish Cardinal Erskine (called to Rome when still a monsignor by Pius VII). Pius had steadfastly refused to entertain such an idea, for by putting himself under English protection he would have given Napoleon grounds for declaring him an enemy of the French. Above all, the notion of escaping from Rome for the safety of his own person was far from the mind of Pius VII, even if in times past some of his predecessors had, in different circumstances, been obliged to take flight. His determination to remain in Rome, cost what it might, was seen as proof of the justice of his cause not only by his own subjects but also by Protestants.

The imperial decree annexing Rome and the Papal States to the French Empire was put into execution in June, 1809. Miollis had the papal flag lowered on Castle St. Angelo and the French Republican Tricolor hoisted in its place with artillery salvos. The rolling of drums accompanied proclamation of the decree throughout the city.

Pacca went to the Pope and found him outwardly unmoved. But both spontaneously expressed their feelings in the words of Christ on the Cross: *"Consummatum est"* — "It is finished."

Pacca's nephew then came in with a copy of the imperial decree, and the Cardinal went with the Pope to read it at the window. Pacca made efforts to read aloud calmly and with the greatest attention. But it was impossible: the thought of the sacrilege being committed, the sight of his Sovereign, Christ's Vicar, having to hear the sentence of dethronement, the false and injurious terms and deafening sound of the cannon proclaiming triumphant usurpation were too much for him.

Pius showed pain and indignation only at the first words of the reading. Little by little his expression regained its customary composure, tranquillity and resignation. He went back to his writing table and, without saying anything, put his signature to a document of protest, which was published that evening.

Pacca asked if he should also give orders for publication of the Bull of Excommunication which had been drawn up against the eventuality of the Holy Father's abduction and deprivation of his temporal sovereignty. The Pope hesitated. Certain expressions against the French government had seemed too severe. Pacca ventured to say he felt the time had come, and that whatever orders Pius gave him, after praying to God, would be in accordance with the divine will. "Very well, then," said the Pope, after lifting his eyes to Heaven, "let it be published. But take care those carrying out your instructions be not discovered, for they would certainly be condemned to death, and I should be inconsolable." Pacca replied he was sure that if God willed this action, He would protect and favor it.

The effect was extraordinary, if not prodigious: copies of the Bull were posted in the usual places—notably the three major basilicas of St. Peter, St. John Lateran and St. Mary Major—in broad daylight as Vespers were being sung, with numbers of people attending. Many said they saw men with brush and pail posting the Bull. Yet not one of them was discovered and arrested either then or afterwards, despite an extraordinary government council called to make minutest and severest investigations.

The formal sentence of excommunication had been drawn up, without naming Napoleon, against all who were in any way responsible for the sacrilegious seizure of Rome. Such was the loyalty of the Roman people that all employed in public administration refused to continue working until they received instructions from the Church, being ready for any sacrifice rather than incur her censure by serving the new government. Customs officials, porters and transport workers, streetsweepers and lamplighters abandoned their jobs. The Roman Penitentiary[3] had to issue instructions to confessors and ecclesiastical tribunals as to categories of persons who might or might not continue in their employment without culpability. The French were bound to admit that "the Pope governs with his fingertips far more than we with our bayonets."

The Emperor received news of the Bull of Excommunication shortly before his decisive victory over the Austrians at the battle of Wagram. He denied responsibility for the further sacrilegious act which had taken place, that of arresting and abducting the Pope; but from his communications this was what Miollis evidently thought he wanted. Miollis' second-in-command, the young General Radet, believed the Emperor wanted this, and when Miollis hesitated, took it upon himself to arrest the Pope and remove him from Rome with Pacca.

These events followed soon upon the promulgation of the

Bull of Excommunication. A month after the promulgation, Pacca, who had shared the Pope's imprisonment in the Quirinal for nearly a year, learned that pickets of cavalry were patrolling the streets leading to the palace. After an anxious day expecting the worst, he kept watch through the night. Toward dawn on July 6, 1809, not hearing any sound, he retired to take a little rest. But no sooner had he gone to bed than a servant came to tell him the French were in the building.

Hastily rising and dressing, he saw people carrying arms and torches trying to get through the doors of the inner courtyard. Others had already broken in by ladders through the upper windows of the servants' quarters. Led by a servant who had been dismissed for stealing, a band of police spies, gendarmes and rebels against the papal government managed to get to the main doors and open them to let in General Radet and his officers.

Pacca went at once to waken Pius, who got up and, fully robed and keeping his serenity, passed into the room where he was accustomed to giving audience. The Pope and Pacca were joined by Cardinal Despuig[4] and other prelates and members of the papal household.

They heard the outer doors of the apartment being smashed, then all the other doors broken down until the assailants arrived before that of the room where they were seated waiting.

The Pope ordered the door to be unlocked, to save further damage and disorder, then went forward and stood in the middle of the room in front of the table where he had been seated. Pacca and Despuig stood on either side of him, flanked by the other prelates, priests and officials.

General Radet was the first to enter, followed by other French officers and gendarmes and one or two of the rebels who had led the intruders. Radet went up to the Pontiff and stood before him, and for some minutes there was absolute silence.

"We stood and looked at one another in bewilderment without uttering a word or making any movement," Pacca recorded in his memoirs. "At last, General Radet, pale and trembling, hardly able to utter the words, told the Pope he had an unpleasant and painful duty to perform, but having sworn fidelity and obedience to the Emperor could not do less than execute it: he had to inform His Holiness he must renounce temporal sovereignty of Rome and his States. If not, he had orders to bring him to General Miollis, who would let him know where he was to be taken."

Pius VII, without losing his composure, in firm and dignified tones, replied that if he, Radet, believed it his duty to execute the Emperor's orders for his oath of loyalty and obedience, how much more was the Sovereign Pontiff, bound by many an oath, obliged to uphold the rights of the Holy See... The Emperor would never obtain what he was demanding. "After all We have done for him," the Holy Father added, "We did not expect this treatment."

"Holy Father," Radet answered, "I know the Emperor is much indebted to you."

"More than you know," Pius told him, in somewhat resentful tones, then asked, "Are we to go alone?"

Radet answered that he could take his minister Pacca with him. While the Pope was getting a few necessary things together in his bedroom, Radet promised that nothing would be touched in his absence. "He who puts little value on his own life values things even less," Pius answered.

Pacca joined the Pope, surrounded by gendarmes, police agents and rebel subjects, walking down the stairs over the remains of splintered doors to the courtyard, from where a band of French troops and more police agents led him to the main gateway and the waiting carriage. A number of Neapolitan troops had been drawn up to assist Radet's enterprise.

Pius was made to get into the carriage, Pacca after him; the blinds were drawn down, both windows locked, and the carriage drove away—but not to General Miollis. At the city gates, the horses were changed and drove off at full speed in the direction of Viterbo.

The Pope reproved Radet for his lie in saying he was taking him to Miollis, and for the way he had been led off alone

Pope Pius VII

with Pacca and without anything. But the young General's only reply was that his orders had been carried out, and no one had been killed or wounded—at which Pacca asked if he thought they had been in a fortress offering armed resistance.

Pius inquired of Pacca if he had brought any money with him; he had not been able to. Pope and Cardinal Secretary of State found that between them they had four small coins in their purses. They could not help laughing, in spite of their predicament.

As they drove on, Pacca was assailed by uneasy thoughts as to whether he had done right in encouraging the Pope to publish the Bull of Excommunication, considering its results. Pius divined his thoughts for, turning to him with a smile, he said comfortingly and with great kindness: "We did well, Your Eminence, to publish the Bull last June 10th..."

On the evening of the same day Pacca also had the consolation of knowing that, on his orders, a moving notification penned by Pius a few moments before leaving was being posted up all over Rome, a loving farewell message from the Common Father at being parted from his sons:

> In peace with all the world but praying also for the peace of every princedom, only an act of violence could separate him from the City of Rome . . . universal center of Catholic unity. . . The perpetrators of his forcible abduction were responsible to God for all the consequences. He for his part desired, counselled and ordered his faithful subjects, in particular those of his flock in Rome, and all his universal flock of the Catholic Church, to imitate the faithful of earliest times, when St. Peter was in chains, and the Church "prayed to God for him without ceasing. (*Acts* 12:5)."

NOTES

1. There had been several variants: besides the early liturgical rites of Gaul (Gallican liturgies) there were the allied Mozarabic and Celtic rites, a Frenchified version of the Roman rite and other surviving French diocesan uses.
2. Napoleon abolished the title of Holy Roman Emperor (and its accompanying title, Protector of the Church) in that year, 1806.
3. Formerly the Roman tribunal dealing with matters of the internal forum, granting absolutions and dispensations, deciding cases of conscience and dealing with the whole matter of indulgences on their practical side.
4. Archbishop Despuig, Spain's unofficial envoy at the Conclave, was created Cardinal by Pius VII in 1804.

~ 7 ~

CAPTIVITY IN SAVONA

The Painful Journey—Homage of the People—
The Armed Guards—The Pope's Daily Life—Our Lady
of Mercy—Struggle over Canonical Institution
of Bishops—Increasing Pressure upon Pius VII

The journey that had begun in Rome an hour after dawn continued until midnight—nineteen hours in the stifling heat of July with the carriage windows closed and only one short stop for a hurried meal. Pius was suffering from dysentery as well as strangury aggravated by the speed kept up over the rutty roads. Almost 67 years old (the year was now 1809), the Pope felt acutely the hardships of the journey.

Neither he nor Pacca had any change of clothing, so when at last they got out, bathed in sweat, at a little inn in the Tuscan hills, they had to let what they had on dry upon them in the cool night air. Pacca helped the only servant make up the Pope's bed, and after a little supper, they lay down in adjoining rooms dressed as they were.

Radet had the grace to thank Pacca for having kept up the Holy Father's spirits during the nearly unendurable journey. Pius had in fact astonished the Cardinal by expressing no regret whatsoever for the strong words of the Bull of Excommunication which had caused their present situation; but he dismayed the Cardinal by his remonstrances to Radet, in severe and resentful tones, so that Pacca felt obliged to beg the Pope to speak with his customary gentleness.

Pius was feverish the next morning after the sudden change of temperature. Radet had orders to go on at once so as to reach Florence by evening, but Pius refused to move until the members of his household who had been allowed to follow arrived. The two carriages that had left Rome later the day before drew up at the inn toward midday with the Pope's private chaplain, his doctor, cook and a servant, plus some necessary baggage; and so the journey continued.

As the carriage drove away too quickly from a locality where the Holy Father had been recognized and people allowed to approach him, a wheel came off and the carriage toppled over. Pius fell to one side of the interior with Pacca above him. Neither were hurt, the carriage was righted, and people ran up to help the Pope and Cardinal out while Radet's officers tried threateningly to keep people off with drawn sabers. Pius replied smilingly to those crowding around him trying to kiss his hands and feet and asking if he had been hurt, thanked them for their sympathy, and spoke almost jokingly of what had happened. The accident had in fact alarmed Radet (who had been thrown into a ditch) and his men far more than the Pope and Pacca.

News of the mishap spread in no time so that, as Pius proceeded in one of the following carriages, groups gathered by the wayside crying out their sympathy and begging his blessing.

Florence was reached by nightfall. At the Charterhouse where the Pope was to be kept for a time, the Prior was waiting at the doors, but none of the monks was allowed to come near him. The Holy Father was assigned the same apartment that Pius VI had been kept in on his way to Valence. Overcome by weariness and suffering, he could not conceal his dejection. An envoy from the court of the Grand Duchess of Tuscany, Elisa Bonaparte, Napoleon's sister, came to pay formal respects, but the Pope was too exhausted to receive him. Hardly able to raise his head, he managed only to mutter a few unintelligible words.

A lavish supper was served but he could not eat it, his

main need being to make up for lost sleep. He was eventually able to retire, but in the middle of the night he was awakened and told that the Grand Duchess had decided he could not remain in Tuscany. He was to be moved on at once, before dawn, to another destination.

Pacca found the Pope all but prostrate, his face a greenish color and expressing deepest desolation. "I realize," he said, "these people mean to kill me by ill-treatment, nor do I think I shall be able to endure life much longer." He was parted from Pacca and driven off in the direction of Genoa without being permitted to say Mass, despite the fact that it was now Sunday.

Grenoble had been chosen by the Governor General of the French "Department beyond the Alps" as the Pope's next destination because it was the well-fortified headquarters of an army division. But Napoleon, disclaiming responsibility for the Pope's removal from Rome, wrote to the Chief of Police, Fouché, in Paris that he did not want him in France. He should be taken back to Italy where a suitable house to lodge him was to be found at Savona pending further developments. "If he stops being so foolish," the Emperor wrote, "I should even have no objection to his being brought back to Rome."

So Pope Pius VII was dragged back over the Alps. His journey from Grenoble to Savona was accompanied by such popular demonstrations of devotion that the destination was only reached by slow stages after two weeks. He passed through Valence, where in captivity and sordid surroundings Pius VI had breathed his last, and the ancient papal city of Avignon, famous for the great "Schism of the West" and "Babylonian Captivity" of the Popes, through Marseilles and along the French Riviera.

At Nice the bridge over the River Varo had to be crossed on foot, and when the Pope got to the other side he was acclaimed by a great crowd of people only lately aware of what had really happened. Some of the military escort were manhandled, and it became impossible to go forward in the midst of the throng surrounding the Pope's carriage.

Rumors that the Pope was approaching Savona and was to remain there had reached the people of the city, though few believed it. But when definite orders came to the Prefect of the Department, Count de Chabrol, and the Bishop was seen driving off with some of the clergy to meet the Pontiff outside the city, they knew it was true. Because of the Holy Father's plight, exhilaration could not be expressed openly: orders had been sent ahead that no bells were to be rung and there were to be no public demonstrations or rejoicing. Mounted police were posted at every street corner with drawn swords and menacing gestures for any who showed signs of defiance.

The people came crowding into the streets leading to the city gates and waited silently and anxiously.

A dusty coach-and-four came in sight flanked by a squad of horsemen with pistols stuck in their saddle-fronts and naked swords held in their hands... and there was the Sovereign Pontiff, locked inside.

In an instant, all heads were bared and respectfully bowed. Most knelt on the ground but no sound came, forbidden as all had been to applaud. A troupe of trumpeters standing on the cathedral steps who dared sound their instruments were brusquely hushed as the Pope's carriage moved silently and rapidly forward to the Mayor's residence, where it had been arranged for him to be lodged.

The building had a melancholy look and the Pope is said to have exclaimed: "My God! Is this really a prison? Is it here I am to end my days?" But the Mayor and his family were waiting inside on their knees, and Pius breathed a sigh of relief as he was led to the rooms made ready for him. In one of these was an altar, where he went and knelt for some minutes in silent prayer, his face buried in his hands.

As Pius prayed he could hear the murmuring of the people outside growing louder, at times sounding threatening, as though they were unwilling anymore to be kept under control. The number of guards was by now insufficient to deal with the swelling crowds gathered from all parts of the city and beyond.

Then suddenly a cry rang out—the voice of a young man: *"Viva il nostro Santo Padre!"* — "Long live our Holy Father!" — signal for all to give vent to their pent-up feelings. In a crescendoing chorus, thousands and thousands of voices took up the cry: "The Holy Father!" "We want the blessing of the Holy Father!"

If that was all the people wanted, the guards desperately trying to keep order thought it best to let them have it—also in the hope of getting them afterward to return to their homes. So orders were given for the balcony window to be opened— and the Pope for an instant appeared, raised his hand and blessed the throngs of kneeling people.

The mayoral residence of the noble Sansoni family was only the Pope's first lodging in Savona. It was not thought safe enough for guarding him, and on Napoleon's orders the Bishop's Palace was prepared, where Pius could be kept in complete isolation under close police supervision.

The palace had been a Franciscan monastery, with cloisters and garden, adjoining the cathedral. The Bishop was now required to move into other quarters. A group of Savonese carpenters, who had begged for the privilege, worked at night fitting up a dais and throne with white silk hangings and gold-embroidered canopy in one of the rooms of the palace.

After a few days spent in the Sansoni mansion, Pius was led on foot by his guards, together with the few attendants that had been allowed him—his chaplain, house steward, physician and one or two servants—to the place where he was to be kept for the next two and a half years.

Here, resigned and thankful that at least for a time the days of being dragged from one place to another were over, he as ever committed all to God. What most weighed on him was the fact that he was cut off from every adviser and minister, with no means of governing the Church. He was not at first allowed to be visited even by the Bishop of Savona or any of the clergy.

His daily visitor was the Prefect, Count Chabrol, a young French nobleman who combined gentlemanly courtesy with the hardness of a jailor in the service of the Emperor. Chabrol was taking no chances with his prisoner, for the week after the Holy Father was installed in the episcopal palace a reinforced guard of 150 infantry and 100 artillery soldiers arrived, with a further detachment of gendarmes, as "guard of honor" for the Pontiff. With a squadron of dragoons soon added, historical records calculate that nearly 1,000 men in arms were guarding the Pope inside and outside the residence. Sentinels kept constant watch at the gates and doors as well as outside the cathedral, and more were at the door of the Holy Father's apartment. General Berthier and his men occupied one wing of the building; Colonel Lagorse was in command of the gendarmes. Plainclothes agents and spies mixed with the people, were present in the chapel while the Holy Father was celebrating Mass and in the throne room when he was permitted to give audiences.

In Savona as everywhere else, strictest orders were enforced prohibiting anything to be published about the Pope in newspapers, magazines, books or pamphlets; and booksellers were forbidden to sell any literature that made reference to him.

Napoleon realized that the machinery of the Church, the spiritual kingdom he aimed to rule as well as the earthly, was vitally hampered by the Pope's no longer confirming bishops in office, after the Emperor had named them. He instructed some of the Church's highest dignitaries—his uncle Cardinal Fesch, Cardinals Maury and Caprara, and others he could count on—to write to the Pope, as if on their own, and set before him the harm he was doing by withholding ratification of bishops to vacant sees.

Pius VII replied to Cardinal Caprara's letter: "After so many innovations fatal to Religion which the Emperor has set afoot, and against which We have long and vainly protested, the exile of many bishops and cardinals, Our arrest in Our own palace and being dragged from place to place so closely guarded that bishops of several dioceses We traversed could not approach Us, how could We consent in this matter to the author of such violent measures? . . . Ponder these things, my Lord Cardinal, not in the way of human wisdom, but in the sanctuary, and you will feel the force of them. . ."

The Pope declined the Prefect's repeated offer to be taken for a drive on the seacoast or in the surrounding countryside, this being an impermissible diversion in his captive state while the Church was suffering. But he did ask during his first days in Savona to visit the Shrine of Our Lady of Mercy—*Nostra Signora della Misericordia*—not far from the city, where the Blessed Virgin was believed to have appeared in 1536.

The Pope's desire was prompted by a singular circumstance that had made him think of Savona before ever knowing he would be taken there. A few days before Radet had broken into the Quirinal, the chaplain of the Genoese church in Rome had managed to enter the palace and get to the Pope disguised as a servant. His purpose was to offer him a picture of Our Lady of Mercy venerated at the shrine near Savona, certain that the Pope's tribulations would be ended through her intercession. He had thanked the priest, greatly touched by his attention, put the holy picture in the pocket of his soutane and kept it with him. Looking at it again, and recalling the confidence of the priest who had given it to him, Pius also now felt certain, exclaiming as he put the picture to his lips: *"Digitus Dei est hic"* — "The finger of God is here."

The Pope's visit to the shrine was duly arranged. After celebrating Mass there, assisted by the Bishop of Savona and another, he venerated the image of Our Lady, praying on his knees for some minutes with his head pressed against the feet.

On September 8, Feast of Our Lady's Nativity, Pius celebrated Mass in Savona Cathedral. The choir sang a motet on the words *Tu es Petrus* with the repeated refrain *et portae inferi non praevalebunt*— "and the Gates of Hell shall not prevail against it." Uneasy looks were exchanged between the Pope's guardians, Chabrol, Berthier and Lagorse present with others. The people, noting this, took up the refrain as they went out of the cathedral, singing *"non praevalebunt...non praevalebunt...."* The police, who had orders to arrest anyone showing signs of too much zeal for the Pontiff, were honest enough to do nothing, as these were only the words of the Gospel being repeated.

But when Pius VII appeared on the balcony adjoining the cathedral and gave his blessing to the gathering in the square, the police felt bound to make a few conscientious arrests, charging persons with too fervent acclamation of the Pope damaging to the imperial government.

Pius VII's first request on arriving at the episcopal palace was to be able to pray daily before the Blessed Sacrament. This was granted, and a tribune was fitted up for him over-looking the cathedral altar and accessible from the cloisters. Here the Pope spent many hours each day in prayer and adoration, asking God's help for the Church and pardon for her persecutors; and here every evening, together with some of his household, he recited the Rosary.

This soon became known to the people of Savona who, visiting the cathedral, would glance up to catch a glimpse of the Pope behind the grating and follow his example by stopping to pray before the Tabernacle and say the Rosary for his intentions.

The Pope otherwise spent his days in the retirement of his room—for which his Benedictine training had well accustomed him—praying, reading and writing, when not giving audience in the throne room, as was for a time permitted him. He meekly expressed his thanks for the least service and every mark of respect that was shown him, calling Savona his little Rome, and the Bishop's palace his little Vatican. He asked for and obtained from the episcopal library a number of spiritual books and the works of Pope St. Leo the Great, drawing courage from his predecessor's saving Rome by intrepidly facing "the Scourge of God," Attila, in the fifth century. His only recreation was a little walk after his main frugal meal, taken at two o'clock, on the terrace or in the cloister garden. The brightness of a flower caught

in a ray of sunshine, the notes of a bird hidden in the shrub-
bery or perched on a branch of an orange tree, made him
pause with intense delight. Once he was seen to stoop and
touch the horns of a snail drawing itself with scarcely per-
ceptible movement along a leaf, a smile on his face and an
expression of wistful meditation.

On one of these daily walks, Pius caught the sound of
someone sobbing above the sound of the fountain at the far
end of the garden. Going near he came upon a woman doing
the washing and crying so much her tears were falling upon
the wet linen. His heart anguished at the sight of such distress,
the Holy Father tenderly asked what was grieving her so
greatly, and the woman told him, in a voice broken with
sobs, that her son had just died.

After letting her cry on for a while, the Pope comforted
her, asking: "My good woman, supposing before this dear
son of yours had died I had been free to return to Rome
and had asked you to let me take him with me, would you
have said no?"

"Ah, your Holiness, what ever are you saying—me refuse
to give you my son? I'd have thanked you on my knees."

"Well, what I could not do, God has done. He has required
your son of you—not to take him to Rome, but to Heaven."
Greatly comforted by these words of the Holy Father, the
poor woman dried her tears.

Pius usually said his morning Mass in the private chapel
assisted by two of the cathedral canons, with a few others
present. Some were occasionally admitted to the hall where
they could see the altar and join in the Holy Sacrifice.

After breaking his fast with a light collation, the Pope passed
into the throne room where a selected number of persons
were waiting to have audience and kiss his hands and feet,
according to the custom. Many, although closely watched
by the ever-present guards, could not conceal their dismay
and indignation at the plight of the Supreme Pontiff and con-
soled him with mute looks that told him of their love, admiration and compassion; the Pope returned this with looks

and gestures of fatherly affection and gratitude.

As time went on, the presence of Pope Pius VII in Savona became more and more known in spite of the silenced press. Not only the clergy, religious and people of the city sought audience or asked to attend his Mass, but also those of other cities and regions, including foreign visitors. Before long, they became thousands; there was no room in any neighboring hotel or inn, and many passed the night under arcades or in the open country where they could find shelter. Tickets of entry to the episcopal palace had to be issued for places inside, if only in the hall and corridors. The piazza was full to overflowing with people who had to be content with receiving the Pope's blessing afterward from the balcony.

Pius had asked the Mayor, Count Sansoni, why it was mostly clergy and religious or members of distinguished families who were admitted and so few ordinary folk of all classes. Soon more were allowed to come and even to speak a few words. Mothers came with children in arms, and men and women dressed in traditional local costumes brought gifts, sometimes with ingenuous requests. One man begged the Pontiff for a plenary indulgence for the sins he had committed—and for those he might still commit as well. The Pope replied he could grant this for past sins, with penance; but for the future it would be best not to commit any more. A simple-minded lay brother asked for faculties to bless rosaries and medals; Pius said, very well, he could bless them with his trowel. A pious lady asked for a plenary indulgence every time she went to Communion. A little too much, the Pope told her: once a month will do, and at the hour of death, for you and your family.

An old peasant woman managed to get near the Pope with a basket of eggs which, she assured him, were absolutely fresh from her own hens. She was about to offer them when an attendant, considering this an unworthy present, tried to take the basket from her. The Pope stopped him, accepted the eggs and told the delighted woman her gift was appreciated.

Favors and miracles of healing attributed to Pius VII's

intercession also multiplied. A maidservant with a septic finger that would not heal held it up before the Pope, who blessed it, told her to dip it in holy water and pray with complete faith. She did so, and the finger was perfectly healed. A boy of twelve squeezed through the crowd trying to reach the audience room and banged his head on a metal banister, causing a deep head wound. He got before the Pope bandaged with a bloody handkerchief. "My poor son!" Pius cried, "I bless you and your head." When he got home the lad told his parents what had happened, but taking off the handkerchief, they found not the slightest trace of any wound.

Besides these miracles of physical healing attributed to Pius VII were greater ones of grace and spiritual conversion: hardened sinners doing penance and receiving the Sacraments, persons who for years had never been into a church returning to the practice of religion, others whose lives had been a public scandal making amends and reforming.

Among the most striking examples was the case of a customs officer, a high-ranking member of a Masonic Lodge, who not long after the Pope's arrival in Savona had asked the Mayor if he could speak with Pius. A few days later, during the Pope's Mass in the cathedral, the official was seen to make his way up to the altar rails and kneel there in an attitude of deep reverence and compunction before receiving Communion. As the Pope came away from the altar, the man threw himself at his feet, publicly imploring forgiveness. He paid for his repentance by being disowned by the Lodge, dismissed from his post and persecuted by the police. But he persevered, and his example was followed by others.

Who knows if the uneasiness apparent in the Emperor Napoleon's correspondence and conduct after Pope Pius VII's abduction from Rome may have partly come—whatever the human and political causes—from a flicker of Catholic conscience which never quite seemed to have left him. He was aware of the Pope's increasing popularity and French unpopularity in Savona. Official reports reaching Paris stated that within a week after the Pope's arrival in Savona, crowds arriving there daily by land and sea swelled to such proportions that the guards had to be doubled. By mid-September, the number of foreign visitors alone had risen to 6,000, half the city's usual total. Reported miracles of healing, grace and conversion spread Pius VII's fame of sanctity far beyond Savona and Italy.

Unsuccessful in stifling all news concerning the Pope, Napoleon changed his tactics. He could not reckon on subduing Catholic consciences in the face of the growing indignation at his treatment of the head of Christendom. He would, then, persuade his subjects and the world that the Pope's sojourn in Savona was a necessary and temporary measure of surveillance and protection, that he was no prisoner, and that he, the Emperor, was the first in showing him due respect and honor.

A count by the name of Salmatoris, who had been honored for his services to Louis XVI but had not hesitated to offer these to Bonaparte after the King's execution, and had been likewise honored, was sent to Savona for this purpose. The Count arrived with a company of horsemen, liveried servants and attendants, with the mission of seeing that Pius VII was royally lodged, treated and surrounded by every kind of magnificence, pomp and ceremony. The Pope was further to be persuaded to form a consistory of cardinals (chosen by the Emperor) and a chancellery staffed by confidential persons (also picked by Napoleon).

Pius listened quietly to what the Count proposed, then answered that, though grateful for the attention lavished on him, he could not accept such honors as long as liberty was denied him. Magnificence did not become a Pontiff in captivity while the Church of God was in sorrow, loss and mourning. The present modest services of his household, whose expenses were paid by voluntary offerings from the faithful, were quite enough for him. If a consistory were to be called, it would have to be with cardinals of his own choosing—but lest he endanger them Pius took care not to name any. Such a consistory, moreover, should be held in

Rome, where he would be reunited with his ministers, all of whom were equally dear to him.

Despite this refusal, a gilded carriage with richly harnessed horses and liveried coachmen, grooms and servants was sent around to the episcopal palace. The Pope was told the cathedral was being decked out in grand style for a papal Mass; he intimated that nothing would induce him to celebrate it under the circumstances.

Not taking no for an answer, on the Emperor's instructions the Prefect Chabrol and Count Salmatoris, with Generals Lagorse and Berthier, came and tried to persuade him—but in vain.

Still intent on his purpose, the Emperor then had the best upholsterers from Genoa and even interior decorators from Paris transform the ex-Franciscan monastery episcopal palace into a royal one. Gold and silver ornaments and vases, crystal chandeliers, red and gold embroidered curtains were put up there and in the cathedral.

But to all the advances daily made him by the Count and Prefect, Pius gently answered that instead of gilding his chains, why did the Emperor not break them? He was finally compelled to declare with severity that, if they did not desist in trying to persuade him, he would have no alternative but to make public protestation, so that the faithful should be left in no doubt as to the true situation.

Even this did not avail. His place of residence was to be known as the Pontifical Palace. Kitchens and stables were built on, and one day, returning to his apartments after his walk in the cloister garden, Pius found that sumptuous silk hangings had replaced the plain window curtains, and a silver chandelier hung glittering from the ceiling. Instead of his modest desk, there was a huge writing table inlaid with gold, along with a gold pen and inkstand.

The Holy Father expressed pained surprise and insisted on its being made known that he had not ordered these things. But he was told by the newly-appointed Governor of the Pontifical Palace, who had taken up residence there with a number of secretaries, valets and liveried servants, that he would gravely offend His Majesty the Emperor if he did not accept and thank him for these honors and attentions.

A concerted attempt was next made to get the Pope to celebrate a weekly "Gala Mass" in the cathedral. He refused. Yet the episcopal chair was taken away and replaced by an ornate papal throne set on a high dais with seats ranged around for the religious, civil and military public authorities. The Bishop of Savona was ordered to substitute for the Pope if he would not come.

Before the first of these "Gala Masses" attended by governmental officials, the cathedral doors were left open and a red carpet laid down for the Pope to pass between military guards to celebrate the publicly announced rite. Pius still refused, though knowing he was perilously offending the Emperor; his anguish was increased by fear that his absence would be misunderstood and would cause perplexity, if not disaffection, among some of the people.

With all this, one advantage did however come to him: a wide marble terrace had been built instead of the older, simple wooden one overlooking the square, thus making a more decorous and dignified setting for the daily blessing he had been accustomed to give; and Pius did not hesitate to appear on it.

A witness at the time described the scene: the opening of the high glass doors of the terrace above the piazza crowded with expectant people standing still as statues and without making a sound, the appearance of the white-vested figure of the Pope, majestic in simplicity, on his face an air of gentle sorrow mingled with great fatherly goodness. A resounding cry came from the throng as if from one person, heartfelt and rising to a mighty shout of acclamation. Then the Pope was seen to change expression, his face lighting up with love at the spontaneous demonstration of devotion. When, after a pause, he raised his hand and sweetly sang the blessing, *Benedicat vos omnipotens Deus, Pater, et Filius et Spiritus Sanctus,* slowly tracing the Sign of the Cross over the heads of the kneeling crowd, many were weeping.

Once, on the Holy Father's coming out onto the balcony, the sky grew suddenly overcast and the rain came streaming down. No one moved, the same great cry of acclamation resounded, so that after the blessing Pius added words of admiration and praise, exclaiming: "God will bless the faith of the good people of Savona."

Chabrol, Salmatoris and the Generals in time gave up trying to induce the Pope to celebrate the "Gala Mass." But respectfully, chivalrously even, the Prefect continued to pay his daily visits asking after the Pope's health and showing him a copy of the *Moniteur*, the strictly censored, government-controlled paper giving news of Napoleon's empire. Pius replied courteously, asking after the Prefect's health and the Emperor's, and inquiring if there were really peace in Europe—something necessary also for the peace of the Church.

The Prefect's efforts next became concentrated on endeavoring to induce Pius VII to approve the incorporation of Rome and the Papal States into the French Empire, where the Pope, he argued, should act as chaplain-in-chief to the Emperor, with residence in France. Invariably and unwearyingly, humbly and patiently before such blinded ambition and incomprehension, Pius repeated that what the monk Barnabas Chiaramonti might consent to, the Sovereign Pontiff could not. The See of Peter had been established at Rome, and as Bishop of Rome his was a sacred trust, handed down through the centuries, and not his to renounce. He reminded Chabrol of the disastrous consequences for the Church and society which had come about with the removal of the papal residence to Avignon in the 14th century.

But deaf to the Holy Father's reasoning and subservient to his master Napoleon's might and glory, Chabrol would not give up; his daily persuasions went on until, during one of them, Pius cut him short, exclaiming with unwonted force and firmness: "What is it you are trying to get from me? I have told you I cannot yield and compromise my conscience. I am left with my back to the wall. God Himself will see to the saving of His Church." And saying no more, the Pope retired to pray alone.

On New Year's Day, 1810, the chief government and municipal public authorities went to pay a courtesy visit to the Holy Father, whom they found shut in his room, having ordered that none should disturb him. Half an hour passed before Pius emerged to receive the delegation and listen to the formal address of homage delivered on behalf of the people of Savona, to which he replied with polite acknowledgement. He did not know that at the very time the Emperor's ministers were paying him these empty compliments, others had burst into the offices of the ecclesiastical tribunals and congregations of the Roman Curia and taken possession of the archives. The Papal Treasury was also invaded. Priceless vestments, altar vessels and works of sacred art were taken away—not for the Pope's use at Savona, as was given out, but to be sent to Paris. Even the papal seals and "Fisherman's Ring" (with which bulls are authenticated) were taken from the delegate in charge of the Church in Rome and deposited with General Radet.

Pius VII, however, did soon learn, from the copy of the *Moniteur* daily shown him, that the imperial decree declaring Rome and the Papal States incorporated into the French Empire was confirmed. Powerless to act, he entrusted his cause and that of the Church to God in the words of the psalm: *"Judica me, Deus, et discerne causam meam de gente non sancta: ab homine iniquo et doloso erue me"* . . . "Show me Thy justice, O God, and distinguish my cause against an unholy people: deliver me from the unjust and deceitful man. . ."

It was at this time that Pius was informed of the Emperor's repudiation of his wife Josephine and attempted remarriage to Marie-Louise, Archduchess of Austria. He also knew of the arrest and banishment of the thirteen cardinals residing in Paris who, together with Consalvi, had not attended the nuptial ceremony. They were convinced the first marriage was not invalid (as claimed by the Emperor and even confirmed by the Parisian archdiocesan courts) and insisted that the matrimonial cases of Catholic sovereigns are the sole competence of the Holy See.

Soon after the Emperor's remarriage, the Austrian Chancellor Metternich proposed sending an envoy to the Pope in Savona with regard to the regulating of certain Church affairs; Napoleon agreed, possibly hoping such an embassy might influence Pius when his own efforts had not been able to. The man chosen was Count Lebzeltern, who had been Austrian ambassador in Rome. Pius, for his part, saw a ray of hope in the mission, and the Austrian envoy's visit was of some comfort to him.

Lebzeltern sent a detailed report to Metternich of his conversation with the Pope, whom he found "considerably aged, but in good health, tranquil and serene," just as he had previously known him.

"There is not the least harshness in his manner of speaking, even when touching on questions most displeasing to him," the Austrian envoy reported. "He is very firm regarding questions upon which he could never give way... Not a single word comes from him concerning those who have usurped his sovereignty. What most weighs on him is Pacca's imprisonment, the dispersion of his ministers and cardinals and the banishment of some of them together with bishops abiding by his instructions."

Pius told Lebzeltern that in his present isolation it was a consolation to speak to him on matters concerning the Church. His great preoccupation was this breaking off of all relations with his ministers and clergy, and the difficulty of communicating even with the French bishops. "We ask nothing for Ourself from the Emperor," the Pope told the envoy. "We are old and need nothing, have nothing to lose and have sacrificed everything in doing Our duty... but We ardently desire reestablishment of communications with the Bishops, clergy and faithful."

To Lebzeltern's amazement, he found that Pius VII felt no resentment concerning his treatment by Napoleon, but only love and pity for him. "None more than We desire the

Emperor's happiness," he said with heartfelt sincerity. "He is a prince of many fine qualities. Would to Heaven he could see where his true interests lie. He has in his hands, if he will yet sincerely befriend the Church, every means of benefiting Religion and drawing down on himself and his descendants the blessing of peoples and posterity and of leaving a really glorious name to the world. . ."

Pius VII several times received the Austrian envoy and spoke openly to him of what was on his mind. He repeated that he had absolutely no thought of taking up residence in Paris or Avignon as the Emperor had urged, but insisted on being allowed to return to Rome and united with his cardinals and counsellors for the necessary government of the Church. The question of the temporal power was touched upon, and the Pope, rising from his chair, said he had expressed his thoughts and feelings as he would not have done with most other persons, certain that Lebzeltern was incapable of abusing or betraying his confidence.

Pius VII ended by saying: "Listen, Lebzeltern. I do not authorize you in reports you may pass to Vienna or Paris to say any more than as follows: that you found me resigned to the decrees of Divine Providence, into whose hands I have entrusted my cause and the God-given rights of my dignity. Say that I am serene and tranquil in my imprisonment, convinced as I am that the evils weighing upon the Church are but attributable to their real author.

"Tell the Emperor I earnestly hope he will draw nearer to the Church and reflect how all the glory of this world will never suffice to win him glory for eternity. Tell him to cease persecuting Us and to give Us the means of free communication with the faithful. . . Tell him that I ardently long for conciliation, but not at the expense of my conscience. . . Assure him I bear him no grudge, that I forgive him what has happened and that nothing would cause me more pain than to know he thinks I bear him resentment, which my heart is incapable of."

The Pope even intimated that, if the Emperor gave clear

evidence of a change of heart, he might even lift the excommunication.

This charity and forbearance never blinded the captive Pope to Napoleon's worst qualities and intentions, which many had accused him of not seeing. He was perfectly aware of them. For the tones of the lamb then became those of the lion: "But if the Emperor, behind the mask of protector, dare strike further blows at Religion, if despite my unwillingness he has me dragged off to Paris, if he goes on giving out that my present impotence is owing to my obstinacy, sacrificing the Church's interests for human and temporal considerations . . . if, at length, he forces me to leave this passive conduct of mine, I would then take up such arms as are still left to me and which he surely would not expect."

After this, Pius' customary gentle manner of speech returned, and noting the surprise and dismay on the face of Lebzeltern, he apologized for having given such strong vent to his thoughts and feelings. "Set your mind at rest," he assured him mildly. "I would never go to such extreme lengths unless positively constrained to by force used against me . . . for I trust that God will continue to give me the courage and strength to bear my cross with patience."

Then, as if still further to ask pardon for his vehement outburst, with lowered eyes Pius concluded: "If you knew what a life of anguish I lead, day and night—the constant grief—you would better understand what at times makes a tempest in my heart."

These messages, contained in the Austrian envoy's reports to Bonaparte, had no apparent effect on him. After dissolving most of the religious orders in France and Italy and exiling or imprisoning bishops not compliant to his will, Napoleon ordered the name and liturgical feast of the great reforming Benedictine Pope Hildebrand, Gregory VII, to be removed from the calendar and his feast day no longer recognized by the Church in France.

An imperial decree followed making the "Gallican Liberties" of 1628 a law of the Empire. According to these

"Liberties" the Pope had no temporal power above princes and was bound in other matters by the constitutions and customs of the French and other "local churches." Many bishops and priests felt they had to respect this law while yet recognizing it as erroneous. Its worst consequence was the Emperor's determination to do without the Pope. The Concordat had conceded him the right to appoint bishops, but granting canonical institution was reserved, as of right and necessity, to the Pope. As a result of the Emperor's invasions of papal territory and unjust demands, Pius VII had refused and continued to refuse ratification of his episcopal nominees. Napoleon now openly declared his intention of taking this vital matter into his own hands. However, an ecclesiastical commission appointed by him for consultation had to report that bishops could not lawfully govern their dioceses without canonical institution accorded by the Pope.

A number of bishops and clergy had refused to accept the law of Gallican Liberties and would not obey the Emperor in these respects. This was a consolation to Pius, who was suffering for his sovereign independence and primacy of jurisdiction over the Universal Church. From the Emperor's point of view, the Austrian envoy's mission had not influenced Pius the way Napoleon wanted. If it was impossible for his episcopal nominees to govern their dioceses without ratification and the Pope would not give it, he would have to force him.

"It must not seem that we are acting capriciously or from desire for innovation," the Emperor wrote to the Minister of Public Worship. "It must appear that action is being taken on account of certain rebellious bishops and disobedient priests [no priest could be ordained without the Emperor's license] and the obstinacy of the Pope, who persists in opposing our will."

So following the unsuccessful mission of Lebzeltern, another deputation was now sent to bend Pius to Napoleon's will; this time it was made up of two cardinals, Spina and Caselli. It was made to appear a casual, courtesy visit to the Sovereign Pontiff on the part of their Eminences. But Pius at once saw through Napoleon's new attempt to put greater pressure on him and make him ratify the bishops he had named for some twenty vacant dioceses of the Empire—bishops more or less subservient, as were both cardinals, to the Emperor. He received the cardinals with icy courtesy and told them he could make no decision unless given his liberty and free choice of counsellors.

The cardinals left Savona mistakenly concluding, from some of the Pope's words, that he would be willing to consider ratifying the bishops in certain special circumstances. But Napoleon was so angry on hearing that his prisoner had still dared to suggest any condition for the settlement of the matter that he lost patience and ordered a number of bishops to assume government without canonical institution.

He offered the Parisian archdiocese to his uncle, Cardinal Fesch. But Fesch had come under the influence of the heroic old Superior of the St. Sulpice Seminary, Monsieur Emery (as he was known), and would not accept without the Pope's ratification. The Emperor then invited Cardinal Maury, who had abandoned his diocese of Montefiascone in Italy, to be Archbishop of Paris, and Maury hastened to accept.

The Emperor's act was countered by an act of Pope Pius. He addressed a brief to the Vicar Capitular[1] of the French capital laying down that any bishop appointed by the Emperor but not confirmed by the Pope was to be regarded as an intruder, without power or jurisdiction. In drawing up this brief, Pius made use of historical documents which the saintly Italian priest Bruno Lanteri (now Venerable Bruno Lanteri) had succeeded in smuggling into the episcopal palace. Fr. Lanteri had already managed to get sums of money to the Pope but knew that, even more than financial help, he needed books and documents.

To send the Pope books, documents or uncensored papers meant exile or death. But one of Fr. Lanteri's penitents had willingly taken the risk. He copied out on small sheets of paper certain documents—Pope Gregory VII's forbidding investiture of bishops by lay princes in 1075, and the Acts of

the First Council of Lyons whereby in 1245 Innocent IV condemned the Emperor Frederick II, who was claiming to be
sole Lord of Christendom, for intrusion on the Church's rights.
Obtaining an audience among other persons, he slipped the
sheets into the folds of the Pope's garments while stooping
to kiss his feet.

It was difficult enough to get documents into the episcopal
palace, still more to get any out. But Pius VII now found
a trusted person to smuggle the brief out in his clothing and
deliver it secretly to the Vicar Capitular of Paris, together
with a letter of remonstrance to Cardinal Maury for having
accepted the archbishopric. The Pope reminded the Cardinal
of the danger of schism caused by his unlawful acceptance,
as well as the grave sanctions incurred by one who, appointed
to govern a diocese, arbitrarily deserts it for another.

The Parisian Vicar Capitular had been opposed to Maury's
appointment and, after receiving the papal brief, was not afraid
to let him know it. During an ordination ceremony in Notre
Dame Cathedral, as Maury was requiring the promise of obedience from the ordinand kneeling before him, the Vicar Capitular said in an audible voice: "Your Eminence should be
reminded he has not the right to demand this promise."

Pius VII realized, from the successful smuggling out of
his brief, that there were others willing to take similar risks.
He then wrote letters to various other dioceses forbidding
obedience to the bishop not ratified by him, and a further
letter to the Vicar Capitular of Paris; the latter, however, was
intercepted, leading to the others being discovered.

The Emperor's fury knew no bounds. He at first ordered
the Vicar Capitular to be shot, but commuted the sentence
to imprisonment. Fr. Lanteri was suspected, but no proof was
found; he was put under house arrest. Before the Emperor
could effectively take more general action, however, Pius
managed to get other letters and messages to persons in Savona
and elsewhere.

An ex-army general secretly sympathizing with the Pope,
whose position entitled him to enter and leave the episcopal

palace freely, became the bearer of dispatches concealed under his uniform. A grocer who supplied the kitchens was permitted to offer some of his produce to the Pope and began getting messages in and out of the palace on slips of paper stuck between lettuce leaves or inside hollowed fruit. A workman who was admitted to the Pope's apartments for repairs hid letters in a double-bottomed tool box. Then there was the servant who sewed messages into the hems of his coat; he was suspected, stopped and thoroughly searched but with no result. On being told, Pius asked if he were not afraid; the reply came: "Afraid of what? Do no ill and have no fear."

The Emperor now proceeded to vent his wrath on Pius. He gave orders he should no longer be treated with respect. His writing table, pens and ink were taken away and all letters coming in or going out from the city held up. The Bishop of Savona himself, after severe interrogation, was sent to Paris. "His Majesty is sufficiently enlightened according to the times," the Prefect Chabrol informed the Pope, "to be able to distinguish between the teaching of Jesus Christ and that of Pope Gregory VII."

Pius was further told that the briefs and letters he had secretly sent out to various persons and "plotting priests" had aroused the indignation of all the theologians of France and Italy. It was his own fault if the Vicar Capitular of Paris and other accomplices were in a place where they could do no more harm.

A list of names and particulars was required of all persons in the Pope's service or those who had in any way access to him, that "the poison might the more easily be prevented from spreading further."

These instructions were quickly carried out. In the middle of the night the Prefect, accompanied by a band of police spies and hirelings specially sent from Paris, burst into the episcopal palace, throwing open all the doors and placing extra guards at every entrance. The Pope, awakened by the noise, was roughly summoned from his bed and subjected to a prolonged and insulting interrogation. But when the questioning became not only impertinent but outrageous, Pius, with holy indignation, refused anymore to answer. With a glance up at the crucifix, he cried out loudly: *"Domine, vim patior, responde pro me!..."* ("Lord, I suffer violence, answer for me!") — at which the Prefect broke off his examination and left the room with the others.

The chief purpose of the interrogation had been to wrest from Pius the names of those who had had a hand in getting letters and messages in and out of the palace. But needless to say, he revealed none. The next day the rooms of his apartment were turned upside down, wardrobes and cupboards broken into, sheets, blankets and coverlets and every article of clothing searched. Mattresses and cushions were unsewn and needles stuck through them.

The moment for a still more rigorous inspection came later during the Pope's daily walk in the garden. He returned to find all his books and papers had disappeared, with every other object of personal use.

The report sent to Napoleon admitted that nothing had been found to prove "rebellion" on the Pope's part or on the part of those in his service. The Emperor was, however, chagrined to learn, from a list that had been found, that among those known to have sent alms to the Pontiff were some members of his own court and government.

In spite of the Pope's proven "guiltlessness," more measures followed. The Pope's steward, his trusted room servant and his chaplain were sent to prison; only his cook and personal physician were allowed to remain. He was no longer allowed to appear and bless the people. Doors were sealed and a window was cut in the wall of his room so that he might be observed at any hour. The work on it was never finished as no builder could be found to undertake so dastardly a job.

From then on Pius was treated worse than a common prisoner. He was given too little food, and sometimes his meals were forgotten.

All Savona knew of the Pontiff's harsh treatment and lack of proper nourishment in the midst of so many physical and mental sufferings. By and by, as Pius walked up and down the paths of the little garden taking his daily exercise, he would be surprised to see little packages or envelopes lying here and there in the flower beds or grass and, stooping to pick one up, would find it was a bar of chocolate, another a packet of biscuits. He never knew that some children, sent by a Savonese family to the top of the cathedral bell tower with instructions to take good aim, had thrown down the welcome packets unsuspected and unobserved.

A young locksmith was sent to close up the window leading from the Pope's apartments to the outer balcony, and while working, felt a light tap on his shoulder. "So you are further locking in the prisoner, eh?" said Pius, gently smiling. The boy, only then realizing what it was he had been told to do, knelt at the Pope's feet. But Pius, lifting him, said kindly: "Do what you have to do, my boy. Get on with your work!" and quietly went back to his room.

Repeatedly reprimanded by the Prefect on his daily visits for his resistance to the Emperor's demands, Pius would now simply reply: "It is no use going over all that again. The present state of affairs will last only as long as it please Divine Providence. As for myself, I am resigned to everything, and if I do not have my reward in this world, I can surely expect it in the next."

"His indifference and resignation are truly extraordinary," Chabrol was obliged to testify in his reports. The same was said by Berthier in a letter to the Minister of Public Worship in Paris: "The gentle and amiable character of the Pope is revealed in his look, his smile, his whole countenance. He has such trust in God that in the midst of so many trials and sufferings he is never discouraged. He continues to raise his thoughts to Heaven, certain that God can permit nothing unless it be for the eventual good of the Church. Persecution itself he sees as a good, and his sufferings as a pledge of salvation; and he says the Church will come out triumphant in the end."

NOTES

1. A Vicar Capitular was a cleric appointed by a cathedral chapter to administer a diocese during a vacancy. His office was occasionally extended into a quasi-permanent one by temporal rulers wanting to influence a diocese but unable to persuade the Pope to grant canonical institution to the bishop of their choice. (The title of Vicar Capitular is no longer used.) A cathedral chapter (of canons) is the college of priests having the duty of carrying out solemn liturgical ceremonies and such tasks as may be entrusted to them by the diocesan bishop. The erection, alteration or suppression of a cathedral chapter is reserved to the Holy See.

~ 8 ~

FURTHER STRUGGLES OVER
CANONICAL INSTITUTION OF BISHOPS

The Pope Resists Napoleon—Napoleon Convokes an
Imperial Council—The Council Bishops Resist
Napoleon—The Bishops Yield Conditionally

In 1811 Napoleon had reached the zenith of his power.
He had conquered most of Europe and was ruling over some
seventy million subjects. The power of the Pope was, hu-
manly speaking, at its lowest; it practically did not exist. But
Pius VII's passive resistance to Napoleon by withholding canonical institution from the bishops of his choosing was proving the most effective check to the Emperor's pretensions.

Napoleon now tried to justify these by adverting to Louis
XIV,[1] who had circumvented the Pope by having his episcopal nominees elected by cathedral chapters. Installed as "ad-
ministrators capitular," they were enabled to administer the
dioceses without canonical status.[2]

Pius VII was shown a copy of the *Moniteur* publishing a
report that all the clergy of France and most of Italy had
signed a statement of loyalty to the Emperor in his claims.
It caused great pain to Pius to see that the clergy of his former
diocese of Imola were included, and also Savona. He hoped,
if the report were true, that many had done this from the
pressure of circumstances and with mental reservation.

The Bishop of Savona was summoned to Paris, where the
Emperor decorated him with the star of the Imperial Legion

of Honor. Receiving him upon his return, Pius asked if the
pectoral cross the Pope had given him at his consecration
was not sufficient.

The Emperor's next idea for settling the question of according canonical institution to his bishops without the Pope,
if he still could not force him to grant this, was the convoking
of a general Imperial Council of State and Church.[3] A consultive ecclesiastical committee advised Napoleon that were
such a council to express the remonstrances of the Church
regarding the Pope's refusal to grant institution, it might have
an effect. But the Emperor wanted to know if an imperial
council would have the necessary authority *in fact*. (According to Gallican theory, a general council was held to be above
the Pope.) If the question would have to be referred back
to the Pope, it would be useless to call a council.

Even Gallican-minded bishops and clergy, however, felt that
whether the council was held to be above the Pope or the
Pope above the council, it would be improper to call one
while ignoring the Church's Head. The only rule that might
justify doing without the Pope in a case of extreme urgency
was *Salus populi suprema lex*—"The good of the people is the
highest law." But was not the Emperor himself responsible
for the urgent situation by denying the Pope liberty and free
choice of counsellors?

This, however, the ecclesiastical committee dared not say
to the Emperor outright. Not satisfied, he determined first
to call an extraordinary preliminary council of bishops and
ministers of state.

The assembly met in the great hall of the imperial Tuileries
Palace. The hero of the occasion was to be M. Emery, who
had been reluctant to attend but had been urged to do so
by Cardinal Fesch. Napoleon kept all waiting for two hours—
he believed long waits softened people's minds—then appeared
with much magnificence, surrounded by the chief officials
and dignitaries of his court. The effect was as calculated, for
there were few who did not feel subdued or dismayed.

The session opened with a diatribe by the Emperor against

Pius VII, whom he denounced as a rebel and stirrer up of revolt against him, causing civil strife.

No bishop dared rise to protest. One witness described their lordships "sitting in cowed silence like oaks beneath their branches in a hailstorm."

Their very silence, though, had an unforeseen effect. For Napoleon, feeling he had overstepped his bounds, suddenly turned to the venerable old Abbé Emery and, in milder tones, demanded his opinion.

All waited with bated breath. After a few moments, with a mute prayer to God and tears in his eyes, the little old priest spoke. "Sire," he began, "I cannot think otherwise than according to what is contained in the catechism, taught by your orders. We read there that the Pope is the visible Head of the Church. Can a society do without its head? Without him to whom obedience is owing by divine right?"

To everyone's astonishment, the Emperor showed visible respect and invited Emery to go on.

He did so by quoting the preamble to the Declaration of the Gallican Articles admitting the primacy of Peter and the Roman pontiffs as instituted by Christ. To convoke a general council without or against the Pope could not produce any good result.

The Emperor objected that Christ gave the Pope the spiritual power but not the temporal. The Emperor Charlemagne had given the Pope that, and he, Charlemagne's successor, determined to take it back because the Pope did not know how to use it, and it was hindering his exercise of the spiritual power.

Emery was not at a loss. "On this point I think as Bossuet," he countered, "whom Your Majesty is often pleased to cite. Bossuet affirmed that full liberty and independence of the Pope is necessary for the exercise of his authority in all the world."

"I accept the authority of Bossuet," the Emperor rejoined. "But that held good for his time, when Europe was divided among many sovereigns and it would have been unjust for the Pope to obey them. But what would be the harm of his obeying me, now that all Europe is under my rule?"

The old priest still found a true answer without offending. "Your Majesty knows the history of revolutions better than I. What is true of today may indeed not be of tomorrow. So a stable order of things ought to be proof against present and future obstacles."

Finally questioned by the Emperor whether canonical institution for elected bishops might, in certain circumstances, be delegated to a local council, Emery answered that the Pope would never consent to this, as it would amount to an annulment of his own right.

"Bravo, my Lords! counselling me to blunder by requiring the Pope to grant what he cannot," cried Napoleon. He declared the assembly closed but on his way out bowed to Emery (who died not long after from the strain of his ordeal).

But although Napoleon respected the old priest's "opinion," and declared that opinion in the matter must be free, he did not change his conduct.

The influence of Emery's words, however, remained, not only upon Cardinal Fesch but also in giving greater assurance and courage to many of the bishops.

Before taking the step of convoking an imperial council, the Emperor made a further attempt to bend the Pope's will to his and wring from him agreement to institute his episcopal nominees. In the spring of 1811 he sent three chosen bishops with special instructions to Savona. The episcopal delegation was to announce to the Pope the convoking of an imperial council, telling him that this could be avoided if he would grant the necessary bulls for the Emperor's thirty bishops. In that event, His Majesty would not only offer the Pope freedom to set up his court in Paris or at Avignon, but alternatively would leave him free to return to Rome, on condition he did so as Bishop and Head of Catholicity, with no pretensions to temporal sovereignty, and on condition he take the oath of loyalty, as the bishops had done, in the hands of Napoleon.

Pius knew the character and standing of the bishops sent to treat with him and was immediately on his guard. As soon as he heard the delegation's proposals, he knew a crucial moment had come.

The three bishops had introduced what they had been instructed to say by drawing a picture of the pitiful state of the Church in so many dioceses that were without bishops because of Pius' refusal to grant institution, with the consequent disorders and danger of schism. After hanging this sword of Damocles over the Pope's head, the bishops broached the question of a general "imperial" council.

Pius heard them with his customary kindness but expressed amazement at the idea of such a council being convoked by a lay sovereign without him; he said there could be no justification in calling such a council. He told the bishops he had always been willing to grant canonical institution, but freely, without constraint, with normal counsel and the rightful means which had been withheld from him.

Their lordships laid before the Pope a score of letters signed by French, Italian and Spanish cardinals, archbishops and bishops begging him to make all possible sacrifice for the good of the Church by granting the required canonical institution.

None were more ready than he, Pius then told the bishops, to make every sacrifice—except that of betraying his own conscience. Taking the letters with him, he ended the audience and went to pray in the tribune of the cathedral, as was his custom. A servant came to tell him the midday meal had long been served, but he did not leave the tribune until three hours later.

Seeing that the bishops had not been able to persuade Pius, the Prefect Chabrol, General Berthier and Lagorse tried to break down his resistance by daily harangues—appeals to his fatherly heart and goodness alternated with threats. The Pope's personal physician, Dr. Porta, joined in this assault. But none could move him.

When the bishops afterwards came back for further audience, Pius told them he could never agree to granting bulls

of institution on the stipulated conditions. He utterly refused
to think of residing in Paris or Avignon. Nor would he ever
return to Rome at the price of swearing fidelity to Napoleon,
which would be tantamount to condoning the Emperor's usurpation of the Pope's own sovereign authority.

At one moment during this audience Pius grew agitated
and spoke of retreating to the catacombs, as some of his
predecessors had done in times of persecution.

The episcopal delegation reported their discouragement to
the Minister of Public Worship in Paris and spoke of their
amazement at the Pope's goodness, gentleness, resignation and
even love toward them. Chabrol reported: "We are doing
everything we yet can, together with Dr. Porta, to unsettle
him... Dr. Porta has served us well." From this it has been
conjectured—although proof has not been forthcoming—
that foul play may have been resorted to even by the Pope's
personal physician.

The bishops returned to find the Pope changed, hesitant,
but still unmoved by their entreaties, and unmovable. Nor
did Chabrol's and the others' renewed assaults on his conscience have any result, although they told him in threatening
tones that he should make up his mind to yield to the Emperor's just demands, otherwise the Church and all the world
would know that, in return for all the generous sacrifices
Napoleon had made in reestablishing Religion, he, the Pope
alone, had shown himself ungrateful and had stopped his ears
to the Emperor's supplications.

The Prefect then changed his tone and tried to touch Pius'
heart by tearful pleading, describing how he had always
pitied the Pope, who was a good and holy man. He sympathized with him in misfortune and fervently begged him
to provide for the Church's needs, *for the sake of his own salvation.* But Pius was not affected.

"I succeeded in softening him," Chabrol reported, "but still
could not change him; it was impossible to make him budge
an inch from his incredibly obstinate position."

The main outcome of the episcopal delegation's proposals

was that Pius, ever amiable but thoroughly wearied and not strong in physical health, unintentionally gave the bishops grounds for hope. They left the draft of modified proposals for a "national" or imperial council in the Pope's hands before taking leave. His lack of comment or objection were presumed to constitute acceptance.

Early in the morning after their departure, the servant who slept in the room adjoining the Holy Father's heard Pius sighing and blaming himself out loud for not having objected. As soon as he had risen and dressed, Pius made hasty inquiries whether the delegation might be caught up with on the road and a message sent. But it was too late; the bishops had left hours before.

The Pope's altered health and physical weakness soon gave place to normal health and spirits. He took up the draft and canceled, corrected and rewrote until it was all but illegible, exclaiming: "Thank God I did not sign!" Then he threatened so severely to raise his voice before the world and reveal what had really happened that Chabrol felt compelled to give his word that the amended copy would be sent after the episcopal delegation with an explanatory note. And this was done.

When Napoleon heard of the delegation's practical failure, he vented his feelings upon the bishops, telling them they had served neither himself nor the Church. He ignored the Pope's rewritten draft and gave out that he had the Pontiff's agreement on the chief issues to be discussed by the Imperial Council.

This general Imperial Council, which the Emperor now persuaded himself he had no reason not to convoke, assembled in Notre Dame Cathedral in June, 1811. The assembly was made up of six cardinals and eighty-nine bishops, forty-two of whom were Italian. It had been planned that Cardinal Maury would preside as Archbishop of Paris, but Cardinal Fesch claimed the right because as Archbishop of Lyons he had the traditional title of Primate of the Gauls. So Napoleon charged Fesch with directing the discussions. He supposed his uncle would uphold his claims. But the Cardinal's Gallican

ideas had been modified under Emery's influence and
Napoleon's hopes were mistaken. He was also to find himself
misled in thinking that the Council would be considered superior to the Pope.

Thus it was that the crowds of people who flocked to Notre
Dame for the Council's opening could hardly believe their
ears when they heard solemnly affirmed, by the impressive
ecclesiastical gathering of the Church's highest authorities,
the Pope's divine right to receive obedience from all princes,
priests and faithful.

This first act of the Council, a council which had been
convoked by the Emperor against the Pope and in his own
interests, was seen by Napoleon as treachery. The press was
forbidden to speak of it, although the people of Paris were
talking of nothing else. He summoned Fesch and poured a
torrent of abuse and threats upon him. With not the least
respect for his eminent dignity, he accused him and the bishops
of designedly fomenting discord in the empire, and it was
all the Cardinal uncle could do to keep his self-control.

The following day the cardinals and bishops assembled in
the archiepiscopal palace for the first general session. They
were dismayed to see two government officials, the Ministers
of Public Worship of France and Italy, enter and seat themselves on either side of Cardinals Maury and Fesch. Amazement grew, mingled with indignation, when the French
Minister calmly took from his portfolio a decree dictated by
the Emperor and proceeded to read it: His Majesty, while
recognizing Fesch and Maury as Director and President of
the Council, had at the same time created a further office,
that of Council Police.

After an indictment of the Pope and complaints that the
Church's present ills were due to the Pope's obstinacy despite
the Emperor's efforts to remedy them, the imperial decree
peremptorily announced that, as Protector of the Church, His
Majesty would not suffer the various dioceses to remain vacant
nor agree to the temporary measure of having diocesan ad-
ministrators installed by cathedral chapters instead of bishops

with canonical status. But any resolution taken by vote would have to be submitted to His Majesty for approval before being passed. The Council Fathers were further required to ask audience of the Emperor and compose an address to be read before the throne, the text of which had also to be submitted for censoring.

The idea came to some of the bishops, including ex-constitutionals, that if they were obliged to ask audience of the Emperor they should take advantage of this opportunity to ask that Pius VII be set at liberty. The proposal was taken up and agreed to by the assembly. The canons of Notre Dame further had the courage to propose that their Vicar Capitular also be released from prison. If they feared the Emperor's anger, how much more did they not fear the anger of God?

Murmurs of assent came from all save the two government ministers. But Cardinal Maury rose to say that before asking the Emperor to free Pius VII, the assembly should object to the sentence of excommunication passed upon all involved in the invasion of the Papal States, for in using his spiritual authority in regard to a temporal matter the Pope had gone beyond the limits of his powers.

These words, impugning the Bull of Excommunication in this way in a council, and coming from a Cardinal of the Church, aroused a storm of protest. It was too much for one of the older Fathers, the Archbishop of Bordeaux, who was Council Secretary. He burst out in a voice trembling with holy indignation: "What, the Holy Father went beyond the limits of his power—have you never read the Council of Trent, Chapter 11, the 22nd session: *If any, whether clergy or layman, of whatever dignity or rank, royal or imperial, permit himself to be so overruled as to usurp or appropriate for his own use or others' the Church's possessions, let him be anathema?*" [4]

"That is true," Maury answered, "in the event of the deed being notorious, the crime ascertained and known for certain."

"Then you mean to say," expostulated the Archbishop, his voice rising, "that the facts in this case are not publicly known? Or need proving? Anyway, who may rightfully make himself judge in regard to the culpability of the acts that provoked the excommunication?"

"A matter of opinion," was all Maury found to reply.

This was more than the Archbishop could stand. Hurling the volume of the Council of Trent down on the middle of the table, "Very well, then," he shouted "read what that says, then judge the Pope, condemn the Church, if you have a mind!"

The majority of bishops were by this time also thoroughly roused and offended. They determined that their address before the throne should be as they wanted it and not cut or corrected by the Emperor who, they now saw, cared nothing for their deliberations, but wanted only an echo of his own will.

Learning of the Bishops' intention, the Emperor furiously told Fesch that their business was to find a way of providing duly authorized occupants of vacant sees. There would be no audience and no address. If a solution were not found in eight days, the Concordat itself would be declared dead and buried.

Back in council, matters were brought to a crisis when one of the bishop-members of the Savona delegation felt bound to reveal to his astounded colleagues that the Pope had not signed any definite agreement, and had afterwards changed and corrected the draft of it. Upon this revelation there was complete silence in the council hall, broken after some minutes by a French Gallican bishop in a sudden tirade against complying with "ultramontane[5] Roman doctrines."

A general cry went up: "Ultramontane? Roman? The Roman doctrines are those of the Universal Church. If we bishops do not believe in the supreme powers of the Supreme Pontiff, we believe still less in our own!"

The majority of bishops then voted that the Council was not competent to pronounce on the question of episcopal institution, whereupon fears were expressed that the Emperor might dissolve it. But by now most of the assembly felt that there would be no harm to the Pope, the Church or any of

them if he did. The session ended with Cardinal Fesch proposing that a further delegation be sent to Pius VII at Savona,
as the best safeguard before any decision whatsoever were
made.

There was another scene between the Emperor and his uncle:
Fesch was called a great ignoramus on his attempting to produce theological reasons in defense of the Sovereign Pontiff's
rights and was told that he, the Emperor, could learn more
theology than that in a couple of months. But the Cardinal
was brave enough to insist, upon which Napoleon bellowed:
"Be done with it, I say! I will not be the loser. I shall dissolve
the Council. My committee of philosophers and jurists will
pronounce the necessary sentence and I shall declare *myself*
competent, despite your Council. The metropolitans⁶ could
institute the bishops by my orders. If they refuse, I shall close
the seminaries, and there will be no more priests!"

Highly offended in his dignity as bishop and cardinal, Fesch
was finally provoked into retorting: "Very well, then! If you
want to make martyrs, you may begin with your own rela-
tive: here I am, ready to give my life for the Faith. For I
would have you know, in my turn, that without the Pope's
consent, I, as a metropolitan, would never grant episcopal
institution to a single one of my suffragans. Moreover, if anyone else dared give it, I would excommunicate him."

The tempestuous two-hour scene was interrupted by the
courtier Bishop Duvoisin, with whom the Emperor retired
for a while in private conversation. Returning, he summoned
the imperial Secretary of State. Calling Fesch and his fellow
cardinals and bishops a pack of idiots who did not know
what they were about, and declaring that it was necessary
for him to get them out of the mess they had landed themselves in, the Emperor then and there proceeded to dictate
a decree based on the lie that the episcopal delegation sent
to Savona had fully accomplished its mission and that the
Pope, at the thought of so many evils afflicting the Church,
had promised to grant canonical institution to Napoleon's
nominees.

The decree was read out the following day to the bewildered Council Fathers. Many came close to falling into the trap. Was it possible the Pope had, after all, consented? Then there was no need for further discussion. They could proceed accordingly and there would at last be reconciliation.

But, on reflection, an uncomfortable query presented itself: if the Pope had agreed, why had this not been made known when the delegation returned from Savona? Also, if the Pope had signed the document, where was it? Why had a copy not been produced at the Council?

The assembly of bishops concluded that a great lie had been presented to them—and this time the lie brought no good to the liar: the imperial decree was rejected outright by the great majority. But before any action could be taken, the Emperor, knowing he was discovered, dissolved the Council. Three of the bishops whom he considered the ringleaders of the conciliar opposition were arrested at night in their beds and dragged off to the Vincennes Paris prison.

In spite of the official silence of the press, news of the arrests was soon known all over Paris and France, and no bishop could foresee the fate in store for him. Faithful Catholics and good citizens everywhere openly expressed their indignation, and many of the Emperor's ministers and friends now began to feel sorry for him. Some left. To call a general imperial council of the Church's highest authorities, then throw into prison bishops who disagreed with the policy of the one who convoked it—clearly the great man had at length proved himself author of a great fiasco. A host of further difficulties now beset him, and it became increasingly evident that it would not be he who would triumph, but rather his adversaries and those he was oppressing and persecuting.

United in council, the Shepherds had shown themselves proof against Napoleon's wiles. Having dispersed them, the exasperated Emperor persisted, setting up a commission of state counsellors to take in hand the crying question of episcopal institution. In the hope of preventing still worse abuse of imperial authority, it was proposed that the Emperor might get the Council Fathers to give consent individually to what they had not been able to agree to as a body.

Cardinal Maury approved this expedient of "bottling wine that had not been found good in the barrel," and it was hastily adopted. Three bishops were in prison, a number had quickly retreated to their dioceses hoping to escape the same fate, but the majority had been kept in Paris. These were called, one by one, to speak with the Minister of Public Worship. This official managed in two weeks, by alternate threats, lying and cajoling, to get sixty-five individual signatures of consent to the imperial decree which had been rejected in council. Many gave in, like Fesch in the end, after days of resistance, but still subject to the Pope's approval.

The Bishop of Dijon, who happened to be the brother of one of Napoleon's best generals, was urged personally by the Emperor to sign. The Bishop asked for time to reflect, as he never made a decision without first consulting the Holy Ghost. Meeting the holy old prelate some days later in a hall of his palace, the Emperor demanded, "Well, Monseigneur! What answer did you get from the Holy Ghost?"

"Sire," came the simple rejoinder, "He gave me exactly the opposite counsel to your Majesty's."

Another bishop told the Minister of Public Worship that, if he put his signature to such a decree, he would lose the confidence of his flock. "They need never know," was the Minister's answer.

"But my conscience would."

"We have proof the Pope has consented."

"It is not authentic."

"Most of your colleagues have signed."

"In that case, one signature more is hardly necessary."

To another bishop, the Minister triumphantly stated, "Only thirteen prelates have refused."

"Then add me, and we shall be fourteen," came the answer.

Finally, however, a sufficient number of signatures was in time obtained. The Emperor declared the Council reopened, and there was collectively affirmed what had been privately obtained. The assembly was then adjourned pending return of the conciliar delegation which had been sent to the Pope in Savona.

NOTES

1. This King of France (1643-1715) had been claiming the revenues of vacant sees as of "royal right." Pope Innocent XI (1676-1689) threatened to excommunicate him, whereupon Louis XIV convoked an assembly of the French clergy, which confirmed the King's claims and reaffirmed the "Gallican Liberties" of 1628, which declared, among other things, that the Pope was bound by the Constitutions of the French and other local churches. Innocent then declared the articles of the Gallican Liberties null and void, and in 1682 refused canonical institutions to thirty-five bishops chosen by Louis from members of the clergy who had taken part in the assembly.

    The Gallican Articles affirmed that the Holy See had no temporal power over princes and was subject to an Ecumenical Council; that the Pope was bound by the Constitutions of the French and other local churches; and that the Pope's judgment was not irreformable unless it had the consent of the Church. Gallicanism was checked at the French Revolution, waned with Pius VII's return to Rome and came to an end with the First Vatican Council (1869-70), at which it was condemned.
2. See note 1, p. 100.
3. The Council was not really a council of the Church at all. It is sometimes called a "national" council, at other times an "imperial" or "general" council, in reference to Napoleon's empire.
4. The Archbishop was probably, in the heat of the moment, quoting from memory, though he had the book before him. The Council of Trent document in question is more detailed and states that the guilty person shall be anathematized until he restores what has been taken and obtains absolution from the Roman Pontiff.
5. The term *ultramontane* (meaning "beyond the mountains," i.e., the Alps) was invented under Gallicanism as depreciatory of papal authority and of Rome's supposedly excessive claims.
6. The title and rank of a metropolitan (Greek *metropolis* = mother city) is that of an archbishop presiding over an entire ecclesiastical province and consequently having suffragan (i.e., supporting) diocesan bishops under him. The powers of a metropolitan were once much more considerable than they are now.

~ 9 ~

THE CONCILIAR DELEGATION TO SAVONA

The Pope Yields Conditionally regarding Canonical
Institution—Napoleon Is Not Satisfied—Further
Pressure—The Pope Stands Firm—His Great Tranquility
and Charity—Pius Is Moved from Savona

The conciliar delegation appointed to go to Savona in the
summer of 1811 was made up of five cardinals and four
bishops, "men best suited to deceive the Pope with their sub-
terfuges and pretences," Consalvi did not hesitate to write
in his *Memoirs*. They were given explicit instructions to obtain Pius VII's approbation of the imperial decree introduced
at the general Council. They were to notify the Pope that,
failing his final consent to grant canonical institution, the concordats hitherto concluded with the Holy See would be
abrogated. The "common right" of instituting episcopal
nominees in an emergency would be resorted to through local
synods and metropolitans.

The members of the delegation carried with them forceful
letters from cardinals and bishops insisting on the need for
the Pope's approving what the Emperor required.

Cardinal Pacca, in his memoirs, asked how it was possible
for not one but five members of the Sacred College to have
resigned themselves to playing the double role of feigned advisors to Pius VII while acting as agents, if not accomplices,
of the man who was holding him captive and oppressing
him and the Church. They had indeed already betrayed the

Purple they wore—symbol of the blood they should be ready
to shed for Christ—because of their tacit consent to the Emperor's unlawful remarriage, thus distinguishing themselves
from the "Black Cardinals" who had not consented and who
were therefore deprived of their Purple and banished.

Pacca charitably found extenuating circumstances in the extreme confusion reigning throughout the Church and society
at the time, a confusion making even the strongest—or those
who ought to have been—give in, seduced by false loyalties
or failing under great political pressure. Pacca also thought
that some of the cardinals and bishops may have been delighted
by the idea of being able to see the Pope again after so long,
and that they may have thought, or persuaded themselves
into thinking, that their double mission as deceiving counsellors would, in the exceptional circumstances, really serve
the Church's cause and that of peace.

Pius himself seemed truly pleased to see them. His suspi-
cions were at first aroused, but such was their apparent sincerity that from initial conversations these were allayed. As
ever, he spoke of the Emperor without resentment and even
with affection. It seems that Pius, in his profound goodness
and with his trusting nature, could even now hardly bring
himself to believe that such a delegation had come to deceive
and force from him what he was surely known to have all
along refused.

But the Pope's first fears were again confirmed when he
found that the Prefect Chabrol, as though acting on instructions, was again adding his voice to the others' and endeavoring
to persuade him of the absolute necessity for now yielding
to the Emperor.

Chabrol argued that episcopal institution had once been
held valid without papal confirmation. Pius answered that
in these cases the Pope exceptionally conceded the faculty
of according institution *in his name,* and he was able to quote
some instances. The Prefect told Pius, showing him what was
written in the press, how public opinion and highest-ranking
churchmen were all against him, and that the present Council

was with the Emperor. Pius answered that he now listened to God and his conscience and allowed no one and nothing to deviate him; that in the time of the Arian heresy, the greater number of bishops themselves fell into error and the Church had suffered terrible shocks; yet God and His saints had upheld and succoured her.

Pius went so far on one occasion as to tell the Prefect, in reply to the latter's reiterated persuasions and amateur theology, that if his return to Rome were denied him he would be prepared to go from city to city, preaching and evangelizing the people, as the first Apostles of Christ had done. For the rest, he committed himself entirely into God's hands and did not fear persecution, well knowing that by persecution the Church is purified and made ready for further victories.

Evidently this did not make sense to the Prefect, who, ignorant as he was of Church history, thought the Pope's words mere extravagance. In his report to the Minister at Paris, he said: "This man has a head all larded with bad theology, and the only history he knows is that in favor of the papacy. His weakness is great in proportion to his dignity, and he is unworthy of the great epoch we live in."

Meanwhile, after the audiences granted to members of the conciliar delegation and alone in his little prison of the episcopal palace, Pius heard the din of official festivities—music and fireworks celebrating the birth of the Emperor's son by Marie-Louise, and he was told of the title conferred on him: "King of Rome." None had dared question this or remind the Emperor that such a title had never been assumed by anyone, Rome being the Sovereign Pontiff's capital and capital of Christendom.

It was at this time—on the Feast of the Assumption of the Blessed Virgin, August 15, 1811—that Pius VII was seen raised from the ground while hearing Mass, his head surrounded by a light of glory. The Pope had previously been seen so raised in ecstasy while celebrating the Mass of Pentecost that same year.

Soon, as by common agreement, a concerted assault was

made upon the Pope's conscience by a constant coming and
going at all hours on the part of the cardinals and bishops,
the Prefect and Dr. Porta, in suitably psychological moments;
and for a fortnight on end he was not given a moment's peace.
When in fearful mental and physical strain Pius admitted to
a most intense interior struggle of conscience, he was laughed
at and told these were shadowy scruples. He came near to
complete breakdown, with his health being undermined, his
appetite gone and his nights sleepless.

At length, utterly worn down, Pius accepted the imperial
decree—although with conditions, as Fesch had done—and
signed a brief agreeing to institution of episcopal nominees
in certain circumstances only and on certain conditions. He
insisted, however, that the Council, held without him, had
no validity.

The triumphant announcement sent thereafter to Paris by
the conciliar delegation contained an appeal for the Emperor
to lighten the Pope's lot, and it concluded with the confident
expectation of His Majesty's complaisance and bounty.

Napoleon was in the North making ready for his titanic
Russian campaign. The papal brief and conditional acceptance
wrested from Pius were at first ignored—then refused. "The
Pope's brief is unacceptable," the Emperor wrote to the Minister of Public Worship. "He refuses validity for the Council
assembly of bishops convoked at Paris, calls the Church of
Rome 'Mistress and Teacher of all the churches' and lays down
that canonical institution of bishops in exceptional circumstances must still be given in the Pope's name. He must correct the brief on these points."

Indescribable was the consternation of the cardinals and
bishops at Savona, who had expected the Emperor's gratitude and applause. But faithful to their mission and abiding
by their instructions, they redoubled their joint efforts and
went so far as to hand the Pope an official ultimatum stating
that the Emperor Napoleon had all the churches of the Empire in his hands. Disaster would ensue for all were he to
withdraw his protection if the Pope finally refused to meet

his wishes. The whole world knew and approved the Emperor's proposals for Church settlement and rejoiced in the prospect of long-desired conciliation. If the Pope would not agree to the Emperor's final requirements, the cardinals and bishops would have to make it known that his refusal alone was the cause of the Church's continuing evils.

But Pius VII—according to the delegation's own report sent to Paris—had by now the tranquility of one who has made an irrevocable decision. Nevertheless, the cardinals and bishops dared still further: they formulated an affirmative agreement and put it into the Pope's hands for him to sign.

With unflinching firmness he refused and, from then on, determined to have no more dealings with the delegation— although he was still willing to receive singly any of the members who desired to speak with him.

By the beginning of 1812 the cardinals and bishops had been in Savona six months and, seeing all hope of succeeding gone, decided to go back to Paris. But before their departure, one last parting shot was aimed at Pius: a note was handed to him saying that the Emperor's forbearance had reached its limits and that they were finally charged by His Majesty to inform the Pope that *the faculty of instituting bishops to their sees had been taken from him.*

Needless to say, this information received no comment from the Pope, who despite everything addressed one more heartfelt and respectful appeal to the Emperor for liberty of counsel and action before any other step could be taken. But there was no reply. Instead, Napoleon dictated a letter to the Minister of Public Worship to be passed on to the conciliar delegation before leaving Savona:

> His Majesty does not judge it fitting to reply to the Pope's personal letter. He will write when he is satisfied with him. The Pope asks for freedom of communication, but how has he lost this freedom except by violating his duties of instilling peace and charity? He has cursed the Emperor with a Bull of Excommunication.

Was it for maligning sovereigns that Christ let Himself be crucified?

Notwithstanding, the Emperor was pleased to scorn the said criminal and ridiculous document and leave the Pope in peace, free to communicate with the faithful in Savona. But what use did he make of that freedom? To send briefs to cathedral chapters secretly and stir up strife against him.

The Pope is always speaking of his conscience. Has not the Emperor a conscience, too? And is not conscience what all have, independently of anyone, each person being bound to enlighten his own? And how is it, then, that the Pope who distrusts his own conscience and enlightenment rejects that of a hundred bishops in council? Or have bishops not also their own conscience?

His Majesty pities the Pope's ignorance and is profoundly distressed to see a Pontiff who might play a magnificent part in the Church be the cause, instead, of calamity.

After stating that the institution of bishops was a right that in the past had been "usurped by the court of Rome. . . appropriated to themselves by astuteness and cavilling on the part of popes down the centuries," the Emperor's missive drew to a close by asserting that "owing to present pontifical ineptitude detrimental to bishops, the latter in spite of him will now be put in possession of all their rights and authority." Finally:

> As the Pope is not sufficiently enlightened by the Holy Spirit, despite unanimous episcopal counsel, *why does he not resign?* For he is evidently incapable of distinguishing dogma from the essentials of religion and cannot see that non-essentials in temporal matters are subject to change and variation.
>
> If the Pope is unable to understand this fairly obvious distinction, easy enough for any young seminarian, let him come down from the Pontifical Chair and make way for a man of better sense and comprehension, who may at last repair the sundry evils that none other than he has brought upon himself and the Church.

As the letter was read to him Pius listened with bowed head and half-closed eyes like one caught without shelter in a hailstorm. But at the words accusing him of stirring up trouble for the Emperor, he raised himself and vigorously protested, "That is not true!" The invitation for him to resign shook his whole frame with indignation, and he rose to his feet, crying out: "That I shall never do!" with so much force that Chabrol retreated from his presence.

Yet in a day or two, he returned again to the attack. Chabrol reported to Paris his ensuing conversation with Pius VII: ". . . I told the Pope that I had come back to cull the fruits of his reflections on the letter I had read, but I found him as obstinate as ever. He would not budge from the Brief and told me he would not take one step further. I told him that to go on refusing to correct it as the Emperor desired was tantamount to abandoning the ship's helm in the height of a storm."

"I am not abandoning the helm," he replied. "I only say that, in my present position, conscience forbids fresh concessions."

"Meanwhile (I observed), the faithful are being abandoned... Your conduct will arouse the discontent of all Christendom. All will cry: 'Let the Pope resign—the Pope should resign!' And the Pope will in duty be obliged to do so."

"Let them cry," was Pius' answer. "But the Pope will not resign."

The Prefect then referred to possible forced deposition, at which Pius silenced him by saying he knew how far the authority of a council can go, even if it be valid and ecumenical. It could do nothing over and above the Pope. The Pope can only resign from the See of Peter freely, of his own will.

Yet this high-placed servant of Napoleon appointed as Pius VII's chief jailer would not give up trying to convince the Pope of his errors. He even entertained hopes that he alone, when all others and the Emperor himself had failed, might in a choice moment succeed in piercing the Pope's armor and wring from him unconditional consent to his master's demands. But in vain. For the Prefect finally had to report:

> I made the remaining members of his household speak
> to him, but he would not even listen to what they had
> to say. I went to him again in despair, beseeching and
> urging the terrible responsibility of going against all the
> cardinals, bishops and clergy, all the disastrous conse-
> quences, the concordats rescinded, episcopal institution
> itself taken from his hands. . . I charged Dr. Porta duly
> to work upon him and repeat these things at meal time
> and warn him he still had time to change his mind. . .
> All in vain.

Reprisals against the Pope were not long in following. Instructions arrived from Paris, for Chabrol's eyes alone, containing orders for the Pope to be treated even more harshly
and disrespectfully. He was allowed no visitors, spied on at
all hours and guarded as a dangerous criminal.

The tranquility and serenity of Pius VII at this most rigorous time of his imprisonment in the episcopal palace of Savona, isolated from everyone and everything, was a puzzle
for the Prefect. "He shows not the slightest sign of affliction
or distress," Chabrol reported. "Yesterday he even *joked* on
hearing of the light shower bath of frozen rain which some
of the departing cardinals and bishops had had on their way
back over the Alps. He appears not in the least annoyed or
bored with the solitary life he is made to lead."

The Emperor himself, meanwhile, was far from possessing
serenity and peace of mind. He was aware of increasing disaffection among all classes of people, especially the clergy.
He issued a series of lightning orders aimed at bishops and
priests he suspected of resistance, especially those in seminaries and religious communities. The Society of priests of St.
Sulpice, which he particularly feared for being imbued with
the spirit of its heroic old superior, M. Emery, was the first
target of his wrath and persecuting measures. St. Vincent de
Paul's Daughters of Charity were dissolved for being unwilling to accept the Emperor's mother, Madame Letizia, as
Superior General, and their spiritual director was sent to prison.

Then, on the eve of embarking on what he was confident

would be his greatest and most decisive victory, the conquest of Russia, Napoleon decided on the security measure of having Pius moved from Savona. There was danger that a hostile power, such as England, might attempt to rescue the Pope (as had been planned in 1807) by sea. It would be safer to have him near Paris. On his return from Russia, the Emperor reckoned, he would at length be in a position to deal with the Pope successfully in person. Fontainebleau was chosen as being near the capital but sufficiently far not to attract popular demonstrations.

Early in June, 1812, Pius was taking his siesta when he was roused and told he was to leave for France that evening. He showed neither surprise nor concern, but raised his eyes to Heaven, then lowered them, without a word. Told he had to change his dress and disguise himself, he remarked that all would recognize him. But Lagorse, his chosen escort, insisted, and he patiently allowed the pectoral cross to be taken off and his white vestments exchanged for black. Shoes could not be found to fit him so the gold-embroidered cross was torn off his white satin shoes, which were smeared with ink and put back onto his feet still damp, without a murmur of complaint from him.

So dressed, the Pope was led out at midnight by a side door where there awaited a coach without lights and with muffled wheels, drawn by unshod horses. He was locked inside, together with a member of his household and Dr. Porta, and the coach slid silently out of the city.

A peasant coming down from the hills the next day told how he had caught sight of the Pope being driven away at high speed and how he had lifted his hand to him in blessing. The man was promptly arrested and escorted out of Savona, after being interrogated. But the story went quickly round so that to keep up pretenses of the Pope's still being in Savona the Prefect resorted to trickery: sentinels were placed as usual at all the doors of the episcopal palace, the candles were lit on the altar at the customary time of the Pope's morning Mass and a sacristan was sent from the cathedral with the hosts. The Prefect himself appeared in full dress for his daily visit, and meals were carried up to the papal apartment.

It was only known for certain that Pius was no longer there when the boys who had climbed the cathedral tower and thrown biscuits and chocolate into the garden were again sent up and told to watch for sight of the Pope through the windows. There was none, the secret came out, and the pretense fell apart before the dismayed and angered people.

By this time Pius was in the Alpine mountain hospice on the heights of Mount Cenis, almost at death's door. For two days and nights, locked in the jolting carriage, he had been raced along at breakneck speed with hardly a stop. He apparently imagined it was intended to kill him, for Lagorse reported that once, unable to endure any more, he said he would throw himself out and ask only to be left to die by the wayside. He was again suffering from the painful urinary complaint brought on by ceaseless travel, reaching Mount Cenis in a state of feverish collapse.

The monks of the Benedictine hospice helped Pius out of the coach; they thought he was dying. He was laid in a bed, and at his request the abbot administered the Last Sacraments. One of those present remarked that the resignation and serenity on the Pope's pallid, worn face at the thought of possibly sacrificing his life in this way could not have been greater than if he had been on the point of returning to Rome in freedom.

His doctor declared he could not travel further without rest. But orders were for the Pope to continue immediately on to Paris. Lagorse, fearing Pius would die on the way, asked for a delay and a surgeon. He was refused, and a telegraphed order from Paris confirmed immediate continuation of the journey.

To his credit, Lagorse ignored them and sent for a surgeon on his own initiative. Dr. Claraz proved not only competent, but valiant. He was told that to reveal whom his patient was would cost him his life. The doctor was unable to prevent the journey being continued, and considering the Pope's prostration, he could not operate. But he administered drugs to ease the pain. On the surgeon's orders Pius was laid in the coach on a bed made of cushions and pillows, and then was again dragged off posthaste.

Dr. Claraz asked to be allowed to accompany the Pope, and Lagorse consented. There were no stops except for one or two brief halts to give the Pope some relief. Claraz nursed him the whole time. The cobbled streets of Lyons were taken at a gallop to get clear of curious crowds. Claraz held the Pope's head in his hands and heard him repeating, between groans he could not suppress: "May God forgive him, as I have forgiven him!...May God forgive him!..."

His Holiness Pope Pius VII lands in Ancona on his way to Rome three months after being elected Pope at the Conclave in Venice on March 14, 1800.

126-1

Discussions in Rome regarding "The French Concordat" between France and the Roman Catholic Church (July 15, 1801).

Pope Pius VII at the coronation of Napoleon and Josephine in Paris (December 11, 1804).

The reconciliation between Pope Pius VII and Scipione de Ricci after the former's return from Florence (May 9, 1805).

Pope Pius VII frees Cardinal Pacca from the hands of French soldiers (September 6, 1808).

126-3

Pope Pius VII refuses to abdicate as ruler of his states (October 27, 1808).

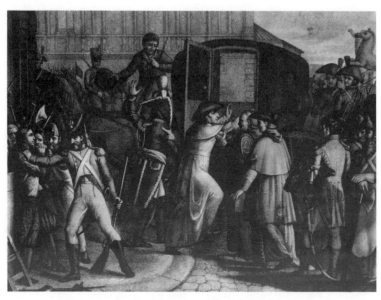

Pius VII is abducted and deported to France (July 6, 1809).

126-4

Pope Pius VII by the Ponte del Varo (near Nice) on the way to Savona (August 7, 1809).

Pope Pius VII as a prisoner in Savona. This imprisonment would last from August 10, 1809 to June 10, 1812.

A French bishop opens a meeting by asking *"Ubi est Petrus?"*—"Where is Peter?" (June, 1811).

Pope Pius VII is ravished in ecstasy while attending Mass (August 15, 1811).

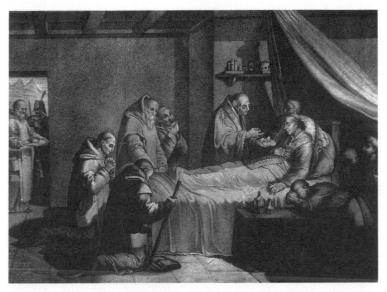

Pope Pius VII receives Holy Viaticum at the Moncenisio Pass on the painful journey from Savona to Fontainebleau, his new place of captivity (June, 1812).

Pope Pius VII, prisoner at Fontainebleau, receiving visitors. This captivity would last from June 29, 1812 to January 23, 1814.

Fontainebleau: A new concordat is requested.

Pope Pius VII negotiates a new concordat with Napoleon (July, 1813).

126-8

Having been released from Fontainebleau, Pope Pius VII begins his journey back to Italy (January 23, 1814).

Joyous welcome of the Pope at Nice, en route to Rome (February 9, 1814).

Pope Pius VII is handed over to the Austrian-Neapolitan Army near Parma (March 25, 1814).

Pope Pius VII travels to Bologna (March 31, 1814).

126-10

Pope Pius VII blesses the people of Imola at Easter (April 10, 1814).

Pope Pius VII is received in Forli in the palace of Conte Gaddi (April 15, 1814).

126-11

Pope Pius VII confirms a child in the palace of Marchese Camillo Spreti, Ravenna (April 18, 1814).

Pius VII baptizes his nephew's child in Cesena (April 20, 1814).

126-12

Pope Pius VII travels back to Rome and establishes the festival of Santa Maria Ausiliatrice (May 24, 1814).

During his second flight from Rome, Pope Pius VII is received by Granduca Ferdinand III (May 29, 1815).

Pius VII takes part in the Corpus Christi procession in the city of Florence (June 1, 1815).

Pope Pius VII comes definitively back to Rome (June 7, 1815).

~ 10 ~

THE POPE AT FONTAINEBLEAU

Further Pressure on Pius VII—Napoleon Visits Him—
The Pope under Duress Signs a Provisional Agreement
with Napoleon—The False Concordat—
The Pope Retracts—Beginning of the End for
Napoleon—Orders to Leave Fontainebleau

The traveling coach at last came to a halt in the June noon-
day heat before the royal palace of Fontainebleau, and Pius
was lifted out, motionless and pale as a corpse. But the keeper
refused to open the doors. The Emperor's orders for the Pope
to be received and lodged in the palace had been bungled;
there were no instructions to admit anyone. Lagorse, however, was able to have the adjacent Senator's palace opened
up, and there Pius was laid until orders from Paris were
confirmed.

For two weeks Pius lay between life and death, too ill to
speak or move, occupying the same rooms assigned him when
he came to Paris to crown the newly elected Emperor in 1804.

When some semblance of normal health returned, the Pope
began receiving courtesy visits from the Minister of Public
Worship, the Chief of Police, the "red" cardinals (who had
not opposed the Emperor's remarriage) residing in Paris, and
courtier bishops.

Pius preferred to say Mass not in the palace chapel but
at an altar set up in the room next to the one he slept in.

Nor would he go out, politely declining the services of the coachman even to drive him through the gardens, so as to avoid the curious gaze of the little crowds that gathered at the gates to get a glimpse of him. He was still a prisoner and he determined to show the world this.

The Pope received patiently and courteously all who came to him. Only Cardinal Maury, who had deserted his diocese of Montefiascone and further disobeyed in accepting the Archbishopric of Paris, succeeded in exasperating him. After listening to his self-justifying arguments for a little while, Pius took him by the arm and led him to the door.

While Pius VII was being transported on that coach journey from Savona to the hospice on Mt. Cenis, then from there to Fontainebleau, Napoleon at the head of his *"Grande Armée"* of 600,000 men had been advancing across Poland into the heart of Russia. The Czar had become his enemy, guilty of the same offense as the Pope's for having refused to close Russian ports against the English ships or declare himself hostile to England.

Napoleon planned another lightning campaign. The Russians had not nearly as many men as he, but they knew how to defend their country. Withdrawing and withdrawing over the endless plains, they drew the French armies after them. Napoleon's troops reached Smolensk in August, but they were not able to catch up with the retreating enemy forces, who had set the city on fire.

The French first did battle with the Russians at Borodino, 100 miles from Moscow; they were victorious but sustained an enormous loss of lives. There Napoleon also heard that his troops had been defeated by Wellington at Salamanca.

No triumphal entry into Moscow awaited him: what was left of the *Grande Armée* marched in and found all deserted. The Kremlin stood before them, the gates wide open, its rooms and halls empty. Napoleon set up headquarters there and addressed peace proposals to Czar Alexander. Then fires broke out all over the city. Supplies failed. There was no reply from Alexander. Winter set in. Napoleon began his retreat.

The retreat from Moscow became harder and harder: snow began to fall, making roads indistinguishable; guns and carriages stuck and had to be abandoned; men and horses dropped down exhausted and were frozen. Napoleon's life was constantly in danger from lurking Cossacks. In 1809, he had asked: *"What does the Pope mean by excommunication? Does he think the arms will fall from from the hands of my soldiers?"* Now in 1812 it was as though God had said: Thus far and no farther.

Napoleon reached Poland only to hear of the (unsuccessful) *coup d'état* planned against him in his absence. He arrived back in Paris in December, leaving behind the remnant of his armies.

One of the Emperor's first acts after his return, seeing the magnitude of the disaster that had overtaken him, was to break his six-year silence and address a personal letter to Pius. He realized it was now more than ever necessary to show the world he had the Pope's support. He assured Pius in affectionate terms that, in spite of all that had happened, he still hoped they would together be able to reach an understanding concerning State and Church differences. He, the Emperor, desired nothing else; but it would depend entirely on His Holiness whether these hopes were realized. His stay at Fontainebleau would afford a suitable occasion for talks.

Pius, for his part, had not ceased to have fatherly love for Napoleon, and such a letter could not fail to please him and revive former hopes. The Pope was unaware, as most still were, of the disastrous retreat from Moscow. He also had no means of knowing the true state of affairs in France: the growing disaffection for the Emperor; the recent *coup d'état*; waning Gallican spirit, especially among the younger clergy, with increasingly wholehearted attachment to the Holy See and sympathy for the prisoner Pope. Nor did Pius yet know of the Emperor's ruthless treatment of bishops who had opposed his will, the disgracing of his uncle Cardinal Fesch, the closing of major seminaries and suppression of religious orders—actions provoking ever greater and wider resentment, making Talleyrand long since foresee his downfall and

Metternich declare the Emperor was now a lost man.

Pius, too, did not fully know how greatly Napoleon misjudged and failed to understand him, the Pope, in his personal character and as a Benedictine religious. The reply the Pope sent in answer to the Emperor's letter was more than gracious; it expressed gratitude, good wishes and willingness to do all he possibly could to meet the Emperor's proposals.

Unknown to Pius, Napoleon's letter to him had been accompanied by a letter to the submissive courtier bishop Duvoisin, who was instructed to pave the way by presenting the Pope with a set of advance proposals and at the same time weaken foreseeable resistance. Bishop Duvoisin was to seek the aid of other prelates for this purpose, among whom were some of those who had vexed and persuaded Pius into signing the provisional Brief at Savona. Then, at the right psychological moment, the Emperor determined to intervene in person, sure that the Pope would finally give in to him.

So once again Pius found himself surrounded and besieged at all hours of the day and night by bishops and cardinals as at Savona; only instead of the modest suite of rooms of the little episcopal palace, the setting was the more propitious-seeming one of the luxurious, royal salons of Fontainebleau. What the delegation urged the Pope now to accept amounted to a renunciation of his temporal power, the conceding of the right of canonical institution, and a condemnation of the cardinals who had refused to acknowledge the Emperor's second marriage.

As before, Pius refused and insisted he must be given his liberty to choose counsellors. His health again broke down, and Bishop Duvoisin reported to the Minister of Public Worship: "The Pope's health is so undermined he is no longer capable of sustaining discussion. He has no confidence in the persons who approach him and does nothing but repeat his desire to satisfy the Emperor's demands, although his conscience will not allow him to decide anything alone..."

The Emperor judged the right moment had come. One evening in mid-January, 1813, Pius was surprised by the sudden appearance of the Emperor, in hunting costume, in the doorway of the room where he was sitting talking with some of the members of his household. A hunting party had been contrived, as eight years before, to make it seem an unplanned meeting; Napoleon was accompanied by the Empress Marie-Louise and the young son she had borne, styled "King of Rome."

Napoleon went straight up to Pius, embraced and kissed him with an effusive demonstration of respect and affection while those present withdrew, leaving Pope and Emperor alone.

Nothing of any importance was at first said. But the next morning, and every day for a week, the Emperor subjected the Sovereign Pontiff to an onslaught of alternate cordiality and coldness, bullying and flattery, charm and threats.

No one was present at the harrowing ordeals, so there was no knowing what exactly took place between Pope and Emperor, except for what Pius afterwards told Cardinal Pacca. Pius denied that the Emperor had laid hands upon his person to intimidate him (as he was capable of doing on occasion to soften an opponent's antagonism), and there is probably no truth in the story of Napoleon's having smashed a Sèvres dinner service to pieces, and certainly not in his having beaten the Pope or dragged him by the hair. But Pius did reveal how Napoleon had not spared him rough and insulting language, once so far forgetting whom he was speaking to as to catch hold of the buttons of his soutane—a typical gesture of his when addressing a military subordinate who gave him trouble.

The Emperor evidently did not hesitate, like his agent Count Chabrol at Savona, to accuse the Pope to his face of ignorance in religious as well as political and social matters, repeating to him over and over again, "Times have changed—*times have changed*! The Church must adapt and be reconciled with the Revolution."

Pius VII is said to have uttered the word "Comedian!" reprovingly at a crucial moment. This was borne out by Msgr. Guzzola, Bishop of Cervia, who referred in his memoirs to

Pius telling him that the colloquies "began with comedy"—the
Emperor's sudden entrance in hunting costume—'and ended
in tragedy'—the Pope's own momentary yielding and signing the articles of the provisional agreement.[1]

For after long resisting and refusing, Pius at last gave in,
as Napoleon had set his mind on making him. Harassed by
cardinals and courtier bishops and members of his own household, he finally took the pen proffered him and, with the
eyes of the Emperor and Empress upon him, put his signature to a provisional agreement to serve as basis for a future
concordat.

Once Napoleon had gone, Pius fell into a mood of utmost
melancholy. His conscience troubled him so much he felt unworthy to celebrate Mass and ceased for a time to do so,
unwilling to take any food other than what was barely necessary to keep him alive. Before the month was out he wrote
in his own hand a declaration with the intention of making
good what he had done, describing himself as "having been
surprised into error" and protesting he had signed not to
spare himself further reprisals from the Emperor, but solely
for fear of the terrible evils that otherwise threatened the
Church. In other words, Pius VII, motivated by the duties
of his ministry, of his own accord and by his own apostolic
authority revoked, abrogated and annulled his act, ordering
that it be considered as not having been done.[2]

This was just what the Emperor, knowing from past experience how the Pontiff could afterward change his mind,
had feared. He immediately had the provisional agreement
promulgated as a concordat, proclaimed it the work of the
Holy Spirit and ordered a *Te Deum* to be sung in Notre Dame
Cathedral and throughout France and the Empire in thanksgiving for the so-called Church-State reconciliation. On hearing of this the Pope could only exclaim: "He has betrayed me."

The granting of freedom to the "black" cardinals, those
whom the Emperor had imprisoned or exiled for not approving his remarriage, was a concession of Napoleon for
the Pope's signing the new provisional agreement. Some of

these cardinals, including Pacca and Consalvi, now began to arrive at Fontainebleau. The latter again became the Pope's first Minister and Secretary of State.

Even before Pius' signing, Cardinal Pacca had had misgivings as soon as he heard that Pius and Napoleon were having prolonged daily conversations. He knew better than most the Pope's modest and compliant character, ever ready to see the best in everyone and everything and go to any lengths to achieve some good, provided Catholic principles were not compromised. He also knew that Pius was surrounded by prelates who had altogether or partially sold themselves to Napoleon or were excessively servile toward him. "I immediately knew there would be a struggle of unequal strength between Gregory Barnabas Chiaramonti and Napoleon Bonaparte, and I foresaw on which side the victory would be," Pacca recorded.

From his northern prison fortress of the Fenestrelle he at once set out for Fontainebleau, and on the way his worst fears were renewed on hearing the parish priest of a little city announce during Mass that a *Te Deum* would be sung in the Cathedral in thanksgiving for the new Concordat between the Pope and the Emperor. Then Pacca learned from the Bishop of Chambéry, loyal and well-informed, of the articles of the so-called new Concordat and of what the Emperor had succeeded in making certain cardinals and bishops do, at Savona and again at Fontainebleau, to force the Pope into agreeing on settling Church-State matters as he wanted.

Reaching Paris, Pacca was shown a copy of the *Moniteur* in which the articles of the provisional agreement had been published as a concordat, and he was told the Pope was contemplating fixing his residence at Avignon.

He hurried on to Fontainebleau, which he found gloomy and deserted on the outside; all the windows were shuttered, and inside, a single sentinel was posted at the top of the great stairs leading up to the royal apartments. The Pope, told of Pacca's arrival, sent for him at once, but greeted him distantly, almost coldly, saying he had not expected him so soon. From this Pacca, with pain, saw under what mental stress Pius was still suffering—bent, pale and emaciated, his eyes sunk into his head, his movements listless like those of a man dazed.

The Cardinal explained how he had made haste, on his release, to come and kneel at the Pope's feet and tell him of his thankfulness and admiration for his heroic constancy in so long a time of suffering and imprisonment.

In a voice full of sorrow, Pius only answered: "But in the end We were defiled... those cardinals, they dragged me to the table and made me sign..." Pacca heard Pius murmur he thought he might die out of his mind, as had Clement XIV.[3]

He said what he could to console the Pope and urged him to put his mind at rest, for of all the ills besetting the Church at the moment, the most disastrous would be his death. He reassured Pius by reminding him he would soon have around him other cardinals who had given proof of their loyalty. Consulting them, he would surely be able to remedy anything he had done in spite of himself.

On hearing the word "remedy," the Holy Father grew serene and said: "Do you really believe it can be remedied?"

"Yes, Most Holy Father," Pacca answered. "Where there's the will there's the way, and almost every evil can be remedied."

Visiting Paris, Pacca found the false Concordat had had the very worst effects even upon some of those remaining good Catholics. Some who had all along kept Pius VII's picture by them, reputing him a saint, had changed their minds and torn it up. But many, if not most in France, despite the *Te Deums* of thanksgiving ordered by the Emperor, had little trust in the new "Concordat," which they felt to be yet one more imposture on the part of the imperial government. In Italy Fr. Lanteri, who had done so much to help the Pope at Savona, realized at once what had happened and, when he had sufficient proof, composed and succeeded in circulating a denunciatory pamphlet convincing people of the truth.

At Fontainebleau it was decided after secret discussions that the only way was for the Pope to deliver to the Emperor a clear and precise retraction of all the articles of the provisional agreement. A number of cardinals opposed this, but Consalvi, with Pacca and di Pietro, were insistent and led the others. Pius himself unhesitatingly agreed, though well knowing the fury this would provoke in the Emperor.

It was agreed that the best way of telling him would be in the form of a personal letter. The difficulty and danger remained of getting the letter out of Fontainebleau palace and delivering it, if indeed it was not discovered before being finished.

Pius was so worn out, mentally and physically, that he was unable to write more than a few lines at a time, which caused added risk and danger. He was constantly watched, and while he was celebrating Mass an official examined what was lying on his writing table and opened drawers and cupboards with a skeleton key. So every morning when the Pope returned from celebrating Mass, Cardinals Consalvi and di Pietro put the sheets of paper on which the letter was being written unobtrusively into the Holy Father's hand for him to continue and afterward took them away hidden in their clothing.

After a week it was finished, signed by the Holy Father and given to Colonel Lagorse, chief keeper of the palace, to take to the Emperor as though it were a normal communication. A visible change came over the Holy Father as soon as the letter was finished and sent to Napoleon: the grief and pain apparent in his face and voice, that seemed to be wearing away his life, gave place once more to his habitual serenity and smile, even joviality. His appetite returned and he no longer had sleepless nights.

The Emperor's reaction to the frustrating of his plans, turning his presumed personal triumph into something little short of ridiculous, was awaited in trepidation. A rumor reached the palace that in a council of State the Emperor had burst out: "If I don't knock the head off the busts of some of those priests at Fontainebleau, matters will never be settled!" To which a certain counsellor noted for his particularly anti-religious principles had said it was time the Emperor declared himself Head of the Church in the French Empire. But

Napoleon had replied: "That would bring things to a further crisis."

The immediate effect of the Pope's retraction was the departure from Fontainebleau of the French bishops in residence there. No one was allowed any longer to be present at the Pope's Mass, nor could anyone from the outside have an audience with him. Then one night, without warning, Cardinal di Pietro was roused from his bed, forced to put on lay clothes and roughly led out of the palace to prison. He was suspected of being the Pope's chief counsellor in the retraction and part author of the letter.

News followed that the false Concordat had been made law throughout the Empire and obligatory for all archbishops, bishops and priests, with severe penalties for transgression. Napoleon ignored the Pope's letter and kept it secret. In order that none should be deceived as to his action, or further cause him to give way unwillingly, Pius then addressed in his own hand a letter to the Sacred College of Cardinals as irrefutable proof of his retraction.[4]

In substance, Pius VII admitted to having made a mistake in a situation of extreme emergency in the hope of avoiding further and greater evils for the Church—but without sufficiently reflecting, also for lack of proper counsel, that the innovation of consenting to a new system would open the door to confusion greater than the evils he hoped to avoid.

Early in the summer of 1813 a Parisian lady, who had had conversations with Pacca during his visit to the capital, came to Fontainebleau seeking approval for a novena of prayers for the Pope's liberation. She and a circle of Catholic friends were hoping the Holy Father would grant an indulgence for all taking part. Pius granted the indulgence by word of mouth only and recommended the novena be kept secret lest it cause trouble from the government. But within a few days Pacca was privately informed of police intervention concerning a novena leaflet being circulated by the most notable Catholics of Paris and claiming to have papal approval and indulgence. The Pope was advised to be more cautious in granting favors of this kind, even orally. The Empress Marie-Louise wrote personally to tell the Pope of the Emperor's victory over the Prussians at Lutzen, "knowing, as she did, his friendly feelings for her husband." A suitable reply to the Empress' letter needed deliberation, lest a phrase be used by the imperial gazette to signify the Pope's favoring Napoleon's campaign in Germany. It was decided to send a formal reply thanking Marie-Louise for her communication but inserting a word of protest at the imprisonment of Cardinal di Pietro, as well as at her husband's treatment of the Sovereign Pontiff.

Then, all unlooked-for, news came of the courtier bishop Duvoisin's deathbed appeal for Napoleon to set the Pope at liberty, in the interests of the Church and faithful and also of the Emperor's own prosperity and happiness. Even Cardinal Fesch, who had brought disgrace on himself for his outspokenness, now wrote from his Lyons archdiocese, of which he was proving an able governor, to Madame Mère, Napoleon's mother: "The Emperor is ruining himself; he is ruining us all. I foresee he will be brought down and utterly defeated. All who touch the Holy Ark, the Supreme Pontiff, suffer the same fate. My nephew is lost, but the Church is saved; for if the Emperor had returned in triumph from Moscow, who knows to what further lengths he would have gone? . . ."

But Napoleon's ambition and self-confidence remained as boundless as the Pontiff's patience, meekness and humility. Instigated by Russia, a fourth allied coalition, with England and Sweden joined in 1813 by Prussia, Austria and some German states, had risen up against him. He was confident he would still overcome them, and further victories followed after Lutzen, enabling his armies to push on to Dresden. But this was the moment chosen by the Austrian Emperor, on the advice of Metternich, to side against his upstart son-in-law, making the French armies' position in Germany untenable. Napoleon wanted to march on Berlin, but his generals would not face it. It was proposed instead to attack Leipzig, in Saxony, officially France's ally. Napoleon reluctantly agreed.

The Saxons saw that the French were likely to lose and joined the other side. The crushing defeat of the French at Leipzig, Battle of the Nations, sent the Emperor back into France. The Allies were closing in on him from all directions, moving steadily on to Paris. It was the beginning of the end.

Napoleon made a last desperate attempt to get the Pope on his side. Instead of again going to Fontainebleau, he determined to send an envoy. A woman—the Marchioness de Brignole, a lady-in-waiting of the Empress Marie-Louise—appeared at Fontainebleau as the Emperor's mediatrix, asking audience of the Pope. But Cardinal Consalvi, ever vigilant in the interests of his sovereign the Supreme Pontiff, had received information through Metternich of Napoleon's recent defeat, news which would have been kept from Pius. He knew it would be needless now to pay attention to any proposal from Napoleon. He told the would-be lady negotiator, on behalf of Pius VII, that he did not consider the time or place favorable for discussing any further treaty concerning affairs of Church and State.

Nevertheless, after the lady there came an ecclesiastic in the person of the Bishop of Piacenza, who had formerly won the Emperor's favor by persuading his clergy to take the oaths of loyalty to the French Republic and the Empire, in spite of the Pope's declaring such acts forbidden and illicit. The Bishop was received by Pius courteously, even with bounty and affection, but also clearly told no further dealings could be thought of until such time as the Pope could return to Rome with full liberty. "The Holy Father told me," this bishop said (in a report after the Emperor's downfall, partly justifying his own embassy), "that he asked nothing but his liberty, that he had need of nothing, and that Providence would soon lead him back to Rome." On the Bishop's remarking that midwinter was not a seasonable time for travel, Pius answered that nothing would stop him, but if his sins made him unworthy of seeing his capital again, he was sure his successor would come into possession of all pertaining to him. The Pope added: "Assure the Emperor I am not his enemy. Religion makes that impossible for me. I love France, and once back in Rome, it will be seen how this is true and I shall do everything needful."

Early in January, 1814, a couple of empty carriages were seen arriving at the gates of Fontainebleau palace and were left empty in the courtyard. At the same time Lagorse returned from Paris, whither he had been summoned, saying he had important news. This he officially announced to the cardinals resident in the palace at the end of the midday meal, which they took together, apart from the Pope. Addressing the Cardinal Dean, Mattei, he revealed he had orders for the Pope to leave Fontainebleau the following day.

The cardinals' first thought was that this was a hasty move merely to get the Holy Father farther away from the allied armies fast approaching Paris. But Lagorse (who himself had tried his hand at mediating between the Emperor and the Pope, as had Chabrol at Savona), perceiving that his announcement had been received by their Eminences with calmly gratified surprise, proceeded truculently: "There's the news, but as far as you are concerned, you are also to leave in four days. If you had acted with more moderation and prudence, everything would already have been settled before now."

To this unlooked-for and gratuitously insulting insinuation the Cardinal Dean Mattei felt bound to give a dignified reply, saying the conduct of the cardinals did not deserve any such reproof, nor could it at any time be said to have been immoderate or imprudent.

Mattei then hastened to inform the Holy Father of the order before Lagorse reached him, and suggested he should strongly urge he be accompanied by at least three members of the Sacred College. But the Pope's request was refused; orders permitted only his chaplain to travel with him.

NOTES

1. The twelve preliminary or provisional articles, signed under duress by Pope Pius VII at Fontainebleau (January 25, 1813)—wrongly termed the "Fontainebleau Concordat"—were seen by the Pope as part of a project for a future Concordat, possibly conceding the faculty of canonical institution of bishops to metropolitan archbishops, with certain conditions, and agreeing to alienation of part of his territorial possessions in exchange for stipulated benefits. This was not definitive but the Emperor deceptively promulgated it as such.

2. Pius VII had a precedent in the act of his predecessor Pascal II (1099-1118), like himself a Benedictine, who, before crowning the German Emperor Henry V, had renounced the Church's lands and temporal jurisdiction on Henry's agreeing to cease investing bishops with their titles and temporal rights. The Roman clergy refused to accept the Pope's renunciation and Henry forced Pascal to grant him the privilege of investing bishops. But at the Lateran Synod of 1112, Pope Pascal withdrew this privilege of investiture which he had granted, and in a further council of 1116 he denounced the compact he had made with the Emperor "for the peace of the Church." He confessed he had failed and asked prayers for God's forgiveness.

    See L. Pasztor, *Per la storia del "Concordato" di Fontainebleau*, in *Chiesa e Stato nell'Ottocento: Miscellanea in onore di Pietro Pirri, II*, Padua, 1962, pp. 597-606; also, J. Leflon-Ch. Perrat: *Les suppressions et édulcorations qu'a fait subir à ses "Mémoires" le Cardinal Pacca*, lvi, pp. 355-382.

3. After signing the Bull suppressing the Society of Jesus in 1773, Pope Clement contracted a strange disease causing intermittent delirium which, according to the papal physicians' report, made the Pope's mind sometimes waver.

4. In this retraction Pius VII again referred to his predecessor Pascal II who, withdrawing his concession to the Emperor Henry V and denouncing the compact he had made with him, wrote: "As We recognized the document to have been ill-done, so We confess it and desire, with the help of the Lord, that it be wholly amended in order that no harm may result for the Church, and no prejudice to Our soul."

~ 11 ~

RETURN TO ROME

Return to Savona—The Intercession of Our Lady
of Mercy—Pius VII Is Freed—Napoleon's
Abdication—The Pope's Journey through Italy
and Tumultuous Welcome in Rome

The morning of January 23, 1814, was the day fixed for
Pius VII's leaving Fontainebleau to return to Savona. After
saying Mass the Pope received the cardinals residing in the
palace and told them he did not know where and when he
would have the consolation of seeing them again. Pius spoke
at first light-heartedly, but changing expression and tone he
went on to recommend that, whether or not they themselves
were separated or dispersed again, wherever they might be,
they would show in their behavior and bearing their sorrow
for the continuing calamitous situation of the Church and
of her head. The Pope then told the cardinals, in tones of
positive command rarely used, that they were not to have
anything to do with discussions or treaties concerning spiritual
or temporal matters without him.

Moved to tears, the cardinals promised faithful obedience
and stayed with Pius while he took a little food. After a short
prayer in the tribune of the palace chapel, the Pope went down
to the courtyard and got into the waiting carriage.

News of Napoleon's increasing reverses began to reach the
people, tired of long submitting to his iron rule, and everywhere crowds gathered in greater numbers to acclaim the

Pontiff on his way. But when the Pope heard occasional curses and cries of "Death to the Emperor!" his expression changed, and his hand raised in blessing was arrested in midair.

From Nice onward into Italy his progress took on the appearance of a triumphal procession. Hundreds of thousands poured down from hillside cities to the seacoast of the Riviera, carrying crosses, lights and banners to where the Pope was due to pass. When darkness came, beacons flared from the hilltops, and the continual movement of people carrying torches resembled streams of light running down to the sea. Church bells rang without ceasing; bells from distant towers and campaniles were taken down and hung on tree boughs over the road so that their ringing might reach the Pope's ears.

Savona and neighboring districts had been transformed into what looked like one great garden of garlands, booths and flowers, with the road into the city paved with floral carpets. The Bishop, clergy and people went out to meet the Pope who had left them after living captive in their midst a year and a half ago. At the city gates the horses were unharnessed from the papal carriage, which was then drawn by silken cords to the cathedral, where Pius imparted the Eucharistic Benediction, afterwards blessing from the balcony those unable to get inside, as he had been accustomed to do.

The mayor, Count Sansoni, came to visit him, asked after his health and whether he needed anything. Pius thanked him, said he felt fairly well and needed nothing, except that the shirt he had on felt rather uncomfortable—he had not had a change of linen since leaving Fontainebleau. A dozen shirts of the finest quality were at once offered.

On March 10, the novena of prayers to Our Lady of Mercy began, as every year, in preparation for the celebrations marking the apparition of the Blessed Virgin near Savona on March 18, 1536. The Pope followed the novena from his tribune above the nave of the cathedral where he had been used to pray for hours during his years of imprisonment. He heard the throngs of people fervently repeating *Mater Misericordiae, ora pro nobis!* and felt that their prayers and supplications were being offered—as they were—for him and his final liberation. He remembered once again how he had been given the little picture of Our Lady of Mercy by the Genoese chaplain who had gained entrance to the Quirinal Palace not long before his abduction, and the chaplain's assurance that Pius' tribulations and the Church's would end through Our Lady under that title.

The Pope also recalled how, on first arriving in Savona, he had felt certain his liberation would come about through the Virgin, whose shrine he had shortly afterward visited. Once more, as he kissed the picture, that feeling of certainty came to him.

It was confirmed quicker than he could have imagined: on the last day of the novena, eve of the festivity, General Lagorse came and breathlessly brought him the news received from Paris: *he was free*—he could return to Rome when he pleased . . .

Lagorse expected this would be the very next day. "No," Pius said: "Tomorrow is the festivity of the Savonese people in honor of Our Lady of Mercy. We shall start the day after. . ."

All at once the Pope's face turned deathly pale; Lagorse, with those standing by, had to support him and prevent his falling. The realization of having his freedom, of being able to return to Rome, momentarily overcame him. His heart, which had long stood up to a series of blows, trials and hardships, nearly failed at the sudden, joyful news.

Upon hearing the news the people of Savona were meanwhile also behaving in an unexpected way: the memory of the Pope's having been taken secretly away, and the deception of his still being there kept up for days, was still fresh in their minds. How were they now to know if the Sovereign Pontiff, once more with them, might not be taken away again? The people had grown used to putting little faith in the imperial government's words and ways. So instead of illuminating the city, as was the custom, individual citizens kept watch all night praying.

Nor was the next day passed in the customary rejoicing and festivities. After the commemorative Masses, it was passed in prayer vigils imploring Heaven's protection for the Pope they had come to know and love in his confinement and suffering.

The crowds that had gathered before the episcopal palace for the Pope's blessing refused to disperse in the evening. Toward midnight a group agreed to watch all night and give the alarm in case of any trickery. Only then were the police able to get the people away.

At dawn the night watch grew to several hundreds, then thousands. No more attempt was made to control the crowds, and the Pope's traveling carriage had difficulty in drawing up before the main doors. When Pius VII appeared, cheerful and smiling, his hand raised in blessing but also signing the people to keep calm and orderly, sighs and sobs were heard as all knelt on the ground and then as the carriage drove slowly away. One present described how, in that moment, the entire throng rose as one person and a mighty shout rang out: *"Viva il Papa!"* "Long live the Pope!" Most thought they would never see him again.

Passing through Modena the Pope was met by General Bentinck, Commander-in-chief of British forces in Italy. Bentinck came to congratulate Pius VII on being able to return to Rome, and he assisted him with funds. The Allies had agreed to demand the Sovereign Pontiff's reinstallment in his capital in complete independence, and this was partly what had prompted Napoleon's move—thus forestalling them by ordering the Pope's liberation. The British government wished also to see the Papal States restored; but although the Foreign Secretary, Castlereagh, declared that in this "the sentiments of all England were Catholic," Protestant Britain could not, in fact, give any guarantee.

Grateful for British good will, Pius appealed to the Austrian Emperor, as the Church's official Protector, to intercede with the Allies regarding the territorial rights of the Holy See. He even contemplated going personally to Paris to plead his cause with the allied sovereigns; they had now taken possession of the city, obliging the defeated Emperor to sign his abdication. This he did at the very table in Fontainebleau Palace at which a short while ago he had constrained the Pope to put his name to the false Concordat.

On his journey southward Pius celebrated Easter at Imola, then stayed at his native city, Cesena. He remained there for some time, hesitating to return to Rome as long as it was occupied by the fallen Emperor's brother-in-law Murat, "King of Naples," who had designs of making himself ruler of all Italy. Metternich had secretly guaranteed Murat territorial aggrandizement on the understanding he would drive the French out of the country.

The Austrian Chancellor now sent his envoy, Lebzeltern, to congratulate the Pope on his regained freedom and urge him to return to Rome immediately. Pius had a high opinion of Lebzeltern and received him again gladly. What Lebzeltern thought of Pius VII was expressed in a report he sent Metternich from Cesena, objecting to Austria's secret agreement with Murat at the expense of the Papal States: "while the Christian world, and in the first place Italy, are filled with enthusiasm at seeing once more at liberty a Pope, looked on as a saint and martyr, whose firmness of conduct has inspired non-Catholics also to respect him. . ."

The Pope told the Austrian envoy he was reluctant to return to his capital while still not in possession of all his States, and that he did not intend to cede one inch of his territory to Murat, who now had arrived in Cesena. Lebzeltern had to threaten Murat before he would agree to withdraw and leave the Pope free passage to his capital. But even then Pius hesitated. A chance word had disclosed Austria's secret agreement with Murat, and the Pope began to wonder whom he could trust completely.

At length Lebzeltern managed to convince Pius that going to Paris to speak with the allied sovereigns was neither useful nor consonant with his dignity, and that he should not, on the other hand, let himself be put off by complications of secondary importance. Pius then resigned himself to setting out for Rome under Austrian escort. He decided to send Consalvi, once more appointed Secretary of State, to Paris.

Consalvi was able to rejoin the Pope at Rimini and set off for Paris at once; but though traveling at top speed, he arrived there too late to have any influence on the allied negotiations: the treaty had just been signed, on the whole unfavorable to the papacy. He therefore decided to follow the allied sovereigns to London, after paying his respects to the restored King Louis XVIII.

Proceeding southward, Pius VII found Napoleon's mother Letizia, with her brother Cardinal Fesch, at Loreto and promised them refuge in Rome. At Macerata the holy Bishop of the city, Msgr. Vincent Strambi, was waiting at the cathedral doors with his clergy and people. Bishop Strambi was among those who had given proof of absolute fidelity to the Sovereign Pontiff by suffering imprisonment.[1] Cardinal Pacca was now also able to rejoin the Pope and travel on with him.

Not far from Rome, Pius was met by Napoleon's brother Joseph, driven from the throne of Spain, and by his sister Elisa, Grand duchess of Tuscany, driven from Florence. Both were also promised safe asylum. Then, nearing his capital, the Pope received the homage of Charles IV, the rightful King of Spain living in exile, who joined the triumphal procession, as did the Dean of the Sacred College, Cardinal Mattei, sitting with Pacca beside the Holy Father in the papal carriage.

At the historic Milvan Bridge over the Tiber, twenty-four young men of noble Roman families unharnessed the horses and drew the carriage as far as St. Peter's Basilica, where King Victor Emmanuel of Savoy was waiting at the doors; he tried to throw himself at the Pope's feet, but was prevented by Pius' fatherly embrace.

From St. Peter's the papal procession made its way up to the Quirinal Palace, from which Pius had been abducted more than five years ago, and where such an acclamation and welcome awaited him as can scarcely be imagined.

Cardinal Pacca recalled how he refrained from endeavoring to describe in his *Memoirs* the re-entry into Rome and the procession through the city for fear of failing to give an adequate picture of so great an event and historical occasion. "I will only say," Pacca wrote, "that as the Pope's carriage went by amid the acclamations and applause, many who would have joined in the joyful shouting and applauding could not do so, for their sobs and tears at the sight of the venerable Pontiff made them speechless. . ."

As the Pope passed through the *Porta del Popolo* city gate and under the triumphal arch set up in the piazza, a host of children in white, waving palm branches, ran out from behind buildings singing: "Hosanna! Blessed is he that comes in the Name of the Lord!" while all Rome's church bells were set pealing and cannon thundered from Castel St. Angelo.

The Pope, who until then had mastered his emotion, was too overcome to keep back the tears. Taking branches from the children's hands, he had the carriage decorated with them as it slowly moved forward over carpets of flowers.

The Quirinal Palace had changed much since he left it for his long imprisonment, as it had been made ready to receive Napoleon. Statues of saints had been replaced by images of Greek and Roman gods and goddesses. Pius VII's apartments, which Radet had promised would not be touched, had been redecorated in the same style. Only his bedroom remained just as it had been.[2]

Among the first to seek audience with the returned Pontiff was one of the leading Roman patricians, who had signed a petition to be presented by Murat to the allied powers asking for a secular sovereign instead of the Pope. Pius pardoned him with the words: "And do you think We are not worthy of reproach in some respects?" adding: "Let us together forget what is past!"

NOTES

1. St. Vincent Mary Strambi, a Passionist, was canonized by Pope Pius XII in 1950.
2. Among the priceless liturgical objects, church ornaments and vestments donated by sovereigns and benefactors to be seen in the Papal Treasure is one item of no material worth whatever but possibly of greater interest as a curio than any other: the tiara made of painted cardboard and colored glass, instead of jewels and precious metal, worn by Pius VII after his return to Rome in 1814 when everything of value had been expropriated.

~ 12 ~

AFTERMATH

Cardinal Consalvi in London—Catholic Emancipation
in England and Ireland—The Congress of Vienna—
The Return of Napoleon—His "Hundred Days"—
The Vienna Congress Gives the Papal Legations Back
to the Pope—Waterloo

Consalvi's decision to go to London was a brave as well
as a bold one: no cardinal had set foot on English soil in 300
years, all diplomatic intercourse between Britain and the Holy
See having been forbidden since the Protestant Reformation.

In London, the Russian Czar and the Prussian Sovereign
were jointly celebrating the allied victory with the English
Prince Regent; the Austrian Emperor had already left. Consalvi's charming personality and unobtrusive strength of
character made him acceptable everywhere and admired by
all. He was formally introduced to the English Prince Regent, the future King George IV, by Castlereagh, the British
Foreign Secretary. Writing to Pacca, he described his first conversation. The future king had indulged in so warm and vehement a eulogy of Pius VII as to leave himself almost
incapable of expressing his most ardent admiration for the
Pope's courage, resistance and self-sacrifice. He gave Consalvi assurance of his support in any eventuality.

The Cardinal Secretary of State felt sufficiently encouraged
to broach the question of restoring the Papal Legations and

other rightful claims of the Holy See. He told the Prince
Regent of the Pope's financial difficulties following the French
Revolution, the Napoleonic wars and foreign occupation of
Rome, and he reminded him how Pius VII had indeed lost
his throne for resisting the unjust demands of Napoleon.

"The Prince Regent and highest aristocracy have overwhelmed me with every kind of attention, the most friendly
and respectful kindness," Consalvi was able to write to the
Sovereign Pontiff. "When I gently turn the conversation to
certain religious questions that are very delicate to touch upon,
the Prince Regent puts his hand to his mouth as if telling
me to be silent, but really encouraging me to speak, and calls
out in inimitable tones of affected fear, but in fact good-
humoredly: 'Hush, hush, Cardinal tempter! Listening to you,
I seem to see Henry VIII and his daughter Elizabeth pursuing
me like avenging spirits.'"

In a letter to Consalvi of June 21, 1814, Pius VII wrote:

> We rejoice with you at the reception accorded you
> in England, and especially the gracious friendship the
> Prince Regent shows you. We beg and command you
> to express to His Royal Highness Our most sincere grati-
> tude. But in the midst of such events, which are so won-
> derful as to be beyond human reason, we must not permit
> them to dazzle us. You are not only charged with a great
> diplomatic mission, you are also the representative of
> Christ's Vicar on earth. In this capacity, We beg you
> to have the heart of a father for those poor English and
> Irish Catholics, who for centuries, from generation to
> generation, have suffered in their possessions, liberties
> and rights so as to stay true to the ancient Faith of their
> ancestors. You are the first cardinal since the reign of
> Elizabeth I to be permitted to land in Great Britain. This
> privilege has its obligations and we must not shut our
> ears to the cry of the persecuted. There is no need to
> tell you what the Church expects of you. We know you
> well enough to feel sure you will take advantage of the
> situation you are placed in with due moderation and

prudence. Let nothing be done precipitately. But at the same time nothing must be left undone that could ease the lot of Catholics. By a favor for which We return thanks to Heaven, the Prince Regent shows you his singular regard and holds you in high esteem. Implant in his heart the desire to show himself just toward subjects who have never failed in their duty as citizens, and you will see this little grain of mustard seed produce abundant fruits. Go on sowing: the reaper will only later know the extent of the harvest.

Heeding the Pope's injunctions and faithfully following them, Consalvi refused to be drawn into the heated discussions concerning the emancipation of English and Irish Catholics from the laws still in force against them. A Catholic Relief Bill had in 1813 offered emancipation on condition that the British government be permitted to exercise a veto on the appointment of bishops. A number of English Catholics felt it would be best to accept this, but many did not, nor did most Irish bishops and Catholics. But the Vice-Prefect of the Roman *Propaganda Fide* Congregation, possibly not fully understanding the situation, and while Pius VII was still a prisoner at Fontainebleau, recommended acceptance of the veto stipulated by the Relief Bill. This was violently opposed by the Irish.

Consalvi was in contact with the English and Irish bishops, heard both sides, and sent a detailed, impartial report to Rome. The English he found too accommodating in their desire to ingratiate themselves with the government; the Irish he found capable of any sacrifice but blinded by dislike of their British Protestant rulers. Since the latter persisted in the conditions required for Catholic emancipation, Consalvi concluded by recommending, with due reserve, the conciliatory position taken by the *Propaganda Fide* Congregation. But Pacca, as Pro-Secretary of State in his absence, disavowed Propaganda's recommendation and came out in favor of the Irish position. Consalvi was violently attacked by the leading young Irish lawyer and patriot, Daniel O'Connell.

In England the Apostolic Vicar, Bishop Milner, was alone in also thinking the Propaganda Congregation and Consalvi's policy mistaken. He decided to go to Rome and speak to Pius VII. Dr. Milner crossed the channel in a little fishing smack, passing through the camps of the Russian, Prussian, Austrian and English allies while peace with France, signed and settled, was still in the making. In Rome he learned that, as he had thought, Pius VII himself had not approved the veto recommended by the Vice-Prefect of Propaganda.

Bishop Milner was received in audience by the Pope and assured that the recommendation ought not to have been given without his authority. The whole question of English and Irish Catholic emancipation was to be reconsidered at the Pope's wish, so that whatever was most just and expedient should be decided.

Dr. Milner recorded some of his impressions of the Eternal City: the Corpus Christi procession, the Feast of Sts. Peter and Paul in St. Peter's, of St. John the Baptist in the Lateran Cathedral, the Assumption of the Blessed Virgin Mary in St. Mary Major's Basilica, celebrated with a solemn magnificence unknown in England, "hallowed and cheered by the benign and consoling presence of our beloved Father Pius VII."

He was present in the Sodality Chapel of the Church of the Gesù a week after the Feast of St. Ignatius Loyola when, after celebrating Mass at the tomb of the Founder, Pius VII "reversed the decree which his predecessor Ganganelli (Clement XIV) had been forced by infidels and bad politicians to issue: and after a slumber of forty-one years reawakened into new life the Society of Jesus. This, I learn," Bishop Milner's record continued, "is considered by some of our London Catholics as the downfall of the Catholic Religion—which shows how different their ideas are from those of the Vicar of Christ."

"But the most edifying spectacle of all I have seen in this, the Christian capital," the English bishop wrote, "is that of the venerable Pontiff himself, *who is truly a saint upon earth.*

Rigorous toward himself and at the same time absorbed by his devotion, he is ever the *Servus servorum Dei*—Servant of the servants of God—indefatigable in his personal attention and labors for the whole Catholic Church, open at all times to the visits of persons who have business with him and charming all who visit him with a patient attention, a benign sweetness and an affecting piety, which exceed my powers of language to describe.

"In fact, my voice was stifled by my sobs and tears during a considerable part of my first audience with His Holiness, and I was *forcibly led to believe the miracles reported of him* since, as well as before, his return to Rome."

Dr. Milner left Rome toward the end of 1814 after earnestly appealing to the Pope for settlement of the conflict concerning British governmental veto of episcopal elections as a condition for Catholic emancipation. The Pope's answer came three months later from Genoa—where he had been obliged to take refuge on Napoleon's escaping from Elba—in a letter signed by the Cardinal Prefect of Propaganda: taking into account Consalvi's report from London as well as his referendum for Castlereagh at the Congress of Vienna, Pius VII laid down that a limited right of government veto had been, and could be, tolerated by the Church, provided there were suitable safeguards.

The Pope's answer from Genoa—the "Genoese Letter" — was not published immediately. Alarmist rumors were soon spread that government veto on episcopal elections had, after all, been unconditionally approved. Most English bishops and Catholics, including Milner, felt satisfied, though having reservations. But the Irish bishops declared that any such powers of interference in episcopal elections conceded to the British government would injure, and even subvert, the Catholic religion in Ireland. O'Connell went so far as publicly to accuse Consalvi and Castlereagh of bargaining to grant effectual British supremacy over the Irish Church. He feared that the Pope, who had resisted the favor of Napoleon, might yield to Consalvi and Castlereagh, and thought the Pope had paid too much attention to the praises of England contained in letters of English bishops, inspiring him with precisely that confidence in the English government he ought not to have.

The powerful and intransigent Irish patriot was determined his country should not give in. He denied that the Pope had any temporal authority in Ireland and even maintained that papal authority there in spiritual matters, too, was limited. Even in non-essentials of discipline, O'Connell asserted, "the Pope cannot vary our Religion without the assent of the Irish Catholic bishops."[1]

The Irish bishops' declarations and O'Connell's speeches were followed by a special mission to Rome of protest and petition entrusted to a priest and two laymen (but the laymen in the end refused to go). The protest was so intemperately worded and the priest in question so undiplomatic and un-mannerly in his behavior that he was required to leave Rome in twenty-four hours and papal territory in three days.

The Pope therefore addressed a further letter to the Irish bishops expressing the pain he had felt over the offensive mis-sion and message, and explaining that the concessions he was prepared to make to the British government were in conform-ity with principles laid down by previous popes in such cases.

Leading Irish papers nevertheless continued to proclaim that Consalvi had made himself obnoxious to every friend of True Religion by his influence over the Pontiff and called him a "perfidious minister and agent of the British."

Pius VII, however, continued to uphold, as he was always to do in every difficult situation, his "perfidious minister." He gave constant assurance of his deep concern for the true welfare of Irish Catholics and of his policy being solely for the advancement of Religion, never motivated by any politi-cal considerations. But the violent opposition and intemper-ate language used by some toward the Roman curial authorities, the Pope said, tended to play into the hands of anti-Catholics and made it impossible, for the time, to arrive at a solution of the vexed question.

The fruits of pacification and reconciliation that Pius VII

and Consalvi were bent on sowing would only grow to harvest later.

Emancipation from long-lingering anti-Catholic laws did not come until 1829. Historians are agreed on the wisdom of allowing time to bring things to fruition instead of attempting to solve problems while passionate discord and opposition last. The campaign launched and led by O'Connell together with the intransigence of the Irish bishops was a decisive factor in delaying a solution. A good degree of freedom could have been attained at the time by the sorely-tried Catholics of Ireland, but they would have had to accept it as a boon conceded by a superior to an inferior lot of persons, and it would have been accompanied and qualified by the veto. But O'Connell's campaign of agitation, and his own election—despite ineligibility as a Roman Catholic—for a seat in the British parliament, eventually forced the government to remove most of the disabilities long preventing Roman Catholics from playing any part in national public life.

More recently, though, the specialized French historian of the period, Jean Leflon, already referred to, has remarked that O'Connell's methods of demagogic agitation and violent protests, scorning ordinary diplomatic channels and parliamentary procedure, against what he considered the interference of the Roman Curia and even of the Pope—methods used with the complaisance of the national episcopate—not merely smacked of Jansenist, Gallican, Febronian[2] and regalist theory, but were "a truly excessive foreshadowing of that recognition in regard to collegiality which would have realization with Vatican Council II."[3]

Consalvi was also in touch in London with some of the French bishops and clergy exiled by the Revolution. Pius VII's heroic resistance to Napoleon and steadfast refusal to close the papal ports against English shipping or adhere to the Emperor's continental system had done much to soften centuries-old anti-Catholic feeling in Britain. The noble example of the French refugee clergy, and pity for their plight, further helped remove ingrained prejudice.

On the other hand, the Pope had had much to suffer back in 1801 when he called upon every bishop of France to resign his see in order to set up an entirely new episcopate according to the Concordat between the Holy See and the French Government: only five of the nineteen bishops residing in England complied. Pius VII's act was one without precedent in Church history, so this was hardly surprising. Even when the Pope wrote later expressing his grief at their refusal and begging them to reconsider their attitude so as to save him from having to take sanctions, they replied with a joint letter of respectful but final refusal. Their main argument was the Gallican view of the episcopate deriving directly from God.[4] The Pope had therefore taken the matter into his own hands by creating a completely new set of dioceses so that all jurisdiction of the ancient bishops would lapse. Some, though, went on sending pastoral letters to their former flocks, as from still lawful pastors.

The Pope and Consalvi had to put up with yet more from priests and laity who refused to accept the French Concordat itself. In France the *Clementines* of Rouen (after their leader Abbé Clément) and *Louisets* of several other places (from their attachment to Louis XVIII) together formed what was known as the *Petite Eglise*[5] — "Little Church."

Most of the French clergy in England had at first accepted the Concordat, though many did so with reserve, considering it a tactical mistake on the part of the Pope; but soon a minority refused to accept it. Some were far more extreme than in France and were known as Blanchardists, from their initiator and leader the Abbé Blanchard, whose preaching and writings had gained him a following. All who accepted the French Concordat were looked on as schismatics, the Pope included. In a pamphlet first issued in 1805 Blanchard had called Pius VII a heretic for having betrayed the Catholic Faith by his concessions to notorious heretics. The Blanchardists rejoiced that those whom they considered the faithful priests and laity of France had separated themselves into a *Petite Eglise,* and in further pamphlets they went on to call for condemnation of the Concordat and for Pius VII to be denounced to the Church. Two of the English bishop Vicars Apostolic made attempts to restrain these anti-Concordatists, but their efforts were resented and unsuccessful. There even came to be formed in England a *Três Petite Eglise*— "Very Little Church" —creating another minor schism. This group was made up of a score of French priests in London who, in sermons and writings, publicly called the Pope a heretic and all those who obeyed him heretics.

One may imagine that Consalvi, during his stay in London in the summer of 1814, steered clear of what remained of these groups or at least avoided discussion with them. All things considered, his English experience, his contacts with the bishops of England and Ireland, above all his talks with Castlereagh and the Sovereign afforded valuable knowledge and preparation for the crucial role he had next to play representing the Pope at the Congress of Vienna, which was to meet in autumn of that year.

The Cardinal Secretary of State's main concern at the Congress of Vienna was for the interests of Pius VII regarding his temporal sovereignty. His chief hope with the assembled European powers in claiming restitution of all territories the Holy See had possessed before the Revolution lay in the generally recognized heroism of the Pope, its victim, in resisting Napoleon. This gave him singular prestige. Consalvi based his arguments on hereditary right and legitimacy, urging that no sovereignty had been so manifestly and grossly usurped as the Pontiff's.

It became clear that the great powers were less concerned with legitimate rights than with bargaining. All tried to increase their own territories, or national security. Consalvi was invited by Talleyrand to assume presidency of a committee of eight: Russia, Prussia, Austria, Britain, France, Spain, Portugal and Switzerland. But he hesitated, reminded by Metternich of the Achilles' heel in the papal claims, the ceding of the Legations to France by Pius VI under the Treaty of Tolentino. Consalvi argued this had been done under duress:

Austria insisted that the Legations nevertheless remained at the disposal of the allied powers.

Czar Alexander I, whose will was absolute in Russia, endeavored to strike his own bargain: the Pope should be given back the Legations but on condition he set up a sole Russian archbishopric with a prelate who should at the same time be Papal Legate and Primate. The Czar's Caesaro-papism aimed at complete control of the Catholic Church in his dominions, and he knew that the prelate of his choosing (disloyal to the Holy See) would be willing to collaborate in his designs. Consalvi had to explain that the Pontiff is Pope before he is Sovereign, and that although it was vital for him to recover his temporal domains, he could not sacrifice spiritual principles nor put temporal concerns before them.

The precedence and rank pertaining to diplomatic representatives had for some time been among the principal concerns of international politics. Consalvi successfully influenced the Congress to make no change in the long-standing precedence given to representatives of the Sovereign Pontiff. He argued that such precedence was not prejudicial to any other state, being accorded to the Head of the Catholic Church on account of his unique position. This was accepted by all the powers—except England. Castlereagh pointed out that though precedence could be accorded to the Pope as a matter of courtesy, English Protestant laws forbade its admission on principle. Consalvi proposed an exception in the case of the Pope's representatives, and the British Minister finally accepted.

One thing all were agreed upon: the Papal Legations, occupied partly by Austria and partly by Murat's Neapolitan forces, should not go to the adventurous and ambitious Joseph, "King of Naples," brother-in-law of the fallen Emperor. Talleyrand and Castlereagh in particular were working for the restoration of the rightful Bourbon King of Naples, Ferdinand. But the wily Murat had once more changed alliance and was secretly in touch with Napoleon on the Island of Elba, planning to raise Italian support in the event of Napoleon's escaping back to France.

News of the Emperor's escape in March 1815 burst like a bombshell upon the Vienna Congress members. Louis XVIII had not been able to govern effectively, and many welcomed the Emperor's return. Most European nations were, however, determined he should not recover his power; and Britain, Russia, Austria and Prussia once more re-armed to defeat him. Murat now backed his brother-in-law Napoleon, against whom he had not long since secretly allied himself with Austria, and demanded free passage for his own troops through Rome while Napoleon marched north to Paris.

Pius refused. But as Murat's troops approached, he thought it best to leave Rome in order to safeguard his sovereign independence. At the invitation of King Victor Emmanuel I of Savoy the Pope withdrew to Genoa with a number of cardinals and members of the diplomatic corps, after protesting at Murat's invasion of his domain and leaving behind a provisional government.

Pius VII reached Genoa toward the end of March, two days after Napoleon had reoccupied his throne in Paris. The French ambassador to the Holy See, representing Louis XVIII, expressed his apprehensions; but Pius told him not to be alarmed, saying it was only a passing storm—a matter of two or three months.

Murat meanwhile took advantage of the situation, inciting the "oppressed people of Rome" and also those of the Marches, Milan, Turin and Venice to rise and demand their "liberation in a free and independent nation." His tactics anticipated those of Mazzini and his "Young Italy" two decades later; but most Italians were still too attached to Pope and King for Murat's war cry to be effective. After some successes on the battlefields of Bologna, he was beaten by the Austrians at Tolentino and fled to France. Abandoned by Napoleon, he made a desperate attempt to reconquer his "Kingdom of Naples," but fell into the hands of his enemies in southern Italy and was shot.

Pius remained deaf to the renewed overtures of the restored Emperor, who assured the Pontiff of his pacific aims, his will to live in peace with the Holy See and his confident hope that the Pope would yet give canonical institution to the bishops of his choosing for the still vacant sees of France. He once more named his uncle Cardinal Fesch ambassador at Rome, but Pius gently intimated he was not accepted.

Napoleon knew that during his time on Elba, when the throne had been restored to the rightful French king, there had been such an explosion of pent-up popular feeling against the bishops whom he had wrongfully appointed that the police had to be called in to quiet the people and restore order. The canons of Notre Dame Cathedral had refused any longer to accept the intruder archbishop, Cardinal Maury, and had signed a declaration of loyalty to the allied sovereigns. They did not obey the order to sing a *Te Deum* in thanksgiving for the Emperor's restoration and refused to take an oath of loyalty; they were left unpunished. A few bishops here and there were found to support the reinstated Emperor, but not a single cardinal came to the ceremony celebrating the proclamation of the new imperial constitution.

Pius VII refused to excommunicate Napoleon by name, as some urged him to. Consalvi explained that it was not possible to renew explicitly the spiritual penalty on temporal grounds, as Napoleon had intended to restore the Pope's territorial possessions at the time of liberating him. It was also, Consalvi explained, a point of honor for the Emperors onetime prisoner not to aid in any particular way the cause of his former persecutor's enemies. Pius refused the pressing invitation of the allied powers to support their declaration that Napoleon was a disturber of world peace and the object of public revenge.

The restoration of the Bourbon King of Naples removed all obstacles in the way of the Pope's journeying back to Rome through his own dominions. He decided to return without waiting for the conclusion of the Congress of Vienna. But before leaving Genoa, he went again to Savona to crown the image of Our Lady of Mercy in fulfillment of his promise to the people that he would do so if ever circumstances permitted. Pius once more saw the hand of God here, in his having been invited by King Victor Emmanuel to take temporary refuge in a city near Savona.

The crowning took place in the presence of the King, ten cardinals, a number of bishops and priests and thousands of people. It happened that at this moment the first news came of the Austrians defeating Murat at Tolentino, compelling him to withdraw from the Papal Legations and leave the way free for the Pope's return. A second time Pius VII had reason to thank Our Lady of Mercy.

After an absence of seventy days and yet another triumphal journey Pius arrived back in Rome, acclaimed with great rejoicing.

The resumption of hostilities on the part of the Allies against Napoleon proved a spur to the plenipotentiaries assembled in Vienna for settling restitution of the Papal States and Legations. Barely a week before Waterloo, a long and stormy final discussion resulted in an agreement—the last act of the Congress—and his territories were formally consigned to Pius VII. "Without the immense personal reputation of the Holy Father," Consalvi wrote to Pacca, "and the view that is held about his sanctity and character, it would have been useless (and God knows I do not lie or flatter), I repeat, useless to have made claims, negotiated and persuaded; or at least, we should have gained very little. . ."

The British commanded by Wellington were first in the field in the renewed campaign against Napoleon, fighting together with the Prussians under Blücher. They decided to attack from the North, in the Netherlands. Napoleon marched from Paris to meet them, beat Blücher and forced him to retreat. Wellington's forces were victorious, but retreated in order to improve their own position.

Wellington got his army securely posted on rising ground above the plain of Waterloo, where the French armies waited for him to attack them. But he held back. He knew he was not strong enough to win alone and without the help promised by Blücher.

The battle of Waterloo began at 11 o'clock on Sunday morning, June 18. Napoleon saw that the British were alone and cried out exultantly: "At last—I have them!" ordering a cannonade and cavalry charge at the same time.

The French horsemen charged up the slopes, but the British drawn up in compact squares repulsed them. The French charged again and again for hours.

Both sides fought valiantly, with terrible losses. Wellington was always where danger was greatest, encouraging his men, whose endurance was wonderful. But by evening they were all but spent and Wellington was heard to say: "Would to God that Blücher were here, or night were come!"

Blücher had been wounded but was determined to keep his promise to his "brother Wellington." At last, before sunset, the Prussian advance guard was seen approaching from east of the plain. Now sure of victory, Wellington let his men leave their posts and charge. The lines of the French army rolled back, caught and pursued by the English and Prussians.

Napoleon saw that all was lost. It was the end of his "hundred days."

He made haste to return to Paris, where he abdicated for the second time, then endeavored to throw himself upon British hospitality.

NOTES

1. Bernard Ward comments that O'Connell "was all along attempting to limit the Pope's authority and magnify that of a national episcopate" (*The Eve of Catholic Emancipation*), and Leflon says that "such principles of modern democracy consecrated by the French Revolution were more in favor of Irish political interests than the claims of the Catholic Church, sole depositary and guardian of revealed religious truth," adding that O'Connell was, or had lately been, Master of a Dublin Masonic Lodge, a fact he admitted, pleading ignorance of the Church's sanctions. (*History of the Church—The Revolutionary Crisis*). (See Bibliographical Notes).

2. Febronianism: The Gallican-influenced teachings of Bishop Johann Nikolaus von Hontheim (1701-1790) using the pseudonym Justinus Febronius. Bishop Hontheim taught, among other things, that the Church's power of the keys was given by Christ to the whole body of faithful, though it is *exercised* through the hierarchy. In Febronian

theory the Pope's primacy of jurisdiction in the Church was denied, with an increase of authority for the bishops; general councils were held to be above the Pope. The purpose of these theories was to loosen the dependence of the various bishops upon the Holy See in order to set up national churches with the bishops becoming subservient to temporal rulers.

3. *History of the Church—The Revolutionary Crisis.* (See Bibliographical Notes).

4. Bishops receive their spiritual jurisdiction not directly from God but mediately through the Pope. (Dogmatic Constitution on the Church of Christ, *Pastor aeternus*, Vatican Council I, 1870, Dz. 1821-1840).

5. The *"Petite Église"* was sustained tenaciously by a *small number* of extreme Gallican-minded bishops and priests of the old regime who refused to accept the 1801 Concordat. Returning to France, they continued in schism with Rome and tried by many means to influence others. They maintained that their jurisdiction was given them directly by God and that therefore the Pope, whom they recognized as supreme authority, had nevertheless not the power to depose them. Some were reconciled, others were not; the *Petite Église* survived long after Pius VII's liberation and the Restoration following 1815.

~ 13 ~

RESTORATION

Catholic Europe in Ruins—Difficulties in Setting Up
a New Roman Government—Secret Societies and
Brigandage—St. Gaspar del Bufalo—Religious
Disorders in Italy, Germanic States and Poland—
St. Clement Mary Hofbauer—Mending of
Relations between the Pope and Austrian Emperor—
A Time of Purging and Strengthening

Pius VII returned to Rome in June of 1815 to face a situation not unlike the one he had found on becoming Pope in 1800. Then, the Church and European society in the immediate aftermath of the French Revolution began to have order of a kind restored by the First Consul Bonaparte; now, after Napoleon's final defeat, the map of Europe was redrawn and a new order designed—chiefly by the Austrian Chancellor Metternich's Congress system. This "Holy Alliance," as it was called under the influence of the Russian Czar Alexander, aimed above all at checking or quelling any recrudescence of revolutionary activity. But the task of rebuilding the Church, everywhere in ruins, was a gigantic one. The immense organization of the religious orders, which for a thousand years had been the papacy's finest instrument, had for the most part been lost in the catastrophe.

During Consalvi's absence in London and Vienna the Pope had set up a provisional government, appointing Pacca as pro-Secretary of State. Among the most pressing questions to be dealt with was that of ecclesiastics and others who had collaborated with the usurping Republican and Imperial régimes. Also, much-needed reforms in the papal government in accord with the changed mentality and times had to be tackled.

After years of foreign occupation many among the clergy, aristocracy and people held divided views. Pacca wanted a return to the old order and aimed at restoring this as quickly as possible. His intransigence and severe methods were backed by old-guard members of the Roman Curia and cardinals and encouraged by remaining popular indignation against the French and Neapolitan occupiers. But this policy was not in accord with the Pope's intentions and was criticized by Consalvi in letters from Vienna.

Pius VII's pastoral experience as Bishop of Imola during the Republican occupations, apart from his personal character and Benedictine formation, enabled him to view the situation more realistically and to see the need for working to reconcile opposing trends in the Church and post-revolutionary society at as deep a level as possible: he recognized the need for a certain suppleness to avoid too authoritarian and rigid methods no longer acceptable to many and liable to provoke explosive counter-reactions.

Pius lacked neither the will nor the strength to moderate his Minister's policy and procedure. But it would seem that, in spite of showing himself unyielding and adamant where religious principles and sovereign independence were at stake, he was reluctant to impose his will in matters of temporal administration. It was certainly a consistent trait of his to refrain from interfering with the methods or measures of trusted ministers once they were appointed, even though these methods might prove at variance with those he had envisaged.

Pacca's measures were not altogether suitable or manifestly effective, but certain actions of his provisional government were justifiable and necessary. A popular uprising had been instigated in Rome against all who had collaborated in Radet's assault upon the Quirinal Palace and the Pope's abduction. Many would have been killed but for the prompt intervention of armed force by the papal government. The papal government condemned the traitors to hard labor or exile, but not to death. Bishops who had accepted sees without canonical institution and priests who had taken oaths of loyalty to the French Republic or the Emperor were required to make formal retraction and give up the benefices they had so acquired. In certain cases, penances and sanctions were imposed. Lay officials who had gone over to the service of the French were dealt with severely, though there was not always a distinction made between those who had betrayed their Sovereign for personal gain or prestige and others who had been forcibly persuaded to do so through weakness, need or force of circumstances.

The severe measures enacted by the provisional papal government under Pacca against lay persons who had worked for the Republican and Imperial governments caused inevitable resentment and gave impetus to the secret societies working to undermine the papal régime and discredit the Pope's authority. Oldest and most widespread of these was the Carbonari, founded in Naples early in the 19th century with the avowed aim of bringing about a united Italy free from papal and foreign rule. Their method was to provoke disorders, instigate acts of terrorism and kill papal gendarmes and public officials. Attempts were made on the lives of the Cardinal-legates who governed the Legations. The Carbonari were organized in companies commanded by a president. They made use of secret emissaries drawn from all ranks of society, the nobility, the middle classes, the army and especially the clergy, if they could corrupt them. They worked in and from small localities as well as large cities, and were favorable to Freemasonry, which at first held aloof, but later, together with other secret societies, joined forces with the Carbonari.

Pacca saw everything to do with the French Revolution as diabolic. He set about abrogating the Napoleonic civil code, objectional for its legalization of divorce. He put into force again the previous complicated legislative system, replacing lay officials and magistrates with clerical, restored the activities of the Roman Inquisition[1] against heresy and revived the Index of Forbidden Books and censorship of harmful publications. Vaccination and street lighting, introduced by the French, were abolished. Begging was again not unlawful. The Jews were once more obliged to return to the ghetto. Protests, discontent and unrest grew, and Consalvi multiplied his own letters of disapproval.

Cardinal Sala, diarist of the 1798 "Roman Republic" and one of the ablest minds of the Sacred College, had drawn up a project for governmental reform in Rome and States of the Church. He was asked to submit a revised version more in keeping with the changed mentality and situation. Points made anew by Sala included, among others, that the papal government had confused sacred and profane matters. It had clung too insistently to past ways, customs and methods, forgetting the art of understanding and dealing with people. "The Pope's spiritual mission is essential," Sala emphasized, "since it is inherent to its character; on the other hand, the temporal one is accidental and accessory. The Holy See's spiritual mission has been hindered by too heavy a burden of temporal concerns which, at the same time, have not in themselves been consistently well managed." Among remedies suggested was the hitherto unheard-of proposal of entrusting to laymen certain secular offices held by the clergy.

Consalvi, unlike Pacca, had from the first seen the Revolution not as something of purely diabolical origin, but as the launching of a movement—though certainly not of Christian inspiration—giving rise to a course of events which would prove irreversible. He was convinced it was no use trying to establish things again as they had been before 1796. He had actually written (to the nuncio in Germany, the future Leo XII, Msgr. Della Genga, in 1800): "If Noah, coming out of the ark after the flood, had insisted on doing all as he had done before, it would have been absurd, for the world was completely changed. Yet Noah had only to reckon with material and physical changes: he and the few survivors with him were of one mind..."

Cardinal Consalvi criticized the Holy Alliance and the Vienna Congress System as an inefficacious attempt on the whole to heal the wounds of post-revolutionary European society, without sufficiently considering the need to direct men's consciences through censorship of the press. He considered unlimited freedom of the press a most dangerous weapon in the hands of the opponents of religion and monarchy, its benefits nullified in the long run by criminal influences infecting entire peoples—a serious problem with which it would one day be necessary to reckon.

Consalvi returned from the Congress of Vienna to Rome in the late summer of 1815 with full powers as Secretary of State. He found it was one thing to have recovered the Papal States of the Church, but another to keep and rule them. Evidently influenced by Sala's project, he set about drawing up a program of reforms, reorganization and remodeling of the papal government. These included, among other innovations, the introduction of a commission of laymen to assist in consultive capacity, each of the papal delegates ruling the four Legations of Ravenna, Bologna, Ferrara and Forli. Consalvi's reforming program took away judicial powers from the clergy; the ecclesiastical courts were to be retained only for judging clerical cases and those connected with canon law. On no account, though, would Consalvi consider even the possibility of introducing a constitutional régime, as some urged. This type of government, he acknowledged, could be effective in a monarchy headed by a lay sovereign, but it was out of the question in a theocracy ruled by an ecclesiastic. The institutional principles of the pontifical régime were incompatible with constitutional ones, Consalvi maintained: for if the Pope were to give up his legislative powers, he might find himself, as Head of the Universal Church, having to protest against and demand the revocation of laws passed by a national government.

"Everyone knows," Consalvi concluded, "how the principles of a constitutional, democratic régime applied to Church government introduce germs of discord and contradiction, generating schism or heresy. For in the Church, which is a divinely founded monarchy, authority over the members comes from the head, while in constitutional, democratic régimes it is exactly the contrary, authority and power proceeding—at least theoretically—from the members and communicated to the head."

Nevertheless, the Cardinal Secretary of State was bent on introducing every possible change compatible with the papal régime. He aimed at a compromise between the ancient good and the modern welfare, maintaining neither too much nor too little of either. The best of both papal and Republican régimes should be conserved, with the aim of getting rid of the abuses and imperfections in both. In the reconstruction of papal government Consalvi allowed for greater centralization and secularization, principles which he had admittedly taken over from the French administration.

Consalvi saw that in particular, young people who had never known the papal régime, or had been given the worst idea of it, were quite unwilling to submit to government by priests. It was consequently necessary to avoid hastiness and proceed by stages, beginning with an intermediary, provisional régime. "One does not change a régime as one changes a shirt," he said. The French themselves had kept the papal system in force for a time at first, so as to accustom the people by degrees to the Republican rule.

Pius VII consented with reserve to Consalvi's governing program, in contrast to Pacca's. The Pope for the time being also thought best, for the sake of conciliation and concord, to allow the French administrative system and the Napoleonic civil and penal codes to remain in force—except for those articles, such as permission to divorce, that were contrary to Christian principle.

Consalvi was much criticized in Rome by those anxious, with Pacca, to see the old ways return. On the other hand, Metternich believed it was Consalvi's more liberal administration that prevented revolts fomented by the secret societies from breaking out, as they were later to do in Naples, Piedmont and the States of the Church during the reigns of Leo XII and Gregory XVI. All the same, Consalvi's program was not altogether effective. This was partly because of the difficulty of finding like-minded prelates and clergy to run the government machinery. Also, as all experienced rulers know, or come to learn, too much leniency is usually more risky than too great severity.

As Sovereign of Rome, Pius VII had also to deal with economic and financial difficulties. The Holy See had been despoiled of its richest domains, and Church property had been seized. The French Republican leaders had contracted enormous debts, which successive Napoleonic and Neapolitan occupiers had done nothing to remedy—or had even increased. Common necessities were lacking; the number of poor and needy in the City of Rome had grown to thousands. Inflation came with monetary devaluation. Pius did what he could by personal example, drastically cutting down expenses in his own court and household. He distributed the greater part of the voluntary offerings he received for his personal use among poor priests and people. The French ambassador reported that the Pope's own fare was frugal in the extreme. But not many others were able to imitate him. The suppression of most religious orders had resulted in numbers of dispersed men and women members having to exist on pittances—and even these the government could ill afford. Poverty-stricken persons of all classes, who had formerly been helped by the charity of the religious orders, were obliged to go about begging. The number of unemployed became legion.

The more Consalvi's remedial program was seen to be coping for the most part unsuccessfully with the situation, the more he was openly criticized and attacked by both the conservative and liberal forces in the Roman Curia and society. The former, fearing for their prestige and position, called him an innovator, accusing him of being too progressive; the latter called him a "reactionary," saying his program was not sufficiently progressive.

At length, in 1817, a general European economic crisis sent prices soaring, and scarcity of goods and unemployment became acute. The hard-hit, long-suffering poorer classes were exploited by the new revolutionaries and secret societies, who provoked a violent anti-clerical campaign against the papal administration, which they accused of complicity with financial speculators and illicit trafficking in contraband goods.

Added to these evils and providing further incentive for both revolutionary and counter-revolutionary activities was the continuing curse of organized banditry, which the ecclesiastical and civil authorities seemed powerless to put a stop to. During the French and Neapolitan occupations, the bands of robbers and murderers quartered in inaccessible mountain hideouts or forests had grown more and more bold and menacing. Their numbers were increased by escaped or released criminals, who thus found an immediate and profitable way of living and of avenging themselves on the society that had punished them.

One band had become so powerful and daring as to swoop down from the mountains in the dead of night and break into a defenseless regional seminary of Latium not far from Rome. The rector, priests and students were carried off and a couple of students sent back with a letter threatening that all would be killed unless a high ransom were paid. The money was raised by the wealthier priests' and students' families, and a group of armed citizens set out to hand over the ransom money. But the brigands mistook the ransoming party for soldiery sent to capture them and took flight with their prisoners, leaving three of the students behind with their throats cut to frighten off the fancied attackers. The ransomers pursued them, and the surviving prisoners were in the end handed over. The Pope personally housed them and had them looked after until they recovered from the shock of their experience.

Not long afterward another band came down at night from

the hills above Frascati, surrounded the lonely Camaldolese hermitage and, after robbing the church of all valuables, dragged the hermits from their cells and carried them away. Three of the older ones, nearly dying from shock and injuries, were left behind but managed to reach Rome. This further outrage prompted the papal government to raise an armed force which, guided by the three hermits, managed to catch up with the brigands. In the struggle with the soldiery the hermits got away—but so did the brigands, who retreated still higher into the hills, where it was impossible to follow them.

Pius VII came to see that the radical cure for this deep-seated evil was to bring the bandits—men who through circumstances had become robbers and murderers—back to religion. Heeding the advice of the saintly missionary priest Gaspar del Bufalo,[2] who advised him not to destroy the mountain city where most of them had quarters but rather endeavor to convert them, he commissioned this priest to go among them. St. Gaspar went alone, armed only with the crucifix, to their mountain hideouts and spoke to them of God as none had spoken before. They listened to him, came to respect, even to love him—and did as he asked. Whole regions were soon redeemed. Yet the curse of banditry was not eliminated for several generations.

The year 1817 brought such a crisis—governmental, social and economic, and also religious on account of the confusion and uncertainty—that Pius VII became ill. To crown all, the combined forces of the Carbonari, Freemasonry and secret societies took advantage of the situation, and of the Pope's illness, in a concerted plan to rouse the Italian people as a nation against the Sovereign Pontiff. The attempt was foiled by timely countermeasures ordered by Consalvi. A high-ranking lay official of the papal government was suspected as a betrayer, and investigations led to his incrimination as a secret instigator and leader of the rebels. In this year of such acute spiritual and material distress for the papacy and Rome, Pope Pius VII extended the Feast of Our Lady of

Sorrows, which had been celebrated locally since the 17th century, throughout the Universal Church (to be observed on September 15).

Pius continued to uphold and defend Consalvi. At the same time, he could not help seeing that Consalvi's reforming program was but partly successful. The Pope acknowledged the self-sacrifice and devotion to duty of his Secretary of State, as well as his great ability; but he felt bound, after prolonged and painful reflection, to find a solution himself to the problems his temporal sovereignty was causing him.

As several times before, when faced with an extremely critical situation, the Pope's health became seriously affected. His malady, brought on by all these causes, made his sanctity, integrity and greatness stand out all the more against the somber background of this second period of his reign, a reign which looked as though it were beginning to draw to a close—so thought the Austrian ambassador, who reported: "His Holiness has no appetite, is extremely feeble and as soon as he lies down is assailed by spasmodic hiccoughing. The glands of his neck are swollen, he does not sleep and has frequent fits of vomiting that leave him as though lifeless. . ."

The Austrian ambassador so far feared the Pope's imminent death as to advise Vienna of the names of cardinals whom he considered should be excluded from becoming Pope in the event of a not far distant conclave.

Pius was only just able to preside in St. Peter's at the long Holy Week ceremonies, conquering his physical weakness by a great effort of will. Those present were dismayed by the Holy Father's changed appearance and saw that, at times, he seemed almost succumbing to his infirmity while visibly trying to master it.

On Easter Sunday he felt so ill during celebration of the Mass that he was forced to retire to a stall behind the papal throne, set up in case of such an emergency, where he remained from after the Elevation of the Host until Communion. He afterward imparted the customary Easter Blessing *Urbi et Orbi*— to the City and to the World— from the outer balcony of St. Peter's seated, as he could no longer stand.

Consalvi was deeply grieved by the suffering and condition of the Holy Father and had no doubt that this had been brought on by the increasingly critical state of affairs in Church and society. He was doubly distressed, aware also that his own reforming policy was not producing the expected results. In his memoirs of this period Consalvi quoted the Austrian ambassador as having told him he felt that the extreme sensitivity of Pius VII had made him brood too much over the troubles inherent in the very nature of his dual cross: of Supreme Pastor and temporal sovereign.

In spite of the Pope's having urged him, Consalvi had never wished to go beyond the office of deacon to receive Holy Orders, not feeling called to be a priest.[3] It seems he all along felt that his sphere of action—always aimed at the Church's highest good—was to be concentrated on the temporal sphere, with all the inevitable worldly dealings and concessions necessary to avoid greater evils.

Pius, on the other hand, true to his Benedictine training and pastoral experience, thought above all of his own sanctification and salvation and the sanctification and salvation of others. Supernatural, religious motives were always first. Now once more he found himself at grips with the agonizing, fundamental question of how best to exercise his temporal sovereignty without prejudice to his own soul and his spiritual mission toward the multitude of souls who were his sons and daughters in God.

Among the various acts of restoration and revival undertaken in Rome at this time was the reopening of the venerable English College, originating from 1362 and founded by Pope Gregory XIII in 1578 as a seminary for priestly training. One of the students of the newly reopened institute was Nicholas Wiseman, who was to become first Cardinal Archbishop of Westminster in the restored Catholic hierarchy of England. Wiseman and his fellow students saw the resurrection of the Holy See after the Pope's return—with all the works of restoration being accomplished following years of suppression, suffering and obscuration—as little short of a miracle.

Soon after arrival in Rome Wiseman and other English priests and students of the College were received in audience by Pius VII; in his book, *Early Impressions of Rome,* he wrote of the occasion. He had long thought of the Pope, the captive and persecuted Pontiff, as having a particular halo of his own. His gentleness and sanctity had won the reverence even of his enemies. The familiar portrait was not that of a great high priest, but of a meek old man bent over the crucifix praying, in words made sacred by constant utterance: "May the holy and adorable will of God be ever done."

The memory of his triumphal and joyful re-entry into Rome less than three years before was still fresh in people's minds. Some spoke of it as though it had taken place just yesterday when, on Christmas Eve of 1818, Wiseman and his friends ascended the great main staircase of the Quirinal Palace and passed through the magnificent Regal Hall to reach the Pope's antechamber.

After a short wait they were summoned into Pius VII's presence. The room was so small it was hardly possible to make the customary genuflections at the door and halfway across the room when approaching the Pontiff. And instead of receiving the Englishmen seated, Pius rose and went toward them to avoid the appearance of a formal presentation.

Whatever they had read or heard about the affability and sweetness of the Pope's manner, speech and expression was revealed and confirmed before them. He gave each a friendly, "almost national" handclasp, after due homage had been most willingly paid.[4]

The next time Wiseman saw the Pope was during the Corpus Christi procession of 1819. The spirit of piety—he afterward wrote[5]—which Pius' saintly mother had engrafted on a sweet and gentle nature was impressed upon his countenance and figure. Bent down by age and suffering, his attitude seemed one of continual prayer, of earnest and unaffected devotion, abstracted from the ceremonial and the multitude that encompassed him.

None who ever saw the Pope in that position—kneeling before the golden monstrance containing the holiest object of Catholic belief and worship borne aloft beneath the silver-embroidered canopy—could forget it: the hands firmly and immovably clasped at the base of the sacred vesssel; the head bent low, not in feebleness but in homage; the eyes closed, seeing nothing of the state and magnificence all around, the world shut out by the calm and silent meditation within; the noble features so composed that no expression of human feeling or earthly thought could be traced upon or gathered from them . . .

★   ★   ★

Restoration in Rome and the States of the Church had been the first task to be undertaken by Pius VII and the papal government; but disorders were rife in many parts of Europe as well as in Italy. Vast territories of Poland had been incorporated into the Russian Empire. Agitation over Catholic Emancipation in Ireland and England continued, although the Pope's resistance to Napoleon had done much to break down anti-Catholic prejudice and turn people's minds again toward Rome.

The United States of America was still mission land. The Irish Dominican Luke Concanen, Prior of St. Clement's, Rome, had been consecrated first Bishop of New York in 1807, but was prevented from setting out for his diocese by prevailing political conditions in Italy. The Sub-prior of St. Clement's, Fr. Connolly, who succeeded Bishop Concanen, was able to take possession of his see as second Bishop of New York.

In most regions of Italy Napoleon had imposed the Italian Concordat of 1803, with its fundamentally anticlerical regulations. Religious orders had been dissolved and Church property appropriated to the civil power. Many episcopal sees remained vacant or were occupied by prelates appointed by the Emperor without the Pope's approval or ratification.

Spain had stayed more or less immune to French Republican influence. The general attitude toward the usurping King Joseph, brother of Napoleon, had been fiercely hostile. Yet the returning rightful King Charles caused Rome utmost embarrassment by reviving the Inquisition, not only as a just means for discovering and trying heresy, but also as an abusive instrument for spying out and condemning political opponents, adding fuel to the fires of anticlericalism and Protestant propaganda.

In France it was said that many exiles returning with the restored King Louis XVIII had forgotten nothing and learned nothing. The King's morals and way of ruling appeared to be inspired more by the Odes of Horace, his favorite author, than by the Gospel. He set up an ecclesiastical commission with the aim of annulling the Concordat of 1801 between France and the Holy See but keeping intact its appended Gallican "Organic Articles," which had caused Pius so much grief.

Louis sent to Rome an ambassador who was not a trained diplomat, with instructions that referred to Pius VII as, among other things, "the butt of Napoleon, who had abusively succeeded in imposing on him the terms of the Concordat and of his own coronation." France's duty to protect the rights and liberties of the Gallican Church was asserted against ultramontane (Roman) pretensions. The ambassador's mission failed.

Another ambassador was sent by the French King, in reply to Pius VII's personal protest, further claiming Louis' royal right to appoint bishops. He was given a polite but chilly reception and Pius himself declared that the King's claims had to be resisted with firmness and courage, adding he had passed years of imprisonment on this account and he was ready to suffer this once more, if necessary.

The Holy See's relations with Austria continued to be clouded by contradictions: agreement with the Emperor and Metternich over general anti-revolutionary policy could not be satisfactory as long as "Josephist"[6] or regalist principles favored a more or less nationalized Church limiting the Pope's authority and jurisdiction.

But difficulties did not end there. In Austria, as also in Germany and Poland, after the Revolution and Napoleonic wars the general confusion of old and new systems and ideas caused false reforms to be set afoot and gain ground at all levels. True Catholic preaching was scarcely heard anymore. A campaign waged *against the Faith* by the "enlightened" press and clergy in the name of national progress had bit by bit replaced sound doctrine by vague and superficial talk of "universal Christianity" and "universal tolerance." Some of the self-styled reformers, supported by state ministers and having little or no real theological or philosophical formation, went so far as to ridicule in their sermons what was preached by their few remaining brethren who were still truly Catholic.

The spirit of Jansenism was still rampant in the form of religious rationalism and had caused infant Baptism to be looked askance at, so that the Sacrament was delayed until a later age when the child could understand—an error widely repeated in our time.[7] The solemnity, beauty and poetry of the liturgical actions, chants, vestments and setting were taken away from the Mass and ceremonies—which were styled "divine service" and said in German. Laws of fasting were reduced or done away with, and the clergy were dispensed from daily reading of the Breviary. Devotion to the Blessed Virgin had all but disappeared, combated by new-style theologians who denigrated what they called "misplaced enthusiasm" for Christ's Mother. Even good Catholic families had given up saying the Rosary together, and it was thought quite extraordinary when a priest was found in Vienna who would bless and distribute rosary beads and encourage people to use them.

This priest was Fr. Clement Mary Hofbauer—St. Clement Mary[8]—the Redemptorist who succeeded, in spite of every kind of opposition and against tremendous odds, in establishing the Congregation of the Most Holy Redeemer (founded by St. Alphonsus Liguori) in Austria, Germany and Poland.

Under the disreputable King Stanislaus II, Warsaw in the post-revolutionary period had become, according to police records, a city sunk in corruption, crime and impurity. The laxity of most of the clergy was such that the religious authorities admitted that scandal and vice had come to a head and it was hard to see how matters could be remedied.

Fr. Hofbauer was convinced the Holy See was not properly aware of the situation. He was able to alert Consalvi at the Congress of Vienna, as well as reporting to the Roman *Propaganda Fide* Congregation: "Germany is in greater danger now than in the time of Luther. The source of all the evil robbing not only the German peoples but many others of the faith, grace and purity of morals is to be found here in streams of iniquity. Our first duty is to bank up and avert the course of these infected, deadly waters. The people are well disposed and could in a short time with little difficulty be won over to the cause of right and truth—if only we were permitted to apply the proper remedy."

It was not only the State but also the ecclesiastical reforming party that no longer recognized the binding force of Church laws or the Pope's jurisdiction over the whole Church. The national episcopate sought to safeguard itself against what was seen as the encroachments and pretensions of the Roman Curia. The universities had become hotbeds of false and subversive teaching. Fr. Hofbauer knew what he was talking about, for as a student at Vienna University he had been obligated to interrupt a professor during his lecture and tell him that what he was saying was contrary to Catholic doctrine. He happened not long after to meet the professor privately. Instead of showing resentment or offense, the professor thanked Hofbauer for the rebuke, which he acknowledged was just and salutary.

The holy Redemptorist's increasing success in bringing people back to true faith and practice could not long escape the attention of the reforming civil authorities and clergy. The church where he preached and celebrated Mass with all the restored beauty and solemnity of Roman Catholic worship was closed. He was prevented from preaching, watched by the police, and various trumped-up charges were brought against him. Pressure was put upon the Archduke, who was representing the Emperor during his absence in Rome, with the intention of getting the saint convicted and expelled from the country. The Archduke's answer was unexpected: "What Vienna needs is not Father Hofbauer's conviction and removal but more priests like him."

Pius VII had for some time felt sure a personal meeting between himself and the Austrian Emperor Francis could do more than any interchange of diplomatic relations, and he had more than once invited the Emperor to visit him in Rome. Metternich was working for an agreement with the Holy See based more on "realistic" political advantages than on Christian principles; and the Pope protested vehemently against the policy of maintaining a kind of national Austrian Church impeding relations with Rome and obstructing the pastoral ministry of bishops and the teaching of Catholic doctrine.

Francis, for his part, tried for a while to defend this policy by referring to the French and Italian Concordats, with their appended articles providing for the State's advantage. But in the end, in spite of Metternich's objections and the persuasions of his bureaucratic ministers, the Austrian Emperor overcame his hesitations and accepted the Pope's invitation.

His Roman visit proved how right Pius VII had been in insisting. It was the first time an Emperor had gone to Rome since Charles V had done so in the 16th century, and the first time Pius was in a position to muster all the resources of his temporal splendor to honor his imperial guest. Loyal Viennese Catholics placed great hopes in Francis' visit to the Pope, although Metternich warned he would not bring a single Jesuit back with him.

The papal nuncio arrived in Rome before the Emperor to brief the Pope on certain matters crucial for religion in Austria and Germany. He told Pius of the heroic apostolate of the Redemptorist Fr. Hofbauer, with a few religious and lay helpers; the Pope made up his mind to intercede on his behalf.

Francis was immediately captivated by the personality and manner of Pius. His extraordinary simplicity, kindness and courtesy, which clearly came from his deep spirituality and holiness, so affected and subdued the Emperor that Pius felt able to open his eyes, with great tact, to some of the theological errors contained in the Josephist views and policy of his counsellors and ministers.

During one of their talks Pius referred casually to the work of Fr. Hofbauer, saying he had heard great things of him as a truly apostolic priest zealous for God's honor. The Emperor begged to disagree. But the Pope had been prepared and knew how to play on certain of his august Germanic guest's pet contentions. He went on to remark, good-humoredly, that he had been informed how Fr. Hofbauer was not satisfied that the Roman Curia properly understood the Germanic character and how to deal with Austrians and Germans. Might not better things be achieved on both sides if those at Rome heeded the Redemptorist's observations?

This frank admission and proposal on the part of the Sovereign Pontiff completely won over the Emperor. He told his confessor afterward, with sincere compunction, how he felt that Fr. Hofbauer had been wronged and asked for some way of making amends. His confessor had a ready answer: perhaps His Majesty might consider satisfying the Redemptorist's dearest desire, that of seeing his congregation established on a firm footing in Austria.

Francis gave immediate proof of his good intentions. In a further talk with Pius VII he promised to attenuate the Josephist imperial policy against religious orders. He would further authorize Fr. Hofbauer to found a religious community in Vienna and allow the Jesuits to reopen schools and colleges.

Josephism thus received a mortal blow. Some Church historians even refer to the last years of Pius VII's reign as "post-Josephist."

Leflon nevertheless comments that however wrong Church

nationalization was—and it was carried out largely through confused motives—and however ruinous its result to true religion, it is also true that Catholicism in Austria and Germany thereby underwent a drastic purging and emerged stronger. God drew a greater good from a great evil.[9]

Thanks chiefly to the foresight, wisdom and conciliatory spirit of Pius VII, plus the true diplomacy of his faithful minister Consalvi, the danger of schismatic national churches was averted and the way paved for real renewal, conciliation and reunion. This has been further acknowledged by the great German papal historian, Ludwig von Pastor, who wrote that the services rendered to German Catholicism by Rome at this time were comparable to those rendered to it nearly three centuries earlier by the Council of Trent. Now once again, as in the past, "the German dioceses were reanimated by the living breath of the papacy, out of the ruins of an upheaved world."[10]

NOTES

1. The Roman Inquisition was founded by Pope Paul III in 1542 as the supreme doctrinal tribunal for all the world to defend the Church against heresy and safeguard faith and morals. It was more lenient than the French and Spanish Inquisitions, which tended to become political. St. Pius X reorganized the Roman Inquisition, or the Congregation of the Universal Inquisition, in 1908 and named it the Holy Office; then in 1965 Pope Paul VI reformed it and gave it its present name, Congregation for the Doctrine of the Faith.
2. St. Gaspar del Bufalo (1786-1837), with the encouragement of Pius VII, founded the Congregation of the Most Precious Blood. St. Gaspar was canonized by Pius XII in 1954. (cf. *Life of St. Gaspar del Bufalo,* freely adapted from the Italian of Msgr. Vincent Sardi by Edwin G. Kaiser, C.P.P.S., Carthagena, Ohio, 1957.)
3. Until not long ago a cardinal (Latin *cardo,* a "hinge"), i.e., a man appointed by the Pope as a counsellor and assistant in the governorship of the Church, could be a layman. The 1918 Code of Canon Law laid down that he must be a priest, and in 1962 Pope John XXIII established that all cardinals should be bishops.
4. Nicholas Cardinal Wiseman, in *Recollections of the Last Four Popes,* London, 1858.

5. *Ibid.*

6. Josephism, or regalism, like Jansenism and Gallicanism, maintained State supremacy over the Church instead of recognizing and supporting the Church's higher, spiritual, sovereign power. Josephism took its name from the Emperor Joseph II (1765-1790), who put it into practice.

7. Since Baptism is necessary for salvation, the Church requires infants to be baptized *within the first weeks after birth.* (Code of Canon Law,1983).

8. Beatified by Leo XIII in 1888, St. Clement Mary Hofbauer was in 1909 canonized by Pius X.

9. *Church History—The Revolutionary Crisis* (French). (See Bibliographical Notes.)

10. Ludwig von Pastor: *History of the Popes,* continued after von Pastor's death as *Papal History of Later Times* (German and French) by his collaborator Joseph Schmidlin, Munich, 1933.

~ 14 ~

FURTHER RESTORATION, RESTITUTION AND REBUILDING

The Society of Jesus—St. Joseph Pignatelli—
The Benedictines—The City of Rome—The Arts

During the Revolution and in the aftermath of Napoleon's Empire, the Jesuits had made efforts toward their own restoration. A "Society of Priests" consisting of Jesuits had been founded with this aim in Belgium in 1794 and then a "Society of Priests of the Faith" in Italy in 1797. Pius VI had ordered the two to unite in 1799 under the name of "Fathers of the Faith."

But from the outset of his reign Pius VII had something more in mind than such partial and disguised recovery. His first act was to reestablish the Society of Jesus in Russia—or rather to confirm its continued existence there—by his brief *Catholicae Fidei* in 1801, derogating insofar as needful from his predecessor's Bull of suppression. Pius VII's act was made possible by the existence in Russia of some 10,000 Jesuits. The Czarina Catherine admired their teaching methods and for reasons of expediency had not allowed Clement XIV's Bull to be published in her dominions.

Pope Pius VII had particular assistance in this act of his from an ancient Jesuit, Father Karau, who was his private secretary. Further circumstances enabled him to recognize local reestablishment of the Jesuits in the Duchy of Parma and in the Kingdom of Naples. But lingering hostility on the part of several Catholic sovereigns, and then his own long captivity, prevented Pius from doing more during the first half of his reign.

Restoration was made possible in Naples due to a heroic little band of Jesuit Fathers who had been exiled from Spain— led by the Spanish prince and Jesuit Fr. Joseph Pignatelli—to undergo every kind of suffering and hardship. Fr. Joseph Pignatelli was canonized by Pius XII in 1954, the Pope calling him "the divinely constituted link between the old and the new Society of Jesus, to be honored as the Society's restorer."

When Joseph Bonaparte invaded Naples in 1806 and was proclaimed King, Fr. Pignatelli had been banished and came with his companions to Rome, where he was received by Pius VII. His emotion in the Pope's presence was so great that he could not speak, but Pius told him he knew all that had happened in Naples, and not to fear. He lodged him and his companions in rooms adjoining the Jesuit Church of the Gesù, but gave a word of fatherly counsel for the Jesuits not to wear their religious habit publicly, in order to avoid attracting hostility and trouble in the still existing circumstances.

Pius himself suffered considerably for his protection of Fr. Pignatelli. Diplomats in Rome representing different countries remained hostile to the Jesuits; but so great was the Pope's esteem and affection that he did not fear to praise Pignatelli publicly. He even thought of making him a member of the Sacred College of Cardinals in order to have him near as a counsellor. But he refrained on account of the holy Jesuit's abhorrence of high office, and lest such conferral of highest ecclesiastical dignity might worsen his already frail health.

Early in 1808, when a second French invasion seemed imminent, Pignatelli became anxious for the Society's archives. After a night passed in prayer he decided to ask the Pope's advice. The priest was dumbfounded to hear the Pope say, as soon as he saw him, that he was glad he had come since he had thought of sending for him concerning a matter of great importance: the safety of the Society's archives. Pius advised him to transfer all as soon as possible to a place of greater safety and gave him money for the expense. Thus it was that the archives of the

Society of Jesus remained in a modest, out-of-the-way house undiscovered all through the second French occupation and avoided the fate of others, such as the Benedictines, that were taken to Paris.

St. Joseph Pignatelli was later able to show his gratitude by sending a considerable sum of money, all he and his companions could put together, to the Pope when he himself was in need, deprived of revenues as a prisoner in the Quirinal Palace. But when Pius learned who had offered the money, he sent most of it back with his thanks and blessing, accepting a small part only.

Cardinal Pacca had several times spoken of the Jesuits with the Pope at Fontainebleau. Returning to Rome in 1814, he reminded Pius of these conversations. At the Pope's request a bull of restoration was drawn up, justified by pressing supplications for the Society's reestablishment. The bull, *Sollicitudo omnium ecclesiarum,* was published on July 31 of that year, 1814.

Pius VII went from the Quirinal Palace to the Jesuit Church of the Gesù where the Bull was read before members of the Sacred College and the few Jesuits remaining in Rome, mostly of great age. As the Pope drove back from the Gesù to the Quirinal, Rome resounded with cries of joy and applause from people who remembered the silence, sadness and dismay of July 17, 1773, when they had heard of the Bull of Suppression. Now, the worldwide Society of Jesus, founded by St. Ignatius Loyola in 1535, which had seemed to die throughout the Church by an act of the Pope, was by the Pope resurrected.[1]

Pius VII's act was all the more remarkable for his having in his student days and as a young priest imbibed some of the prevalent objections against the Jesuits from certain of his Jansenist-minded teachers and from his reading of the *Provincial Letters* of Pascal and works of other authors impregnated with anti-Jesuit notions.

Consalvi received a copy of the Bull of Restoration while still at the Congress of Vienna. He called it a masterpiece of content and style and wrote his praise and thanks to Pacca, who had drafted it. It later became clear, from letters and documents,

how much Consalvi himself had had the Jesuits' reestablishment at heart and how he had from the first worked for this,
with greatest caution, vigilance and diplomacy. He considered
the Society of Jesus essential as a force preventing the recrudescence of revolutionary ideology and activity.

When the French invaded Naples in 1806, religious orders
were suppressed, but Monte Cassino Abbey was spared as a
cultural establishment and repository of works of art. The
Benedictine community, however, was reduced to penury and
suffered every sort of privation and indignity.

On Pius VII's return to Rome in 1814 the monks lit up their
abbey so that at night the hilltop shone as a visible beacon of
rejoicing for the whole countryside to see. They sent a delegation to felicitate the Pope and received assurance of his special
consideration. The restored Bourbon King of Naples, Ferdinand II, promised help and protection, and Pius intervened
directly with the Sovereign on behalf of the Benedictines. But
financial resources were lacking to both Pope and King. Only
slowly and painfully could the world-famed abbey, founded
in the 6th century by St. Benedict and containing his mortal
remains,[2] begin again to thrive in all its ancient beauty and age-
old monastic tradition.[3]

Pius VII is remembered as a builder and beautifier of the City
of Rome as well as a patron of the arts. St. Peter's Square was
disencumbered of mean dwellings, which were replaced by ones
more in harmony with its dignity and worthier of human habi-
tation; the great square before the Quirinal Palace overlooking
the City was enlarged and given a magnificent fountain; the
Piazza del Popolo as it is now seen and the street leading from
it between the twin churches of St. Mary in Monte Santo and
Our Lady of Miracles date from his reign; the Coliseum, which
was falling into ruin in places, was repaired and buttressed,
among other major works of the kind.

As a student, priest, bishop and cardinal, Pius VII had always been of deeply studious mind and habits. As Pope he became the advocate and inspirer of research and study in the
fields of literature and the arts. He saw these not merely as

ornaments of civilized society, but also and mainly as precious means for imparting true knowledge and raising men's minds to a lofty, balanced view of the world's affairs, as well as an aid to the cultivation of virtue. Academies and institutes of learning, letters, archaeology and painting were revived and patronized by him.

Pius called Msgr. Angelo Mai to Rome and appointed him Keeper of the Vatican Library, encouraging him in his literary labors and researches. Mai became Cardinal Librarian of Holy Roman Church and enriched the library with precious manuscripts, Egyptian papyri and ancient codices. Some of these, including a part of Cicero's *Republic*, he discovered himself.

Pius added new rooms to the Vatican Museum and the new wing known as the Chiaramonti Gallery.

In regard to the visual arts Pius' reign has been compared to the rule of Pericles in Athens. The great Athenian statesman had the Grecian sculptor Phydias to carry out many of his magnificent projects; Pius had the Venetian Canova, who was known as the Phydias of his time.

Soon after his return to Rome in 1814, Pius VII had determined on seeking restitution of some of the many masterpieces that had been taken away to Paris from Italy's churches, museums and galleries. None was better fitted for such action than Canova, and the Pope entrusted him with this special mission. Canova left Rome for the French capital in 1816 with letters to King Louis XVIII and the Foreign Minister Talleyrand.

Every obstacle was at first put in his way by the French government, which was unwilling to part with priceless treasures, however ill-acquired. But with the help of diplomats of different countries, as well as Metternich and the Prince Regent of England, Canova managed to persuade Louis XVIII that Rome was the rightful place. Still, nothing was actually done.

Finally, Sir William Hamilton and the Duke of Wellington asked the British Foreign Minister, Castlereagh, to make

Canova's request on behalf of Pius VII a national question. The British government sent a vigorous note to the French King, who at length ordered action to be taken.

Canova had instructions from the Pope not to insist on the return of every one of the works of art that had been expropriated, but to leave certain of them in the national museums of France as a sign of good will and gift of Pius VII. Even so, the King's order was not carried out. It was not until the English Prince Regent had personally undertaken to pay for the transport of the statues and paintings to Rome—as a further proof of British gratitude to the Pope who had withstood Napoleon and as a mark of singular admiration for Canova—that the long and difficult operation got underway.

Crowds of Roman people gathered at the city gates to watch and applaud the arrival of the convoy carrying the huge crates and boxes of art treasures returning to their city. The Pope rewarded Canova with a Marquis' title and a handsome yearly pension. Canova accepted the title with gratitude but turned over the pension for the endowment and upkeep of Roman academies of art and letters, and to hospitals and hospices caring for poor and needy persons.

An event of considerable religious and historical importance during this latter part of Pius VII's reign was the finding and identifying of the mortal remains of St. Francis of Assisi. Their first resting place after the Founder's death in 1226 was the Church of San Giorgio. St. Francis was canonized by Gregory IX in 1228 and in 1230 his body, laid in a stone urn, was entombed in a sepulchral chamber hewn from live rock in the basilica built by Brother Elias, second successor of St. Francis.

The urn remained partly visible for over two centuries until 1442, when Assisi was attacked and conquered by the Guelphs of Perugia who sacked the city, claimed the body of St. Francis and appealed to Pope Eugene IV for possession. The Pope forbade removal of the body and, to prevent its being taken away by force, ordered the tomb to be closed and concealed with cement and stone, with care not to damage the urn. Successive popes were petitioned to open the tomb, but they refused. Finally St. Pius V gave permission, but he died (in 1572) as work was started, and this gave rise to the legend that any opening the tomb would die. No further attempts were made, and with the passing of centuries confused traditions and legends grew up concerning the tomb's location, and even doubts as to whether the Founder's remains were really there.

At length the Franciscan General Giuseppe Maria De Bonis (who suffered imprisonment for resisting Napoleon) urged the need for discovering and identifying the sacred remains; in 1806 he applied to Pius VII for permission to excavate. This the Pope gave, but work was delayed by the Napoleonic invasion and the Pope's captivity. Not until 1818 were the tomb and urn discovered; a human skeleton was found inside.

Pius VII appointed five bishops, papal delegates, to preside over the process of establishing identity, which was contested by many, including some Franciscans. The bishops were assisted by a team of experts—two architects, two doctors, two surgeons and two archaeologists. Then, after consulting the generals of all branches of the Franciscan Order, the Pope charged a commission of cardinals with examining and deliberating on the findings.

A miracle was finally implored to place the seal of absolute certainty on the cardinals' positive judgment; this was granted, several persons being instantaneously cured of grave diseases by contact with the tomb. Then in 1820 Pius VII issued the decree *Assisiensem basilicam* declaring the bones were really those of St. Francis. He had a medal struck commemorating this event which had caused great rejoicing all over the world.[4]

NOTES

1. There were several links between the Jesuits and Benedictines, the order to which Pius belonged: St. Ignatius had hung his sword, on conversion, in the Benedictine sanctuary Church of Montserrat, pronounced

his first vows in Montmartre, Paris, and solemn ones in St. Paul's, Rome. He meditated on his Society's Constitutions in Monte Cassino.

2. In the bombing and total destruction of 1943, St. Benedict's cell was undamaged. Reconstruction of Monte Cassino was completed in the 1950's.

3. At the time of the first centenary of Pius VII's death in 1923, he was remembered as the restorer of Monte Cassino Abbey, as well as of St. Mary of the Mount, Cesena, which had been restored in 1817.

4. A further recognition of St. Francis' mortal remains took place in 1978. After close examination of the tomb Franciscan General Fr. Vitale Antonio Bonmarco had found, among other things, defects in the surrounding grille, affording insufficient protection, with consequent danger of profanation of the sacred remains. Pope Paul VI accordingly appointed an ecclesiastical and technical consultative commission, presided over by the papal legate for the Assisi Basilica, Cardinal Silvio Oddi. The same year the Pope published a brief, *Patriarchalem Basilicam Assisiensem,* ensuring better protection and conservation of St. Francis' remains.

By order of the Franciscan General, all these events and also everything connected with the tomb of St. Francis from his death to the present time were documented in a volume written by the director of the Order's archive in Rome, Fr. Isidore Liberale Gatti. Thus all formerly existing uncertainties and conflicting accounts were finally and authentically dispelled and clarified. This volume is entitled *La Tomba di S. Francesco nei Secoli,* 528 pages, fully illustrated, published by Casa Editrice Francescana, Assisi.

~ 15 ~

THE END OF A
TWENTY-THREE-YEAR REIGN

Final Consolations and Sorrows for Pius VII—
His Intervention on Behalf of Napoleon—
Death of the Emperor—The Pope's Last Weeks and
Peaceful Death—Monument in St. Peter's—
The Character & Virtues of Pope Pius VII

Toward the end of his long reign of nearly a quarter of a century, Pius VII had many consolations along with continuing griefs and pains. Revolutionary movements and secret societies, organized in the North and South, were made more or less inactive in the Papal States, thanks to Consalvi's policy of clemency and pacification. Nevertheless in Rome itself Carbonarism—designed to overthrow monarchical government—had penetrated the law courts, the schools and universities, the army and police, even the nobility and clergy.

In France, in spite of anti-clerical opposition, religious orders and congregations began to be reestablished, long-vacant sees received bishops and other sees were set up. Gallicanism was on the wane, if not dead.

The Austrian Emperor, now better disposed toward Rome, modified his "Josephist" policy of State supremacy. Thanks chiefly to St. Clement Mary Hofbauer and his followers, spiritual and supernatural interests gained ascendency once more over material and worldly ones. The evil of an independent Germanic Church was avoided and ecclesiastical affairs put on a more satisfactory footing—although Protestantism had benefited from the Napoleonic aftermath of the Revolution and continued to do so.

The Russian Czar, after wavering, published the Pope's brief directed against false mystical sects and clandestine societies; and it was said that he had professed the Roman Catholic Faith on his deathbed.

In Britain and Ireland, progress of the movement toward Catholic emancipation owed much to the foresight and conciliatory policy of the Pope and Consalvi, as well as to the action of Daniel O'Connell.

In the New World, Baltimore was a metropolitan see with New York, Boston, Philadelphia and Bardstown (now the diocese of Louisville, Kentucky) its first suffragans, giving promise for Catholic life and expansion in North America.

A special apostolic mission to South America, and Chile in particular, was entrusted to the young ecclesiastic Count John Mary Mastai, future Bishop of Imola, who was to become Pope Pius IX. Difficult and dangerous conditions prevailed in those regions following Chile's independence from the Spanish Crown, but with prophetic vision Pius VII had assured Mastai's anxious mother of her son's safe return.

Spain was a cause of vexation. Loath to lose the South American colony of Chile, the revolutionary government embarrassed the Holy See with reiterated claims that could not be recognized. A fanatical Jansenist priest was sent as ambassador to Rome, but Pius VII would not receive him.

Also at this time, the Pope had the personal sorrow of seeing his well-loved and faithful Secretary of State, Consalvi, suffering from a painful illness.

Toward the end of his exile on the Island of St. Helena, Napoleon had petitioned Pius for a priest who might help him die. The Pope sent as chaplain the young Fr. Vignali, who assisted the fallen Emperor until his death in May, 1821. It came as a very particular consolation for Pius to know, from trustworthy accounts, that Napoleon had died a Catholic death.

Pope Pius VII restores the Society of Jesus in the Jesuit Church of the Gesù in Rome on August 7, 1814, after it had been suppressed for 40 years. (*Painting from the catafalque at the funeral of Pius VII.*)

St. Clement Mary Hofbauer, the Redemptorist priest who played such an important role in restoring the Church in Austria, Germany and Poland during the reign of Pope Pius VII after the terrible disorders of the Revolution. Pius heard of St. Clement Mary's work and helped clear away political obstacles and harassment so that he could proceed unhindered. This is the only known authentic portrait of the Saint.

Picture courtesy of Mt. St. Alphonsus Library, Esopus, New York.

194-1

Scene of horror among the brigands near Rome in the aftermath of the Revolution. (*Woodcut by Pinelli, circa 1820.*)

Pope Pius VII assigns St. Gaspar del Bufalo (accompanied by Bonanni) to the missions as a remedy for the social evils of the time and aids him in founding the Congregation of the Most Precious Blood.

Commissioned by Pope Pius VII, St. Gaspar del Bufalo speaks to the brigands about God in a mountain cave. They came to respect and love him. St. Gaspar del Bufalo had advised the Pope not to destroy the brigands' mountain city, as others had counselled, but rather to endeavor to convert them. Many repented and were converted.

Pope Pius VII and the excavations at the Roman Forum in 1817. The Pontiff encouraged rebuilding and improvements in the City of Rome.

The restoration of the Papal Legations to the Pope. The four figures at the left represent the four Legations: Ferrara, Ravenna, Roma, Bologna; then are pictured Cardinal Consalvi and Pope Pius VII; the last three figures depict Strength, Meekness and History. (*From the catafalque at the funeral of Pope Pius VII.*)

Pius VII at the founding of the museum and art gallery in the Campidoglio, the capitol building in Rome; this took place in 1818.

Pius VII approves the plan of the new wing of the Vatican Museum and Gallery, the Chiaramonti Museum, in 1818.

Pius VII's mother, the Venerable Giovanna Ghini Chiaramonti, who in her widowhood entered the Carmelite convent at Fano, northern Italy, receiving the name Sister Teresa Aimée of Jesus and Mary. The Pontiff celebrated Mass near his mother's tomb on his journey from Ancona to Rome in 1800.

Luigi Rossini dis. e inc.

St. Paul's-Outside-the-Walls, Rome, after the fire of July 16, 1823.

194-6

The great catafalque erected in St. Peter's Basilica for the funeral rites of Pope Pius VII, August, 1823.

Bust of Pope Pius VII by Antonio Canova in the Capitoline Palace, Rome.

194-7

A symbolic representation of St. Peter and Pope Pius VII, the 1st and 253rd Supreme Pontiffs of the Catholic Church.

During the years of the Emperor's exile Pius used sometimes to meet the Emperor's mother, to whom he had given
refuge in Rome, driving on the Palatine Hill or Appian Way.
The Pope would get out of his carriage and together they
would walk up and down, talking of "the good Emperor."
Pius had intervened, through Consalvi, with the Prince Regent
of England and the allied Sovereigns to soften the rigors of
Napoleon's confinement, which he felt in a most keen way.
Through Consalvi, Pius had written:

> The reestablishment of religion in the great kingdom
> of France was principally owing, after God, to him. The
> dutiful and courageous initiative of 1801 made Us long
> forget and forgive subsequent injuries. Savona and Fon-
> tainebleau were but actions of a misled mind, aberra-
> tions of human ambition; whilst the Concordat was a
> saving act undertaken in a Christian and heroic spirit.

Madame Mère Letizia, the Emperor's mother, wrote
thanking the Pontiff:

> The mother of kings has become the mother of sor-
> rows. The one consolation that remains is the thought
> of the Holy Father's having forgotten the past and
> remembering only the affection he has shown us all.
> Under the pontifical government alone have we found
> support and shelter. Our gratitude is as great as the bene-
> fit conferred. His Holiness and Your Eminence are the
> only ones who have sought to mitigate the sufferings
> of him whose life is ebbing away on that desert rock
> island. I thank you with all my mother's heart.

Her brother, Cardinal Fesch, said: "God did not break
Napoleon, He humbled him; and in humility lies salvation."
Certainly no humiliation was spared the fallen Emperor. His
exile corresponded almost exactly to the six years he had kept
the Pope prisoner in Rome, Savona and Fontainebleau—only
his own captivity and treatment were harsher: the roof of
his ramshackle residence, infested by rats and bugs, let in rain;

his food was not of the right kind and severely rationed; his correspondence was intercepted or withheld. After a time he was not allowed out of the house, then not out of his room, and finally was unable to show himself at the window without being insulted.

Blessed Anna Maria Taigi in Rome saw Napoleon's death and knew, from her mysterious, supernatural sun, his eternal destiny. But the 7,000 pages officially documenting the Beata's visions, prophecies and miracles contain no reference to it.[2]

Was it possible that the Catholic Faith his mother had reared him in, made dormant by military and worldly glory, was reawakened in suffering and confinement? The memoirs of Montholon, head of the fallen Emperor's household, of his officer Gourgaud, his doctor O'Meara and others are contradictory, as indeed appears to have been Napoleon's very behavior. But he certainly heard Mass with evident attention, confessed to Father Vignali and asked for the Last Sacraments. Who can tell how much the memory of Pius VII's goodness, patience and charity in persecution and, above all, the Pope's prayers, contributed in effecting, at the last, a true conversion?

⋆   ⋆   ⋆

On July 6, 1823, which happened to be the 14th anniversary of the assault on the Quirinal and the Pope's abduction from Rome, Pius VII fell and broke a thigh bone, which injury was to cause his death. In his decreasing physical strength Pius had had two previous falls, but without serious consequences. Consalvi had given orders that the Pope was always to be accompanied when moving from one place to another. As an extra precaution, a rope for him to hold onto had been fixed along the walls of his study and the corridor leading to his bedroom.

On this day, alone in the dim light of the room as it grew dusk, the Pope, rising from his chair, had reached for the rope but failed to catch hold of it. His cry of pain as he fell full length upon the marble floor brought attendants and members of the household running to his aid. He was put to bed, and his physician diagnosed a fracture.

Consalvi was distraught and would not leave the Pope's bedside until late that night, when Pius begged him to take some rest.

The Pope lay in great pain for a week. A major operation could not be undertaken at his age and because of his greatly weakened health. He understood there was no hope of recovery and with complete serenity asked for the Last Sacraments.

He bore acute suffering for a further six weeks without complaint, often in high fever, at times delirious. The French King sent a patent adjustable bed which brought some relief; the Austrian Emperor sent bottles of his best Tokay wine.

Aware that members of his household who had gathered around his bed were speaking in subdued tones of world events, the Pope signed them to raise their voices so that he could hear. He was told of the fervent prayers being offered for him in Rome and throughout the world; he expressed his thankfulness, smiled, lifted a hand in blessing.

Meanwhile, during the night of July 16, the most ancient and beautiful Roman Basilica after St. Peter's, St. Paul's-outside-the-walls, through the carelessness of a couple of workmen repairing the roof's wooden rafters, was reduced in a few hours to a pile of smoking ruins. The Basilica and monastery were particularly dear to Pius, who had spent years there as a young Benedictine. He was not told of the disaster so as to spare him further suffering. But some reports say he was heard murmuring, *"St. Paul's—St. Paul's!. . ."*

The following day he became at intervals delirious. The news that the Pope was not expected to live was communicated by Consalvi to the Sacred College of Cardinals. The Blessed Sacrament was exposed in Rome's major Basilicas, parish churches, monasteries and convents, where prayers and sacrifices were offered day and night for the dying Pontiff. The French Ambassador, Chateaubriand, wrote to his court that all Rome, clergy, princes and people, seemed immersed in only one thought—of soon losing a much-loved and venerated head and Sovereign.

On August 19 the Pope's condition grew considerably worse and he suffered intensely. One who spoke comforting words, calling him "Your Holiness," heard him faintly say, with a little sigh: "Holiness? Holiness?. . . I am only a poor sinner. . ."

Other last words distinctly heard repeated, as his lips moved constantly in prayer, were: *"Savona!. . . Fontainebleau!. . ."*

Pius VII's agony began at midnight and lasted until 5 in the morning of August 20 when he peacefully died.

The Pope's embalmed body lay in state in the Consistory Hall of the Quirinal Palace before being borne in procession the following day to the Vatican: first to the Sistine Chapel, then St. Peter's Basilica, where the people came to pay their last respects.

A catafalque over sixty feet high, designed by the famous architect Valadier, was put up in the center of St. Peter's, where it stood during the customary nine-day ceremonies and Masses—the novendial—that follow the death of a pontiff. Bas-reliefs on the four sides at the base of the catafalque showed memorable moments of Pius VII's reign: his return to Rome after long captivity; the restitution of the Papal States of the Church; the restoration of the Society of Jesus; his protection and patronage of the arts.

The Cardinals of the Sacred College assembled to provide for the conclave electing a successor. Letters dictated by Pius VII while still Napoleon's prisoner at Fontainebleau were unsealed and read aloud by the Cardinal Dean. Surrounded by manifold dangers and feeling his death might be near, Pius had set down orders for the members of the Sacred College in this event to assemble at the very first possible moment in the presence of the Cardinal Dean to elect his successor, waiving all customary procedure and formalities.

A further sealed instruction dictated and entrusted to Cardinal Consalvi in the year 1821, when Pius VII had publicly excommunicated all belonging to or abetting the secret Carbonari society, was also read aloud. The instruction contained orders, in the event of the Pope's death, for the Cardinals

to proceed immediately to elect his successor, by way of acclamation,³ if possible "before his dead body, while it was
still warm," and with the utmost secrecy. Not a soul was
to be notified, not even heads of State or ambassadors. The
usual nine-day ceremonies following death were to be omit-
ted and the conclave held without waiting for cardinals away
from Rome or abroad.

This instruction ended by recommending union and concord among all for the good of the Church and religion, in
truth and brotherly love, and it greatly moved the assembled
cardinals, almost all of whom—they were reminded—were
of the late Pope's creating. But since changed circumstances
no longer warranted any such special precautions, it was
decided to proceed in the customary way for the preparing
of the conclave.

Consalvi had said that he and Pius VII would die together.
After the Pope's death he suffered from the open hostility
of certain of his colleagues for what they considered his too
liberal attitude and concessions to the new mentality of post-
revolutionary times. He outlived Pius five months, dying in
January the following year, 1824.

He left a large sum of money in his will to pay for a worthy
monument to the memory of Pius VII, his great friend and
benefactor. The artist first chosen by Consalvi was Canova,
but he had died in 1822 and Consalvi's next choice had fallen
on the Danish sculptor Thorwaldsen, an imitator of Canova's
pure, classical style.

The Danish artist, a Protestant, was greatly surprised by
the Cardinal's choice of him. But he accepted and set to work
at once. After Consalvi's death, Thorwaldsen suffered from
the envy of other artists who thought they ought to have
been chosen. There were even intrigues to hinder his work
or prevent its realization. But he persevered and had the monument ready, according to Consalvi's testamentary wish, by
1831.

Pius VII's mausoleum in St. Peter's, next to the altar of
St. Gregory the Great, shows the Pope seated on the pontifical

throne, his right hand slightly raised in blessing. The countenance expresses characteristic gentleness and reflection, austerity and noble suffering. The attitude is one of meekness, mercy and forgiveness, attitudes constantly shown by Pius VII to those who persecuted and ill-treated him. The laurel-crowned figure of Wisdom stands to the right below the throne, Bible in hand, meditating on Holy Scripture; on the left is Fortitude, clothed in a lion's skin, gazing heavenward, a club thrown down at the feet symbolizing trust in the power of God rather than in earthly might. Two winged genii seated above to the right and left were added, representing Time, holding an hourglass, and History, writing in a book.

★   ★   ★

Pius VII was of rather short stature, slim and slightly round-shouldered. He had an aquiline nose and well-shaped, upturned lips. His hair was thick, black and copious, as were his eyebrows over large, deep-set dark eyes. His physiognomy and figure remained nobly attractive, gentle and open, reflecting his spirit also in old age.

Goodness, meekness, simplicity and piety were his most characteristic qualities. He was incapable of really hard feelings or rancor. Pius' singular virtues, learning, natural gaiety and common sense made him generally loved.

As Pope he continued to live, as far as possible, the retiring, prayerful and studious life of a Benedictine monk. His life, work and policy were imbued with the spirit of charity, humility and moderation taught by St. Benedict's Holy Rule,[1] whose principal objects are prayer and the acquiring and cultivation of the inner, spiritual life, through obedience, vigilance and self-denial.

Pius VII at times showed a certain weakness commonly associated with extreme mildness and gentleness of character; but personal dignity was never lacking, nor underlying strength, which comes of patience and resignation in suffering and trial.

Hesitant in temporal matters when left to himself, with good counsel he found decisiveness and courage. Once clearly seeing where his duty lay, he became unyielding and adamant. His expression and bearing in crucial moments assumed a most severe, almost fierce aspect. He usually entrusted temporal matters to his ministers, placing complete trust in them; in spiritual matters, as Head of the Church he as a rule consulted none but God.

Pius' benign endurance of prolonged and harsh captivity and persecution amounted to a martyrdom of soul—almost a martyrdom of blood. The introduction of a cause for canonization has been unofficially discussed in times past, and recently, by Jesuits and Benedictines.

Contemplating the humiliations, indignities, persecution and captivity of Pius VII, and seeing the papacy emerge victorious, one can echo the words pronounced by this Pontiff in his Allocution on September 26, 1814, not long after his liberation and return to Rome: "An essential truth which we acknowledge of the Holy Catholic Church, instituted by Christ, is that trouble serves to give greater strength, and oppression to produce greater glory."

NOTES

1. The Benedictine Rule, Latin in spirit—practical, efficient and contemplative at the same time—made for a life of rectitude guided by moral principle and purity of heart, overflowing in a variety of works of benefit to others. Mind and heart are grounded on unshakable convictions according to the Gospel of Christ, heedless of human respect; these convictions are the mainspring of all exterior works, whose motive power is thus love of God. Closely identified with the very life of the Church itself in earlier centuries, building the City of God on earth, the Benedictine Order has given the Church forty popes, of whom sixteen are venerated as saints or beati.
2. Msgr. Carlo Salotti, *La Beata Anna Maria Taigi, Storia e Critica,* Rome, 1922.
3. *Acclamation,* also known as *quasi-inspiration,* is the method of choosing a new Pope in which the cardinals unanimously proclaim one name without discussion or voting. The last Pope so chosen was Blessed Innocent XI (1676-1689).

PRINCIPAL DATES IN THE LIFE OF
POPE PIUS VII

1742   Birth.

1756   Takes the Benedictine habit at Mount St. Mary's, Cesena.

1758   Religious profession.

1761   Ordination. Studies philosophy at St. Justa's Abbey, Padua.

1763   Recalled to Rome to complete theological formation.

1766   Professor of theology at St. John the Evangelist's College, Parma.

1773   Suppression of the Society of Jesus.

1775   Death of Clement XIV. Accession of Pius VI. Professor of theology at St. Anselm's College (St. Paul's Abbey), Rome.

1782   Titular abbot of St. Mary of the Mount, Cesena.

1783   Bishop of Tivoli.

1784   Bishop of Imola.

1785   Created Cardinal.

1789   Convocation of French Estates General. The Constituent Assembly.

1793   King Louis XVI and Queen Marie Antoinette guillotined. The "Reign of Terror."

1796   The French "Directory" orders invasion of Italy under General Bonaparte. Bonaparte in Milan. The French Republicans in Imola. Cardinal Chiaramonti is called by Pius VI to Rome.

1797   Interim peace after the Treaty of Tolentino. Cardinal Chiaramonti returns to Imola. He delivers his "Christmas Homily."

1799   General Berthier occupies Rome. Abduction of Pius VI and his death in France. Cardinal Chiaramonti travels to Venice for the Conclave.

1800   Cardinal Chiaramonti elected Pope. He returns to Rome. Napoleon Bonaparte First Consul of France.

1801   The French Concordat.

1802   The Italian Concordat.

1804   Napoleon crowned Emperor of the French. The Pope in Paris.

1805   Pius refuses to ratify Napoleon's episcopal nominees or to ban English subjects from the Papal States.

1806   He further refuses to ally himself with the Emperor's policies or to adhere to his continental blockade of Britain.

1808   General Miollis occupies Rome. Pope Pius is confined in the Quirinal Palace.

1809   Rome is declared a "free imperial city" and the Papal States are incorporated into Napoleon's empire. The Pope publishes Bull of Excommunication of all concerned. He is arrested and taken to Savona.

1810   He refuses to recognize Napoleon's remarriage with Marie-Louise of Austria.

1811   Napoleon convokes an "Imperial Council" of Bishops. Under duress, the Pope grants certain concessions regarding the Emperor's episcopal nominees to an ecclesiastical delegation sent from Paris.

1812   The Emperor orders the Pope's transfer to Fontainebleau. Napoleon's retreat from Moscow, his armies defeated.

1813   The Emperor visits the Pope at Fontainebleau and wrests from him the "False Concordat." Napoleon is defeated at Leipzig "Battle of the Nations." The Pope is permitted to return to Rome, via Savona. Pius crowns the image of Our Lady of Mercy. Napoleon is forced to abdicate.

1814   The Pope's triumphal return to Rome. Restoration of the Society of Jesus.

1815   The Congress of Vienna gives back the Papal Legations. Napoleon escapes from Elba. Pius takes refuge in Genoa. Waterloo. Napoleon is sent to St. Helena. Pius returns to Rome.

1817   Plot to overthrow the papal government forestalled. Economic and social crisis. The Pope falls seriously ill.

1819   He is visited at the Vatican by Emperor Francis I of Austria.

1821   Death of Napoleon.

1823   St. Paul's Basilica, Rome, destroyed by fire. Death of Pius VII.

BIBLIOGRAPHICAL NOTES
AND ACKNOWLEDGMENTS

Many of the main published and unpublished sources of this work are referred to in the text or in notes. Others consulted, mostly in French and Italian, are too numerous to list. For example, some sixteen accounts of the 1800 Conclave that elected Pius VII were studied in Italian, French and German. Among these were that of Cipolletta (Milan, 1863), Petrucelli (Paris, 1865), Cappello (Florence, 1900), Celani (Vatican, 1913), Apollonio (in the First Centenary Publications of Pius VII's death, Ravenna, 1923) and Gallarati-Scotti (Florence, 1961). Moroni's great Dictionary of Ecclesiastical History (Italian) gives authentic indications as to the clearest and most objective accounts.

Jean Leflon revised his work *La crise révolutionnaire, 1789-1815*, published in Fliche-Martin's *History of the Church*, for the second edition published in 1976 (Volume 21, Italian translation G. Zaccaria, Turin, updated bibliography, 10 pages, by Fr. Isidore de Villa-padierna, O.F.M., Cap.)

Regarding the Conclave, Leflon in his previous work on the life of Pius VII (unfinished) before becoming Pope, *Pie VII* (Paris, 1958), traced the part played in Cardinal Chiaramonti's election by Spain's unofficial envoy, Archbishop Despuig, from the Archbishop's diary *Libro de los viajes* (Palma Majorca family archives, unpublished). Leflon's revised work, *La crise révolutionnaire* (referred to above) gives a somewhat different account of the Conclave, indicating Msgr. Despuig only as the "inspirer of maneuvres" that led to the election of Pius VII through a campaign conducted by Cardinal Ruffo and Msgr. Consalvi, the Conclave Secretary. Vatican archivist Prof. L. Pasztor published Consalvi's *Diary* of the Conclave, with comments, in 1962, as also Consalvi's *Memoir* of the Conclave, again with comments, in 1965. The two accounts differ, and Leflon in his work points out inexplicable omissions, notably on the part played by Msgr. Despuig. The *Diary* of the marshal of the Conclave, Count Chigi, was published only in 1962 by the Giorgio Cini Foundation of Venice; and that of Cardinal Flangini, one of the voting cardinals at the Conclave, in G. Damerini's book on St. George's Island Abbey, Venice (2nd edition, Venice, 1969).

The Pope's first biographer, Pistolesi (Rome, 1824), and later Giucci in his *Life of Pope Pius, Vita di Pio VII* (Rome, 1857), deal briefly, but somewhat diversely also, with the Conclave and election. Many other authentic histories of the period, notably those of Gendry, de la Gorce, d'Haussonville, Latreille, Hayward, Welschinger and Mayol de Lupé treat of the reign of Pius VII, the latter treating of his captivity in particular. There is also the Benedictine Dom Charles Poulet's *History of the Catholic Church,* translated by the Rev. Sidney A. Raemers (Volume II), published by B. Herder, St. Louis, 1945, which deals in detail with the reign of Pius VII.

Fr. Domenico Martinengo wrote fully about the period of Pius VII's captivity in his city of Savona. After his death, his unfinished book was completed by his brother Francisco, who died in 1875. A third edition of this work was published in Savona in 1936, entitled *Pio VII in Savona.* Among other specialized works are Paolo Calliari's *Life and Times of Bruno Lanteri,* the priest of the Congregation of the Oblates of the Virgin Mary who smuggled vital documents into the episcopal palace of Savona for the use of the imprisoned Pope— published in Turin, 1968; and by the same author, *Pio Bruno Lanteri* (1759-1830) *e la Controrivoluzione* (Turin 1976); G. Testore's *Il Restauratore* (Rome, 1954) and D. A. Hanly's *Blessed Joseph Pignatelli, S.J.* (New York 1937) on the restoration of the Jesuits; Bernard Ward's *The Eve of Catholic Emancipation* (3 volumes, London, 1911); and J. Hofer's *St. Clement Mary*

Hofbauer, English translation by J. Haas, C.C.S.R. (New York, 1926).

Heartfelt gratitude is due to Dom Stefano Baiocchi, O.S.B., of St. Paul's, Rome, for providential indications, as also to the Benedictines of Mount St. Mary's Abbey, Cesena, where Barnabas Chiaramonti entered religion, and to those of St. George's Abbey—*Abbazia di San Giorgio*—Venice, where Pius VII was elected. Thanks are due in particular to the Prior, Dom Floriano Tognolo, for his constant interest, help and much-needed encouragement. Mrs. Elsa M. Hurschler, S.F.O., must finally be thanked for her work in producing a typescript of the revised manuscript of this book, a project proposed to me in 1977 by John J. Cardinal Wright.

SELECTED BIBLIOGRAPHY

Pope Pius VI

Baldassari, P. *Relazione delle avversità e patimenti del glorioso Papa Pio VI negli ultimi tre anni del suo pontificato.* Vol. 4. Modena, 1840-43.

Gendry, J. *Pie VI, sa vie, son pontificat.* 2 Vols. Paris, 1905.

von Pastor, Ludwig. *History of the Popes.* Vols. 39 & 40 (English trans.). London, 1951.

Pope Pius VII

Bechini, D.G., O.S.B. *I natali di Pio VII (Chiaramonti) nel primo centenario della morte.* Ravenna, 1928.

Bolletino La Madonna del Monte, 150 anno della morte di Pio VII. Cesena, 1974.

Cronaca dell'Abbazia di San Giorgio. Venice, 1900 (First Centenary of Election).

d'Haussonville, Le Comte. *L'Église romaine et le Premier Empire.* Paris, 1870.

Galli, Romeo. *Il Cardinale Gregorio Barnaba Chiaramonti, Vescovo di Imola.* R. Istituto per la Storia del Risorgimento italiano (Congresso 23 Bologna). Rome, 1935— Delfico: pp. 159-169.

Hayward, Fernand. *Le Dernier Siècle de la Rome Pontificale (Clément XIV, Pie VI, Pie VII).* Paris, 1927.

Memoria: Imola-Venezia. Ms. account (Italian) of journey from Imola to Venice of Cardinal Chiaramonti in 1799 for Conclave. Vatican State Archive, Vat. Instr. Misc. n. 7809.

Papers Relating to the Papal States (1808-1811)—including account of the abduction of the Pope from Rome. London, 1833-34, British Museum ms. nos. 157, 158.

Pistolesi, E. *Vita del Sommo Pontefice Pio VII.* Rome, 1824.

Welschinger, H. *Le Pape et L'Empéreur.* Paris, 1905.

Wiseman, N. (Cardinal). *Recollections of Rome, and of the Last Four Popes.* London, 1858 & 1936.

Napoleon

Correspondence de Napoléon. Vols. XI, XII & XIX. Paris, 1858-1870.

Rosebery, Lord. *Napoleon—The Last Phase.* London, 1900. (Includes literature on Napoleon).

Rothenberg, G. *Napoleon's Adversaries.* London, 1980.

Thompson, J. M. *Napoleon Bonaparte.* Oxford, 1951.

Cardinal Consalvi

Daudet. E. *Le Cardinal Consalvi, 1800-1824.* Paris, 1866.

di Corneliano, Mario Nasalli Rocca (later Cardinal). *Memorie del Cardinale Ercole Consalvi* (translated from the French, except for the account of the Conclave [original ms. untraced] printed in the French of Crétinau-Joly). Rome, 1950.

Memorie (Rheims, 1812), published in French translation by J. Crétinau-Joly as *Mémoires du Cardinal Consalvi.* Paris, 1864, with Introduction, 2nd. ed., 1866.

Momenti di Storia Pontificia tra il 1799 ed il 1800, Archivio della Società Romana di Storia patria. 83, 1960.

Pasztor, L. (Vatican archivist). *Diario di Ercole Consalvi, pro-Segretario del Conclave di Venezia* (1800).

Pasztor, L. *Memorie di Cardinal Consalvi,* with Introduction, published from copy of untraced original found in Vatican Library, ms. Vat. lat. 14605, in *Archivium Historiae Pontificiae,* 3, 1965.

Cardinal York

Anderson, R. *Rome Churches of Special Interest for English-Speaking People.* (St. Mary in Portico, Rome; Cardinal York, Cathedral of San Pietro, Frascati). Vatican City (3rd ed., enlarged), 1982.

Bindelli, P. *Enrico Stuart Cardinale Duca di York.* Frascati, 1983.

Fothergill, B. *The Cardinal King.* London, 1958.

Seton, W. W. *The Relations of Henry Cardinal York with the British Government.* London, 1817-1819.

Shield, A. *Cardinal York and His Times.* London, 1908.

Vaughan, A. M. *Henry Cardinal Duke of York, The Last of the Royal Stuarts.* London, 1906.

Cardinal Pacca

Mémoirs—Conversations à Fontainebleau (trans.). Paris, 1846.

Pacca, Bartolomeo Cardinale. *Memorie storiche.* Rome, 1830.

Other Historical Figures

Antignani, Gerardo. *Anna Maria Taigi, Storia di una mamma dai documenti e del diario inediti.* Rome (2nd. ed., rev.), 1983.

Battilori, M. *El cardinal Despuig y su tiempo.* Palma de Mallorca, 1964.

Bessières, P. Albert, S. J. *Wife, Mother and Mystic.* (trans. Rev. Stephen Rigby). London, 1952 & Rockford, U.S.A., 1970.

Cristiani, L. *Un prêtre redouté de Napoléon, P. B. Lanteri.* Nice, 1957.

Other Historical Figures (cont.)

de Lévis-Mirepoix, E. *Un collaborateur de Metternich: Mémoires et papiers du comte Lebzeltern.* Paris, 1949.

de Salamon, Ch. *Mémoires de l'Internonce pendant la Révolution.* Paris, 1850.

Lanteri, B. *Sul supposto concordato (di Fontainebleau).* La Grangia, 1813.

Leflon, J. *M. Emery.* Paris, 1947.

Piatti, T. *Bruno Lanteri.* Turin-Rome, 1954.

Salotti, Msgr. Carlo. *La Beata Anna Maria Taigi, Secondo la Storia e la Critica.* Rome, 1922.

Salva, J. *El Cardinal Despuig.* Palma de Mallorca, 1964.

General

Acton, H. M. M. *The Bourbons of Naples.* London, 1956.

Berthelet, G. *Conclavi del Secolo XIX.* Rome, 1903.

Charles-Roux, F. *Rome, Asile des Bonapartes.* Paris, 1952.

Crétinau-Joly, J. *L'Église romaine en face de la Révolution* (2 Vols.). Paris, 1860.

d'Haussonville, le Comte. *L'Église catholique et la Révolution française* (5 Vols.). Paris, 1868-69.

Latreille, A. *Napoléon et le Saint-Siége, 1801-1808.* Paris, 1935.

Lefebvre, Georges. *La Révolution Française* (trans. Italian, *La Rivoluzione francese*). Rome, 1981.

Memorie del Sagro Monistero di S. Paolo di Roma. Rome, 1783.

Palmer, R. *The World of the French Revolution.* London, 1971.

Proclin, E. *Les Jansenistes du XVIII Siècle et la Constitution Civile du Clergé.* Paris, 1929.

Rohrbacher, Abbé. *Histoire Universelle de l'Église Catholique—L'Empire et chute de Napoléon Bonaparte* (Vol. 28). Paris, 1852.

INDEX

If you have enjoyed this book, consider making your next selection from among the following . . .

Prices subject to change.

Moments Divine—Before the Blessed Sacrament. *Reuter* 8.50
Miraculous Images of Our Lady. *Cruz* 20.00
Miraculous Images of Our Lord. *Cruz* 13.50
Raised from the Dead. *Fr. Hebert*............................... 16.50
Love and Service of God, Infinite Love. *Mother Louise Margaret* 12.50
Life and Work of Mother Louise Margaret. *Fr. O'Connell* 12.50
Autobiography of St. Margaret Mary.............................. 6.00
Thoughts and Sayings of St. Margaret Mary........................ 5.00
The Voice of the Saints. *Comp. by Francis Johnston* 7.00
The 12 Steps to Holiness and Salvation. *St. Alphonsus*............... 7.50
The Rosary and the Crisis of Faith. *Cirrincione & Nelson* 2.00
Sin and Its Consequences. *Cardinal Manning* 7.00
St. Francis of Paola. *Simi & Segreti* 8.00
Dialogue of St. Catherine of Siena. *Transl. Algar Thorold* 10.00
Catholic Answer to Jehovah's Witnesses. *D'Angelo* 12.00
Twelve Promises of the Sacred Heart. (100 cards)..................... 5.00
Life of St. Aloysius Gonzaga. *Fr. Meschler* 12.00
The Love of Mary. *D. Roberto*................................. 8.00
Begone Satan. *Fr. Vogl* 3.00
The Prophets and Our Times. *Fr. R. G. Culleton*..................... 13.50
St. Therese, The Little Flower. *John Beevers* 6.00
St. Joseph of Copertino. *Fr. Angelo Pastrovicchi*.................... 6.00
Mary, The Second Eve. *Cardinal Newman*......................... 3.00
Devotion to Infant Jesus of Prague. *Booklet*....................... .75
Reign of Christ the King in Public & Private Life. *Davies* 1.25
The Wonder of Guadalupe. *Francis Johnston*....................... 9.00
Apologetics. *Msgr. Paul Glenn*................................. 10.00
Baltimore Catechism No. 1..................................... 3.50
Baltimore Catechism No. 2..................................... 4.50
Baltimore Catechism No. 3..................................... 8.00
An Explanation of the Baltimore Catechism. *Fr. Kinkead*............... 16.50
Bethlehem. *Fr. Faber*.. 18.00
Bible History. *Schuster*....................................... 13.50
Blessed Eucharist. *Fr. Mueller* 10.00
Catholic Catechism. *Fr. Faerber*................................ 7.00
The Devil. *Fr. Delaporte* 6.00
Dogmatic Theology for the Laity. *Fr. Premm*...................... 20.00
Evidence of Satan in the Modern World. *Cristiani* 10.00
Fifteen Promises of Mary. (100 cards)............................. 5.00
Life of Anne Catherine Emmerich. 2 vols. *Schmoeger* 37.50
Life of the Blessed Virgin Mary. *Emmerich* 16.50
Manual of Practical Devotion to St. Joseph. *Patrignani* 15.00
Prayer to St. Michael. (100 leaflets) 5.00
Prayerbook of Favorite Litanies. *Fr. Hebert* 10.00
Preparation for Death. (Abridged). *St. Alphonsus*................... 8.00
Purgatory Explained. *Schouppe* 13.50
Purgatory Explained. (pocket, unabr.). *Schouppe* 9.00
Fundamentals of Catholic Dogma. *Ludwig Ott*...................... 21.00
Spiritual Conferences. *Faber* 15.00
Trustful Surrender to Divine Providence. *Bl. Claude* 5.00
Wife, Mother and Mystic. *Bessieres*............................. 8.00
The Agony of Jesus. *Padre Pio*................................. 2.00

Prices subject to change.

Prices subject to change.

Prices subject to change.

The Life of Father De Smet. *Fr. Laveille, S.J.* 18.00
Glories of Divine Grace. *Fr. Matthias Scheeben* 18.00
Hail Holy Queen (from *Glories of Mary*). *St. Alphonsus* 8.00
Novena of Holy Communions. *Lovasik* 2.00
Brief Catechism for Adults. *Cogan*................................... 11.00
The Cath. Religion—Illus./Expl. for Child, Adult, Convert. *Burbach* 9.00
Eucharistic Miracles. *Joan Carroll Cruz*............................. 15.00
The Incorruptibles. *Joan Carroll Cruz* 15.00
Secular Saints: 250 Lay Men, Women & Children. PB. *Cruz*............. 30.00
Pope St. Pius X. *F. A. Forbes* 8.00
St. Alphonsus Liguori. *Frs. Miller and Aubin*........................ 16.50
Self-Abandonment to Divine Providence. *Fr. de Caussade, S.J.* 18.00
The Song of Songs—A Mystical Exposition. *Fr. Arintero, O.P.* 20.00
Prophecy for Today. *Edward Connor* 5.50
Saint Michael and the Angels. *Approved Sources* 9.00
Dolorous Passion of Our Lord. *Anne C. Emmerich*.................... 16.50
Modern Saints—Their Lives & Faces, Book I. *Ann Ball*................ 18.00
Modern Saints—Their Lives & Faces, Book II. *Ann Ball*............... 20.00
Our Lady of Fatima's Peace Plan from Heaven. *Booklet*................. .75
Divine Favors Granted to St. Joseph. *Père Binet*..................... 5.00
St. Joseph Cafasso—Priest of the Gallows. *St. John Bosco*.............. 5.00
Catechism of the Council of Trent. *McHugh/Callan*................... 24.00
The Foot of the Cross. *Fr. Faber*.................................... 16.50
The Rosary in Action. *John Johnson* 9.00
Padre Pio—The Stigmatist. *Fr. Charles Carty* 16.50
Why Squander Illness? *Frs. Rumble & Carty*......................... 2.50
The Sacred Heart and the Priesthood. *de la Touche* 9.00
Fatima—The Great Sign. *Francis Johnston* 8.00
Heliotropium—Conformity of Human Will to Divine. *Drexelius* 13.00
Charity for the Suffering Souls. *Fr. John Nageleisen* 16.50
Devotion to the Sacred Heart of Jesus. *Verheylezoon* 15.00
Who Is Padre Pio? *Radio Replies Press* 2.00
The Stigmata and Modern Science. *Fr. Charles Carty* 1.50
St. Anthony—The Wonder Worker of Padua. *Stoddard*................. 5.00
The Precious Blood. *Fr. Faber* 13.50
The Holy Shroud & Four Visions. *Fr. O'Connell* 2.00
Clean Love in Courtship. *Fr. Lawrence Lovasik* 2.50
The Secret of the Rosary. *St. Louis De Montfort*...................... 5.00
The History of Antichrist. *Rev. P. Huchede*.......................... 4.00
St. Catherine of Siena. *Alice Curtayne* 13.50
Where We Got the Bible. *Fr. Henry Graham* 6.00
Hidden Treasure—Holy Mass. *St. Leonard*........................... 5.00
Imitation of the Sacred Heart of Jesus. *Fr. Arnoudt* 15.00
The Life & Glories of St. Joseph. *Edward Thompson*.................. 15.00
Père Lamy. *Biver*.. 12.00
Humility of Heart. *Fr. Cajetan da Bergamo* 9.00
The Curé D'Ars. *Abbé Francis Trochu*............................... 21.50
Love, Peace and Joy. (St. Gertrude). *Prévot* 7.00

At your Bookdealer or direct from the Publisher.
Toll-Free 1-800-437-5876   *Fax 815-226-7770*

Prices subject to change.

Professor Robin Anderson

Robin Anderson was born in London in 1913. His father, of Scottish ancestry, who was a colonel in the Indian Political Service, published stories of British Imperial India. His mother, of Irish descent, was an amateur painter and pianist. Educated at Marlborough College, Robin Anderson studied at the London Royal Academy of Dramatic Art. In 1936, he married the German-Jewish dancer and actress, Valeska Gert, a refugee from Nazi Germany. During the war years, he worked as a stage manager to Shakespearean actor Sir John Gielgud. His first short story was published in 1946 by England's top literary magazine, *Horizon*.

Converted to Catholicism under the influence of Gerard Manley Hopkins and John Henry Cardinal Newman, Anderson went in 1953 to Rome, where he has lived ever since, working as speaker for Vatican Radio and teacher of languages. Elected fellow of the Institute of Linguists in 1961, he has published articles and poetry and lectured on religious and cultural subjects in Italy, England, the United States and other countries. Among his published works are *The Quiet Grave* (Journals), *Rome Churches for English-Speaking People*, *St. Pius V*, *Between Two Wars— The Life of Pope Pius XI*, *Pope Pius VII* and *Gleams of English-Language Literature*. Collected prose and poetry, with Italian and French translations, appeared in 1983. *Crisis Popes* (on Popes reigning in times of particular crisis) was computer-printed for private circulation in 1997. During the Jubilee Year 2000, Anderson was named candidate for decoration with the Spanish *Isabella Catolica* Cross for his activity in promoting the cause for beatification of the Servant of God Raphael Cardinal Merry del Val, who served as Secretary of State to Pope St. Pius X.